IMAGE, ICON, ECONOMY

Cultural Memory

in 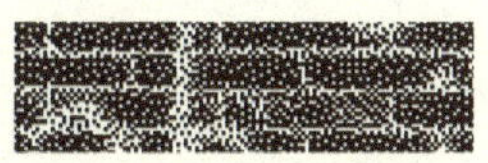

the

Present

Mieke Bal and Hent de Vries, Editors

IMAGE, ICON, ECONOMY

The Byzantine Origins of the Contemporary Imaginary

Marie-José Mondzain

Translated by Rico Franses

STANFORD UNIVERSITY PRESS

STANFORD, CALIFORNIA

Stanford University Press
Stanford, California

Image, Icon, Economy was originally published in French in 1996 under the title *Image, Icône, Économie: Les sources Byzantines de l'imaginaire contemporain* © 1996, Éditions du Seuil.

This work, published as part of a program of aid for publication, received support from the French Ministry of Foreign Affairs and the Cultural Services of the French Embassy in the United States.

Printed in the United States of America on acid-free, archival-quality paper

Library of Congress Cataloging-in-Publication Data

Mondzain, Marie-José.
[Image, icône, économie. English]
Image, icon, economy : the Byzantine origins of the contemporary economy / Marie-José Mondzain ; translated by Rico Franses.
p. cm. — (Cultural memory in the present)
Includes bibliographical references and index.
ISBN 0-8047-4100-X (cloth : alk. paper)
ISBN 0-8047-4101-8 (pbk. : alk. paper)
1. Icons, Byzantine. 2. Semiotics. I. Title. II. Series.
N8187.5.M6513 2004
306.4'7—DC22

2004000088

Original Printing 2005

Contents

Translator's Note

A word needs to be said about the term *imaginary* as it appears in the title of this work and then periodically throughout the book. I have followed the discipline of psychoanalysis in its rendering of the French term *l'imaginaire*, because the word as used by the author retains many of the connotations that it has in that field. Most importantly, it never simply means *fictive* as opposed to *real* or *true*. Although it does relate, on the one hand, to *imagination* in that what it deals with is a field of mental functioning, it refers more specifically to the particular faculty of the psyche for thinking in images. To quote Alan Sheridan, the translator of Jacques Lacan's *The Four Fundamental Concepts of Psychoanalysis*, the imaginary is "the world, the register, the dimension of images, conscious or unconscious, perceived or imagined." Similarly, the term *imaginal*, which is the translation of the identical word in French, also relates to this domain of images.

Acknowledgments

First, I owe a debt of gratitude to Alexandra Hauchecorne, who provided me with many solutions to problems that had appeared formidably intractable. Grateful thanks go out as well to the following for help covering a wide array of technical fields: Glenn Peers, Grant McCrea, Stefan Grant, Paul Duro, Penny Deutscher, and Katarina Posch. I am fortunate to be able to count such expertise among the attributes of friendship. Many thanks as well to the author, Marie-José Mondzain, for her careful reading of this translation, and several crucial qualifications.

Extracts from the *Antirrhetics* of Nikephoros were translated by Vassiliki Dimitropoulou.

Not only Christ but the whole universe disappears if neither circumscribability nor image exist.

—Patriarch Nikephoros, *Antirrhetics,* I, 244 D.

Heresy renders legible in doctrinal terms both social conflict and the binary form of a mode by which a society defines itself by excluding what it turns into its other. It links the ideology of the social to the visibility of the process by which the social body is constituted.

—Michel de Certeau, *La Fable mystique*

Foreword

One day, an extremely knowledgeable Byzantinist, religiously hoping to discourage me, declared that only history, geography, and religion existed in Byzantium, but not philosophy. It was then that I understood how urgent it was to prove the opposite, not only in the interest of philosophy, but to demonstrate that the whole question of history, geography, and religion in Byzantium was nothing other than the very stakes of philosophy itself. From the outset I was helped by another Byzantinist, no doubt more knowledgeable than the first, and whom a freer spirit rendered deeply generous, Jean Gouillard, who is unfortunately no longer with us. He introduced me to the texts of Nikephoros and lent me his support during the years devoted to the translation of the *Antirrhetics.*

In addition to the difficulty of the subject itself, I also had to overcome the obstacles of the derisive disapproval of theologians, as well as that strange custom current among certain historians of jealously reserving for themselves proprietary rights to the centuries while dreading like the plague any theoretical inquiry relating to issues of modernity. One can readily imagine the degree to which I appreciated the help, support, information, and useful criticism provided to me by historian and philosopher friends like Jean Gouillard and Michel de Certeau, as well as Paul Audi, Emmanuel Martineau, Marie-France Auzépy, Françoise Armengaud, Ithzak Goldberg, and Jacques Mercier. I thank them all.

Paradoxically, it also proved necessary for me to resist the sudden fluency made available by the recent fascination of image theorists with iconicity, in which the champions of modern and postmodern (?) invisibility have picked up the scent of a redemptive truffle in an "idolatrous" world. This goes for all those who speak of the icon of the Holy Shroud, of real presence, and the erogenous giddiness of lack and absence. The demon of wild analogy has committed as many misdeeds as the one of monopolistic erudition and ecclesiastic protectionism.

Considering all of the foregoing, an account of my own path through iconic thought might be appropriate at this juncture. I have been studying it now for the last fifteen years and have discovered even among its most difficult aspects an infinitely rich and subtle system of thought. In this book, I have simply attempted to clarify those of its features that are fertile for the philosophy of the image today.

Because the corpus that I was working on revealed itself to be ever more coherent, I decided to put it to use it as simply as possible. This meditation thus begins with an examination of the term *economy*, then turns more specifically to the icon, taking up certain of my earlier studies written at the same time as I was translating the *Antirrhetics.* It then concludes with several reflections on the idol, followed by a revised collection of texts concerning the icons of our contemporary world that still seem to me to bear the mark of iconic thought.

The prophetic tone of an "icon kit," replete with preconceived notions and ready-made answers, which has prevailed since some have begun to talk about art, image, God, the face of others, or the new face of the Slavic world in Holy Russia has no place in this book. Ever since the Other is no longer to be found anywhere, its icon has been paraded everywhere, from the church to the computer, from the museum to the analytic couch. It feeds the mystique of the virtuosi of the virtual and those of the democratic fraternity who have been gravely wounded. A new artifact of presence and of hopes for salvation, the icon nevertheless still needs to reencounter the foundations of its own true theoretical and political power, which it derives from the patristic system of thought concerning the economy.

This study attempts to provide a specific reading of the iconoclastic conflict inasmuch as it closely and intensely concerns a political and philosophical problem that is still with us now. What interests me about it is the genesis of a way of thinking about the image that we are still heirs of today. It is also no exaggeration to use the word *reading* here, because it is to the reading of a major text, written during the iconoclastic crisis, that this book owes its very subject matter. The text in question is the *Antirrhetics* of Patriarch Nikephoros of Constantinople, written between 818 and 820 while he was in exile during the second iconoclastic crisis.

Throughout the twentieth century, the image has been at the heart of our concern for the safeguarding of liberty and thought. However, since a visual and audiovisual imperialism has invaded the planet and reduced all critical reflection and discussion to a state of servile stupor and acephalic fascination, it has become incumbent on us to attempt to understand the elements of a genealogy whose ultimate offspring is the carrier of the best as well as the worst of things. Perhaps no great disaster is brewing other than the always threatening one of the abdication of thought, but the image is not responsible for that. Rather, it awaits consideration in terms of both its present crushing vitality and its history.

I have attempted in this work to return to that intuition of the church fathers concerning the fundamental interdependence that ties the fate of the artificial image, or icon, to the transfigured flesh of the natural, invisible image and to our living, corporeal reality as desiring, political, and mortal beings. By using the concept of the economy, the church fathers attempted to think through the relation of the imaginary to life and to consider what happens to truth when one's primary concern, as a matter of urgency, is to act effectively in the real world; and all this while confronting the difficulty that results from rejecting idolatry, even while it was inevitably necessary to reckon with it.

The philosophical and anthropological complexity of this problem lent a physical and symbolic violence to the debate, one from which those who are interested in the period have not always escaped. One still sides either with or against the iconoclasts. To the extent that the iconophiles won and deprived us of all the documents that would have enlightened us about their adversaries, the tendency of the researcher is to privilege those whom the history of the triumph have injured most. A system of thought that has come down to us only in the form of lies and caricatures has had to be reconstituted through scraps. True, such a procedure is both a technical and moral necessity, yet while recognizing this, this book pursues the issues on entirely different grounds from the initial polemic: two currents of thought that cannot be understood without each other are set in relation to each other, until we finally discover that *contradiction is intrinsic to the nature of the image itself.* The image and the icon lie at the heart of all considerations of the symbol and the sign, as well as their relation to the problematic of being and appearing, seeing and believing, strength and power. When emperor and patriarch confront each other, each in turn wanting to convince us that this confrontation is a fight against the devil, our only choice is to investigate the question of how the figures of salvation and damnation have been constructed through the course of history, and how the image became the cornerstone of various excommunications and inclusions. Both camps are passionate; each is fascinating. Iconophilia has drawn us along in the wake of its violent adherences, but the voice of iconoclasm has never been killed, for all that. As for the idolaters, who were unanimously condemned by everyone—they still prosper and continue to offer us the most seductive pictures of our own desires to worship and destroy.

Introduction

The iconoclastic crisis in Byzantium was essentially a Constantinopolitan political crisis, which is to say, a crisis over the symbolic foundation of authority. This concerned the very conception of power at the highest level of hierarchical authority. More precisely, it could be said that the crisis was an economic one, provided that the word *economy* is given the meaning that it had in Byzantium, and it is this that forms the subject of the first part of our study. Here we will demonstrate how, and in what sense, the debate between the iconophiles and iconoclasts is knotted around a certain number of keywords. Our method will consist of attempting to understand the structure of the lexical constellation that forms the unflagging armature of the debate by means of the texts that defend images and refute those that attack them. The crisis will be analyzed on the basis of the polemic, the play of questions and answers, that was formulated in certain texts, particularly in the *Antirrhetics* of Nikephoros. These questions concern, on the one hand, theoretical issues, such as relationships, mimesis, the line,[1] the imaginal voice, and the transfiguration of form, and on the other, political issues such as pedagogy, strategy, and the appropriation of territory. These two sets of issues define the operational field of the concept of economy as it was applied to the image and the icon. For such is the ambivalence of the question posed by the terms *eikôn* and *oikonomia*: in question is the natural image and the fate of the artificial image.

To privilege the icon in the study of a crisis referred to as the "crisis of iconoclasm" would seem to be obvious, but good sense sometimes appears vulgar to the wise. Thus, even though they have acknowledged that a dogmatic debate of a decidedly theological nature was indeed able to shake an empire to its roots, scholars have preferred to suppose that such a crisis, even though bearing the name of iconoclasm, concerned, in truth, something else completely.[2] The historical study of the economic, social, and military circumstances pertaining at the time has often led commentators to hypothesize that the debate over the icon was only a pretext and that the reality was entirely different. Thus the interpretation of the crisis has been oriented either toward an explanation of a rather interior sort (a struggle against monarchical power), or it has insisted on the empire's reinforcement of its borders, economic recovery, the militarization and decentralization of power, or even the influence of the oriental provinces that lived in contact with aniconic cultures. The empire was undergoing a political crisis; therefore it was thought necessary to furnish a political explanation for it, and in consequence, relegate the question of the icon to the rank of secondary causes, or put it in the role of a doctrinal screen that hid reality. But what if this political crisis was precisely a crisis of iconicity—provided, of course, that one examine this iconicity in the terms in which it was then linked to the overall effects of symbolization in general, and therefore also to effects that are political in nature? It is this hypothesis that underpins this investigation.

What, then, was the doctrine of the icon, this philosophy of the image that for the first time not only overcame within monotheist thought certain theological prohibitions, but even surmounted those difficulties born within Greek thought of the ontological speculation about *doxa*, *mimēsis*, and the phenomenon? For a Greek system of thought it most definitely is that we are dealing with here, and it can be summarized in the following formulation: *an economic conception of the natural image founds the artificial image, and an economic conception of the artificial image, in turn, founds temporal power.* It is this that will be explained in the following pages.

Greece is usually considered to be the birthplace of all philosophical questions concerning being and language. Its paternity in the domain of the image, however, has hardly ever been recognized because this philosophical development occurred at the heart of Christian thought, far from Athens. Because Byzantine Christianity was defined as oriental, it was too quickly forgotten that the thought of the church fathers was nothing other than a long debate on the compatibility of Greek thought with the new dogmas of the faith. A scholar such as Ladner, therefore, stressed the philosophical relationships that gave birth to iconic thought, but his work has not been given the attention that it deserves among philosophers.[3] Christian scholars and clergy trying to give an account of the origins of Christian thought are the only ones who pause over it. Today, however, this consideration of the subject of the icon is of concern to all of us in the lay and profane world, even though it does not necessarily matter to us in its apologetic or doctrinal sense. Nevertheless, the ideological use that has been made of these iconic themes obliges us to return to its sources in order to demonstrate that the philosophical field is in fact fully independent of the specifically religious domain. For someone like Nikephoros, it is the very cause of thought itself that is sacred, and if the icon is sacred, it is because it founds the very possibility of thinking.

Consideration of the image is still a sacred cause today only because the fate of thought and liberty are at stake in it. The visible world, the one that is given to us to see: is it liberty or enslavement? In order to be able to envisage a world radically founded on visibility, and starting from the conviction that whatever constitutes its essence and meaning is itself invisible, it proved essential to establish a system of thought that set the visible and invisible in relation to each other. This relation was based on the distinction between the image and the icon. The image is invisible, the icon is visible. The economy was the concept of their *living* linkage. The image is a mystery. The icon is an enigma. The economy was the concept of their *relation* and their *intimacy.* The image is eternal similitude, the icon is temporal resemblance. The economy was the theory of the *transfiguration of history.*

The concept of economy has been studied in depth in the theological and juridical domain. Its strange and insistent polysemy, however, has never aroused much more than a mild attention, leading those speaking of it to see it as a blurred concept, without much systematic content. That a word so frequently employed might mean so many disparate, indeed almost contradictory, things has not pushed those who deal with it to search within it for a deeper unity, but rather to attribute instability and indeterminacy to the word itself.

How, then, could a word, whose resonances were primarily administrative and juridical, and that was intended for the proper management of the affairs of the real world, come to concern, without any sense of inconsistency or contradiction, the mystery of the Trinity, of the incarnation and redemption?

The answer to this question arose of itself at a moment of conceptual crisis—that is, at the time of the iconoclastic crisis. The question of the economy cannot be separated from the question of the image itself. "Whoever rejects the icon rejects the totality of the economy." This is the leitmotif of the texts that defend the legitimacy of the icon. Thinking about the subject of the icon does not in the least indicate a new meaning for a word that already possessed innumerable ones. On the contrary, it concerns the arrival on the scene of what unites all these meanings without modifying any of the previous ones at all. The term *economy* is therefore not the subject of a new and specific discourse during the iconoclastic crisis; rather, it supports the whole of the edifice of which the icon constitutes the final stakes, at once intellectually, spiritually, and politically. Indeed, it is at the moment of the crisis that the term finally acquires its systematicity. From this perspective, it is important to determine what was at stake theoretically in the polemic between the emperor and the patriarch as they attempted to impose their own conceptions of symbolic hegemony, and we will attempt to recreate the theoretical architecture of what might be called first the imaginal economy and then the iconic economy. This "economic" doctrine of the icon is a veritable plea for a new conception of the symbol. Something in the system of thought changes as a result of the political convulsion of iconoclasm. As Paul Lemerle said, "Whatever one's philosophical opinion about images and the cult of images, there was a moment when their defenders, even though they were far from aware of it, held in their hands the fate of the form of humanism that is still ours today."[4]

I would alter this claim in only one respect: the Byzantines were undoubtedly perfectly aware of what was happening, and it is rather we, subjects of the Christian West, who have over the centuries been unaware of what then hung in the balance regarding our future. We may be even less aware of it because the ecclesiastic authorities were busy hiding it, for it concerned ensuring the legitimacy of their temporal power. More generally as well, the wholly modern temptation to qualify as unconscious each collective phenomenon of symbolic reorganization may well end up hiding the conscious mode in which the protagonists of a revolution think about the change. The concept of economy is a good example because it would be completely untenable to maintain that so complex and subtle an elaboration could have troubled the ecclesiastical body without its knowing about it. On the contrary, the impression one receives is of a flawless structure in which whatever concerns the most obscure forces is taken into account and subjected to an enlightened management. Perhaps the church was more aware than we suppose of the fact that it had to administer the unconscious of its subjects. I have often been tempted to think that the resistance to philosophical consideration of the concept of economy concerns an unconscious refusal of modern subjects to recognize the common foundations of our thinking about the image and the institutions that govern us in an ecclesiastic manner.

Is it not significant that at each great convulsion of religious and political thought, the question of the legitimacy of the image was raised yet again? Thus, was it not the case that the iconoclastic crisis was not studied until very late, and only then specifically in the context of the Reformation, which involved a calling into question of pontifical power, and consequently a fight against the ecclesiastic iconocracy that supported that power? This limited and belated success due to doctrinal and political circumstances, however, had a distorting effect on the subject, in the sense that it was sometimes believed that Byzantine iconoclasm was itself inspired by a rationalist spirit open to biblical exegesis and the return to scriptural sources. It is certainly true that the iconoclasts invoked the biblical texts that prohibited the painted or carved image in the name of the battle against idolatry; nonetheless, their position was driven by a concern more political than spiritual, because from a doctrinal point of view, they considered themselves to be perfect Christians. Because they were trying to separate spiritual power from temporal power, they did not exploit the possible foundations for a doctrinal and political unity of the Christian state. It is only the notional edifice built on the term *economy* that allowed for the simultaneous administration and management of the law, of belief, and of the goods of this world. Only the image and the icon together could become its cornerstone.

In relation to iconoclast thought, the *damnatio memoriae* that befell the camp of the defeated limits us only to quotes of the second council of Nicaea,[5] when it became necessary to refute the theses of the iconoclast council of 754 and fragments transmitted by Nikephoros, who was himself also concerned with their refutation. These fragments, or *Questions*,[6] are the work of Emperor Constantine V, obviously a true thinker in relation to iconoclasm, who was also surrounded by thoroughly competent theologians. It is therefore only on the testimony of its adversaries that we can reconstitute the thought hostile to artificial images. This iconoclast thought can in turn be defined as a *noneconomic conception of the natural image.* It could also provisionally be said that once the doctrine of the icon, or artificial image, had decreed the economic distance separating the visible from ontology, iconoclast thought fought ferociously against it. Iconoclasm rejected precisely the systematic unity of the concept of the economy, and that is perhaps the reason for its failure.

The continual passage from pretext to reality, from conscious to unconscious, from explicit to implicit in the interpretation of the conflict allows us to assume that we are dealing with a crisis in which the relationships between each and every symbol and the real, the imaginary, the fictitious, the deceitful, and the true were all at stake. We are here in a universe of guile,[7] which should remind us of what the Islamic tradition knew and developed under the name of *hila*,[8] the traits of which are practically the same as those of the economy in its political and pedagogical sense. But it is also the Machiavellian guile that in turn takes us back to the political strategy of speech in its relation to actions. When the image is operative, it does something that speech does not. And speech about the image and the icon can only take oblique and twisted routes to explain itself. Because if speech could say everything that the image is able to do, it would substitute itself for the image and would be its superior by being its theory as well. It is precisely because the icon is endowed with a power specific to it that it mattered so much to the emperor to deprive the church of it, and to reserve for himself its exclusive rights and benefits; for iconoclast images do indeed exist, and it was by using them that the emperor intended to rule. The conceptual power of the economy makes the theoretical stakes and the profane objectives of conquest inseparable from each other. Nikephoros reminds us that the image is a Gospel and that there is a perfect equivalence between the scriptural message and the iconic message. Nonetheless, he never loses sight of the fact that teaching and persuading by means of the icon are superior to hearing as a result of the speed with which they operate, and their emotional effectiveness.

Who, then, was Nikephoros?[9] For the personality of the patriarch and the iconoclastic crisis in general, readers are referred to the preface that accompanies the translation of the *Antirrhetics*. The full bibliography concerning this period of the Byzantine empire can be found at the end of that work as well. Here we will merely summarize a few of the major characteristics relevant to the present study. Nikephoros was born in 758, during the reign of Constantine V, and received a lay education at the imperial court that destined him for the career of a civil servant. During the first iconoclastic crisis—that is, the one that preceded the second Nicene council in 787—Nikephoros's father fell victim to his loyalty to the holy images, lost his job, and died in exile. Nikephoros, still a youth, nevertheless pursued his studies at the imperial university and appeared bound for an administrative and political career at the Constantinopolitan court. He was interested in theology by curiosity and personal inclination, particularly when the political turbulence of Constantinople drove him to withdraw and isolate himself for some time far from the tumult of the capital. On several occasions, he seems to have been a man of prudence and negotiation, opposing himself to the intransigent attitude of the monks of Stoudios in the affair of the adulterous marriage of Constantine VI, son of Empress Irene. Economic thought, by which we should understand here a way of thinking about prudent adaptation to circumstances, prevailed for him over the demands of *akribeia*, which is to say, a rigorous and uncompromising faithfulness to canonical precepts. In other words, a sort of realist relativism that evaluated the cost of victory and the willingness to pay it prevailed for him over inflexible ideas that could only lead to failure. Nevertheless, the time would come when, engaged in a remorseless struggle that opposed him to the iconoclast Emperor Leo V, he would find the strength to resist, to the point of exile and death, in order to defend the cause of the icon. Was this a return to the strict doctrinal rigor that the church fathers called *akribeia*, in opposition to the accommodations inspired by the economy? Certainly not. Nikephoros always remained an unfailing champion of the economy. Was it, then, vengeful loyalty to the memory of his father, and a spiritual and philosophical conviction to defend a just and true cause? Without doubt, but it was certainly also a perfect evaluation of what was at stake and of the circumstances that provided an opportunity to fight in exile at a moment when the intransigence of the martyr would be most effective. It is possible to be perfectly "economic," by which we mean opportune and well thought out, by being a radical when the adversary weakens or when one senses that victory is approaching. The strictly historical nature of the concept of the economy allows us to understand the completely historic, that is, circumstantial, scope of the requirements even of universality and timelessness.

What makes Nikephoros's personality both modern and so fascinating is of two different orders. He is passionate, vehement, and partial, to the point of the most perfect bad faith. Using by turns the most subtle rhetoric and the most libelous insult, he nonetheless remains the only truly philosophical writer of this century of crisis. John of Damascus, in the previous century, and Theodore of Stoudios, who was his contemporary, also put their talent at the service of the icon, but their writings are strongly Christological, and their inspiration is essentially doctrinal. For them, the issue is one of defending the dogma of the incarnation and the unity of the church. The defense of the production of icons is always a spiritual obligation connected directly to the thought of the evangelists and church fathers. In Nikephoros, however, contemplation of the issue has an entirely different breadth: *it concerns the nature of all images and the impossibility of thinking and ruling without them.* As we will see, he draws up a portrait of his imperial adversary that is, *a contrario,* highly significant: its intention is to deprive the iconoclast emperor of all aptitude for thought and government. The stakes of the image are therefore not only of concern to Christological orthodoxy; they are political and philosophical, and of the first magnitude.

Who, in the end, will be master of the images? He who will be spiritually faithful to the natural image, he who will respect the natural image within the artificial image, or, finally, he who will continuously practice guile between faithfulness and unfaithfulness, in order to draw from that artifice all possible benefits? In all things it is God who sets the example, *and it is he whom one imitates.*

PART I

THE ECONOMY

1

Principal Themes

The term *economy* has either been regarded as a vague idea, without content, or it has been reduced to a sheer effect of rhetorical opportunism. "I do not believe," writes Gilbert Dagron, "that it is necessary to go beyond summary definitions and see in the economy a well constructed concept. Despite certain striking formulations, a fine rhetorical dressing, and some moral connotations, the notion remains blurred. Above all it is purely negative because it is satisfied to merely note and accept a definitive disjunction between ideal standards and a social space over which they henceforth have no hold." And he continues a little further on: "If the notion of economy had a positive content, we would have a real confrontation of ideas, a dialectic; but as the concept is empty, we only have two poles between which a sort of equilibrium is established."[1] To talk of an "empty concept" or a "negative concept," however, in relation to a term that in Christian texts refers both to the incarnation and Christ himself cannot but cause us some surprise. Moreover, to claim a definitive disjunction between the real and the ideal within the very concept that is responsible for linking them together with the minimum of contradiction by means of the imaginal and iconic system is once again to undo the effects of polysemy, as have all those who reject the linking of spiritual and temporal power in the stakes of the doctrinal debate of iconoclasm.

In what follows, I will endeavor to draw the economy out of this vagueness, but I would add that if the issue is one of rhetoric, the stakes are high for both word and thought. If talking economically consists in reducing every speech act to a manner of speaking, this is of the greatest importance, considering that it takes hold of the very content of thought, in accordance with the wording that it adopts in the manifestation of the truth. Could a theory of relativity be summarized by making every model a simple rhetorical choice? Yet the economy in Byzantium was exactly a pragmatic model that took into account the real historical situation of the person who was acting within that model, and by the same stroke led him to rearrange the truth itself in a different manner. Therefore, if rhetoric there is, it is not a pejorative consequence of a sophisticated use of discourse, but a model of mediation inseparable from the trajectory of the Word in the historical fulfillment of its Parousia. In the same way that God chose a manner of showing himself in order to make himself better understood, his servants, in imitation of him, will make instrumental, specifically focused choices of word and image in demonstrating the foundations and legitimacy of the cause they are defending. One must return to Aristotle's *Rhetoric* in order to understand the quasi-judicial usage that Nikephoros makes of signs, indices, and proofs in the reasoning and structuring of arguments. We are dealing here with a speech for the defense, perhaps even a special pleading, that aims as much at condemning the iconoclast as exonerating the iconophile from the formidable charge of idolatry.

The rhetorical conception of the iconophile economy relates to the ternary relation of the sacred, nature, and reason. It is a "manner of speaking" that is existentially tied to the living character of the word and its involvement in the very effectiveness of the things that it talks about, as well as the effects that it sets out to obtain. It is therefore a science of effects in the most radical sense of the term. But inasmuch as it is a concept that subsumes the manner in which truth emerges, it is rather the cause and condition of possibility of its manifestation for everyone. It is the science of the advocate convinced of the justice of the cause that he is defending and of the guilt of the adversary that he is attacking. It is therefore not the rhetorical science of the sophist, always ready to prove one thing and its opposite indifferently. Rhetoric is the use of persuasive speech, the driving force of which is not cynicism or doubt as to the existence of truth, but the taking into account of the listener and of the very possibility of communication on the moving ground of everyday reality. It is an adaptive, specifically focused *tekhné*, as every true *tekhné* is. The great novelty of the patristic economy is to have abandoned the word *rhetoric*, which for the church fathers designated nothing more than a species of an infinitely larger genus: the manifestation of truth in life. Rhetoric no longer reduces to modes of reasoning and tropes of speech: once it has become economy, it concerns the tropes of our relation with the Logos of God, who is its model. For the economy is first of all God's art for the convincing and saving of humankind. Because the economy is an art, and because it is not an art that is exempt from guile or that results from mimetic thought, whoever masters it invites us to imitate him. Rhetoric is a secondary effect of the economy, not the reverse.

In this respect, Aristotelian thought seems to have been invaded by the notions of similitude and resemblance. The orator who is mimetic of Christ conforms to the choices and behavior of his divine model in his own choice of proofs and argument. On the other hand, his enemy will be taken for a sophist even if he utilizes the same *tekhné*, because he is different to and separated from that model, and we will shortly witness a key example of this in terms of the description of the iconoclast emperor's body. This "manner of speaking" and describing prefigures exactly what will be revealed in our examination of the polysemy of the term *oikonomia*. The proof of the adversary's malice is drawn from his very body because it resembles—or we should rather say, it is in the image of—his own rejection of the image. The rhetoric that underpins this "description" of the indescribable partisan of the uncircumscribable is in keeping with the power of inscription of what he who writes and inscribes defends.

In the most learned translations, the word *economy* is rendered by different terms such as *incarnation, plan, design, administration, providence, responsibility, duties, compromise, lie*, or *guile*, as is relevant, without the reader being warned of the return of the same Greek word—*oikonomia*—in each case. Nevertheless, the translator signals his embarrassment in a note or explains the liberty that he has taken in keeping the word *economy* in quotation marks or italics, accompanying his initiative with a remark about the homonymy of a term deprived of any semantic continuity; some examples of this will be provided shortly. In the following section, therefore, we will attempt to uncover the organic unity of meanings whose apparent unrelatedness arises only by homonymic accident.

The term *oikonomia* is found in Paul, the "inventor" of the natural filial image, in order to talk about the plan of the incarnation.[2] After Paul, it was used almost uninterruptedly from the third century onward—that is, from the moment when patristic and conciliar thought first elaborated a truly Christian philosophy. At the time of the iconoclastic controversy, it became the leitmotif of iconic defense, setting in play an entire semantic ensemble, which it then proved necessary to provide with a conceptual unity, and which in turn brought it to its highest degree of theoretical development. The term recurs thirty-nine times in Nikephoros's *Antirrhetics* and is found commonly in the texts of John of Damascus and Theodore of Stoudios. It is also clearly invoked in the conciliar acts that defend the legitimacy of icons as well as in the iconoclastic *Horos*, which claims to be faithful to that same economy. There can be no shadow of a doubt that the concept of economy played a determining and structural role in the icon's defense, and its effects will be examined further on.

When the iconophiles utilize the word, therefore, they are already preceded by several centuries of common and familiar usage in patristic texts. In the Latin texts it is sometimes translated as *dispensatio* and sometimes as *dispositio*, which well confers upon it its distributive, organic, and functional sense. In the case of the trinitarian economy, Tertullian maintains the Greek term alongside the Latin words, as though to preserve the global nature of its implications that the Latin translation may have reduced.

Not only did the term not cease to be used by all the church fathers to refer both to the entirety of the incarnational plan and to divine providence, but its meaning also expanded considerably thanks to the crisis. It became the central nervous system of the iconophiles' arguments about the management of the relation of the sacred and profane, the visible and the invisible, the intangible truth at the heart of an undulating and relative reality, the relations between the visible and the legible, as well as between the rigor of the law and the adaptability of the rule. Owing to the economy it was possible to escape condemnation for transgression, because the spirit of the law was safe in its circumstantial and practical application. Without the economy there was no middle term between *akribeia* (*akribeïa*), which designated respect for the inflexible rigor of the law, and its transgression (*parabasis*). From human nature to miracle, from sin-commitment to the religious mysteries, it would be possible to make the journey without a break. The economy is the solution to inconsistency; it is the art of enlightened flexibility.

That the doctrine of the incarnation underlies the edifice of iconic thought there is not the least doubt for the church fathers, who clearly set it down as a principle. All of them state it repeatedly: *whoever rejects the icon rejects the economy*, that is, Christ himself and the totality of the incarnational plan in history. Yet no matter what they say, nothing could be less clear, because the iconoclasts who rejected the image also considered themselves to be true Christians, faithful to the evangelic message and Christology as a whole. There were always those who believed that one could perfectly well be Christian and reject the icon, but there was no one who claimed that one could rule without it. Thus the iconoclasts themselves never renounced its services to assist them in their reign; on the contrary, they wanted rather to monopolize it themselves and deprive the ecclesiastic powers of it, which they did by means of theological argument, strictly limiting the interpretation of the economy to Christology only.

Moreover, imperial iconography was abundant—in full bloom, even—during the crisis. At the very moment when the emperor was ordering the destruction of religious images, he was spreading his own portrait as well as the signs of his pomp, pleasures, and glories throughout the empire. Only the images of Christ, his mother, and the saints were forbidden and destroyed. Yet the iconoclasts lost the battle, and the explanation may be that they lacked the use and enlightened manipulation of the concept that gave victory to the other side, *oikonomia*, thanks to which even a break with the law could be interpreted as its fulfillment.

Several questions thus present themselves for our inquiry: how the doctrine of the incarnation and the icon are one and the same, an identity that the concept of *oikonomia* subsumes; and how the question of the appropriation of temporal power hinges on the interpretation of a concept that, officially speaking, should have had only a spiritual calling.

To answer these questions, it is necessary to examine the semantic organization of economic thought. The concept of the economy is an organicist, functionalist one that simultaneously concerns the flesh of the body, the flesh of speech, and the flesh of the image. Thanks to it, the church itself would be identified with the body of Christ, which must in turn be capable of being rendered visible in order for the terrestrial kingdom to constitute itself in the image of the celestial kingdom, whose providential manifestation it would incarnate here below.

In a Christian society there can be no political legitimacy without the constitution of a doctrine flawlessly linking doctrinal adherence to the institutional system that legitimates temporal power. Belief and obedience are the two sides of the same symbolic assembly that makes use of the equivalence between engendering belief and ruling. Today this appears to us to be if not trivial, then at least secularly achieved. Yet how was it possible for one specific system to set in place the philosophical conditions for this fact that is so obvious? It is a little like Euclidian geometry: it seems to respond to so natural a description of immediate experience that it took several centuries to discover and admit that it only derived its validity from the implicit acceptance of the premises that gave it its legitimacy, yet which also marked its conditions and limits. One passes unawares from "only believing in what one sees" to "only obeying what one believes in," that is to say, in accepting to have *relatively* lost from view whatever might become the object of knowledge or, even more, of doubt. The economy functions as a gnosis of the enigma. Without reference to the unity brought about by economic thought of the image in the patristic sense, the stakes of the iconoclastic crisis remain incomprehensible.

In the work of even a Byzantine author, with *oikonomia* being used in several senses by turns, only context allows us to discern the meaning to be chosen, or rather, to privilege. But one must never lose sight of the fact that for the Byzantine reader or listener, all the semantic levels resonated together in a sort of symphonic unity, and all related to the founding and unifying principle of the natural image of the Father in the person of the Son. This, however, does not contradict the juridical and administrative tradition that turned the same word into the concept covering all its functional, pedagogic, and political adaptations. For this reason, it is hoped that the present work will allow the conservation of the word *economy* in all circumstances, as we have done here in the texts cited. It is the only liberty taken regarding the translations, and that liberty has its reason within our purview.

The distensions possible between certain levels, as for example the fact that the term *oikonomia* may designate here trinitarian relations or the Person of Christ and there artifice, concession, or the piously purposeful lie oblige us to note the fact that we are dealing with a conceptual agent that founds a science of context, opportunity, and art, in a word, of the adaptation of the law to its manifestation or its application in living reality. Far from ratifying the disjunction of truth and reality, the economy would become the operator of their functional reconciliation.

The semantic tree generated by the term also shows an organic unity that is subsumed by a concept that counts among its significations the natural order of living organisms.

In Part I, we will examine a few of the fundamental references that will allow us to establish that the *oikonomia* is neither a disparate mosaic nor a fragmented term, but a type of intelligible edifice with coherent interweavings, or perhaps even a homogenous continent where the temporal power of the church is founded by the carnal, visceral, and providential economy of Christ, which leads us from the Word to the legitimacy of its icon, as well as to the strategic opportunity of guile or the lie. It is almost as though the long detour taken by New Testament scripture was only there to prove that God had a historical need for the Son, the Son for the church, and the church for temporal power, always and everywhere, in function of the same coherent and logical principle: the *oikonomia.*

2

A Semantic Study of the Term *Economy*

Before the Church Fathers

Oikonomia does not appear in Homer, Hesiod, Herodotos, or Thucydides, or in the lyric or tragic poets. The noun seems to appear for the first time in Xenophon, where it forms an object of inquiry, as it also does in Aristotle. In both, economic discourse is a logos that lends its epistemic status and purpose to a meditation on the administration and management of domestic life, specifically the philosophical and practical consideration of the management of private fortune, particularly in the rural domain. Very soon, however, the extensive applications raised by these issues become closely tied to the administration of goods and services in the public domain.

In the Classical authors, economic discourse is closely linked to a consideration of profit and utility. Consequently, the issue is not only one of rationalizing the operations relating to goods and people and defining an estate, but of optimizing expected benefits as well. This optimization can be thought of in quantitative terms (increase in wealth) or in qualitative terms (procurement of well-being or the approach of the sovereign good). Economic science thus comes to have something in common with philosophy.

Without entering fully into the details of Aristotle's *Economics*, let us highlight some of the relevant points found there, and which were undoubtedly familiar to patristic thought as well. Its traces will be encountered again on many subsequent occasions.

Aristotle attributes to economics the acquiring of a domestic life and its good functioning, without which, he says, there cannot be any social cohesion. Without this prior cohesion, there is no place for politics, and economics therefore comes before politics. In the second place, economics must conform to nature, not only in that it is based first on agriculture, but also inasmuch as nature has already distributed roles and duties within the species themselves. Implicit within the economy is the notion of an organic objective and functional harmony. There is therefore a providential and natural order to be respected while acting in the service of the greatest cohesion of utility and well-being.

To these thoughts, however, Aristotle also adds many examples taking into account the different strategies and diverse opportunistic schemes put in place by civil and military chiefs in order to increase their profits or, more trivially, to supply money when needed: "We have further made a collection of all the methods that we conceived to be worth mentioning, which men of former days have employed or cunningly devised in order to provide themselves with money."[1] The concept therefore concerns an ensemble of means implemented with an immediate material end in mind. All these dimensions of economic thought will be found again in the church fathers, although in unprecedented scope, because it is the whole of providential nature, the incarnational plan, and the strategic adoption of means to ends that will be subsumed by the selfsame concept.

In Hippocrates, economics is used as a pragmatic concept to discuss the arrangements to be made concerning the sick.[2] In Polybius, it refers to political administration and even the course of events, or the way in which they evolve, whereas in Dionysios of Halicarnassus, it concerns the manner in which a literary work is organized.[3] The noun occurs later than the verb *oikonomein*, which appears in Sophocles's *Electra*, used by Electra herself.[4] Mazon translates the line in question as "I am a servant at my father's palace," by which Electra means that she has been reduced to the servile activity of a steward at her father's palace. The task of the steward[5] is that of every servant charged with household administration, just as Aeschylus symbolically refers to anger as the steward of Agamemnon's palace.[6] This pejorative tone is even more clear in Plato, when Socrates describes to Phaedrus the mischievous and lethal way in which the affairs of love are run by he who does not love.[7] Thus in Greek, the semantic field is from the outset tied as much to material as to symbolic goods, to which the idea of service is added as well.

Generally speaking, then, the Classical *oikonomia* implies the functional organization of an order that has profit in mind, whether material or not. The model of this order is natural, but the good management of this economy in society requires the analysis of situations and human intervention in order to serve the goals at hand in the best way possible.

Also related to the economy are issues regarding the natural law, where questions arise concerning the relationship of an absolute legislative model to the application and efficiency of the law and justice. This juridical signification of the *oikonomia*, however, cannot be seen in isolation: whatever the domain concerned, it always returns to a reflection on the law, its interpretation, and legitimacy. Making justice reign amidst humanity cannot be achieved by the pure and simple application of a transcendent law. An adaptive concept is needed that is charged with ensuring that the law is respected, while taking into account the particularity of every case and of what will conform best both to the law and the interests of life in all its senses. The economy always supposes the consideration of ends, without thereby becoming a sophistic or cynical concept that is preoccupied only with results in full disregard of the foundations of justice and the law. The economy is a science of relations and relative terms, but in no sense is it a relativist concept. It is a notion that simultaneously renders a service and takes account of the very idea of service. Its "servile" resonance will be encountered again, even in the economic interpretation of the incarnation, where he who gives himself to save us takes the "form of a slave."

Patristic Polysemy

The economy in question here is an infinitely sacred one that, following the incarnation, had come to be inscribed in opposition to theology. This opposition had served as the foundation for two systems: the trinitarian economy and the Christological economy. Resulting from the theorization of relations that are specifically purposive in nature, the economy made possible the formulation of both divine unity and divine plurality. It naturally became the principle of all unitary relations within a plurality of parts or functions. It is for this reason that Hippolytus and Tertullian had recourse to the economy to account for trinitarian relations as considered with respect to history. In this respect, there is a temporality involved that concerns the historic, immanent manifestation of the eternal, divine, and transcendent model. All further occurrences of relations of any sort will be derived from this manner of thinking about the relation of God to history.

Since the trinitarian economy had introduced both the Person of the Son and his imaginal and historic nature, it comes as no surprise to see the incarnate Son conceived as an "economy of the Father." Yet this usage of the economy, which is not at all obvious, is nevertheless the one that posed the fewest problems to Christian commentators and translators, for whom the word thus retained its religious and sacred specificity.

From Paul onward, the economy designated not only the Second Person of the Trinity, but the whole of the redemptive plan, from the conception of the Virgin to the resurrection, including Christ's evangelical life and the passion. The notion of a divine plan with the aim of administering and managing fallen creation, and thus of saving it, makes the economy interdependent with the whole of creation from the beginning of time. Because of this, the economy is as much Nature as Providence. The divine economy watches over the harmonious conservation of the world and the preservation of all its parts as it runs in a well-adjusted, purposive manner. The incarnational economy is nothing other than the spreading out of the Father's image in its historic manifestation, which is made possible by the economy of the maternal body. That passage establishes the entry of the visible and the flesh into the concept of economy. In all cases, it concerns an organism or an internal arrangement whose visibility becomes accessible to us. Yet the powerful bond that holds the economy and visible appearance together must not make people believe that they are dealing with the simple and intelligible visibility of reality; the economy is everything except a naive idea. Rather, whatever is mysterious in the Trinity and the designs of providence will have the status of an enigma within the domain of the visible.

If God reveals his salvational plan and intends it to be effective, its economy will make use of all the means familiar to a father in order to bring his wayward son back to him, all the subterfuges of the doctor to heal the patient despite himself, all the seductions dear to the teacher who must make the most difficult knowledge loved. Speech, remedy, guile, condescension, punishment, or lie . . . all the means of the economy are good when one uses them with economy, that is to say, while remaining loyal to the spirit of the divine, providential economy.

Because it encompasses the strategy and tactics necessary for the management of a real, historic situation in their totality, the economy always returns to its classic vocation: to be the concept of the management and administration of temporal realities, whether they be spiritual, intellectual, or material. Such will be the path that will lead us to the image and the icon, intrinsically bound to the economy, and with which they in turn share sacredness, naturalness, and the full range of pragmatic goals.

The consequence of this economic access to the visible leads to a management of the totality of the visible under the sign of the economy. It is no doubt this reason that made the *oikonomia* such an important concept in the debate on the image during the iconoclast crisis. The virgin pregnancy and birth of the living image of the Father gathers together all the aspects of economic thought. From there, there is but one last step to take: someone who identifies the maternal body with the body of the church, an identification for which the icon is the structural relay, because it makes possible a formal treatment of the flesh in a relation of relative similitude, which eucharistic consubstantiality would not.

Theology and Economy

The point here, my dear, is not theology, on the subject of which there can be no question of effigy or thought of similitude, but the economy, thanks to which the prototype and its derivation can be seen; again you must admit that the Word has taken on a flesh similar to ours.[8]

By theology, Theodore of Stoudios means here the discourse of tradition as it weighs over history and as it deals with divine substance and the legitimacy of the names by which that divine substance is known. Theological discourse, whether it be cataphatic or apophatic, always meets up with the end wall of what escapes every word and all comprehension, even if this is in a sparkling powerlessness that will only dispense the grace of silence and light beyond all gnosis. The axis of theology, dear to the iconoclasts, finds its strongest formulation in Pseudo-Dionysios: "Since the way of negation appears to be more suitable to the realm of the divine and since positive affirmations are always unfitting to the hiddenness of the inexpressible, a manifestation through dissimilar shapes is more correctly to be applied to the invisible."[9] This end wall of theology is precisely what the philosophic, iconic, and discursive solution of the economy tries to respond to. Its opposition to theology underlies the foundation of the modernity of iconic thought and allows an approach to it in terms other than those of a single doctrine and religion. It is a thinking in symbolic terms.

The God of the economy distributes himself out, exerts himself, makes himself known. Once he has become visible, he declares himself with a face—*prosôpon*, the term by which the Persons of the Holy Trinity are designated. This is the hypostatic economy of divinity. In connection with the always sought and always impossible meeting between God and humans that characterizes the Old Testament, this is the opening of the historical field: a face-to-face meeting, an exchange of looks henceforth possible, and qualified as enigmatic.

Strangely, therefore, the question of the trinitarian economy, while being situated interior to theology in the general sense of the term, finds itself sensu stricto opposed to theology. The discourse of divine substance, of its eternal, transcendent essence that surpasses all comprehension and escapes all visibility, can only be hostile to all possibilities of portrayal and even to each of the historic figures of the redemption. The economy's role will consist in finding a way to introduce the figure and history into theological thought. This is why the church fathers continuously remind their heretical adversaries (Arians, Montanists, Sabellians . . .) each time that it proves necessary that it is important to distinguish the discourse that speaks according to theology from the one that is situated within the economy. This reminder will be fundamental during the iconoclastic crisis, because each combatant will accuse his adversary of not having respected this distinction. However, the introduction of trinitarian thought overcomes this distinction nicely. "For who will not say that there is only one God? For all that, he still does not deny the economy."[10] Hippolytos, who inaugurates (so to speak) the first systematization of divine triplehood, thus reminds Noetos that according to the economy, there are not three gods.

This double functionality of the concept is striking: it states what the mystery is and simultaneously introduces what that mystery offers in terms of figurative potentiality. For all that, however, there is still no question of the image constituting the definite flesh of the incarnational economy, yet one still senses that the ground is slowly being prepared. This suggests that the use of the concept of the economy will become most widespread during the debate over the image. In effect, it is in opposition to the rupture that separates us from the transcendence of divinity in theology that the economy will establish the conditions of possibility of a discourse concerning God and a certain kind of knowledge of the creator by humankind. Consequently, it would become possible for trinitarian discourse to be made more open, at just the time when the shock caused by the development of heresies made the explanation of what should have remained a mystery inevitable.

The defense of the trinitarian economy and its definition is closely linked to the debate that brought the church fathers into conflict with the Arian heresy. The "pneumatomachs," or adversaries of the Holy Spirit, had made dangerous doctrinal decisions concerning consubstantiality and triune unity. Because the economy was the very concept of relations within the divine, providential management of the visible world, it also became necessary to entrust it with the formulation of the relations that coordinate between themselves the three Persons of the Father, the Son, and the Holy Ghost.

Yet the mystery of divinity must remain whole, and it is worth repeating that it is impious to scrutinize it and to ask too many questions. That is the sin of "indiscreet and curious thought" of which John Chrysostom speaks so magnificently in his tract *On the Providence of God.*[11] Despite this recommendation, however, which is appropriate for all mysteries, the church fathers had difficulty in foregoing all argumentation, and it is there that their speculations reached their most fertile heights for the future of iconicity. As St. Augustine wrote in *The Trinity*: "This wisdom, then, which is God, how do we understand it to be a Trinity? I did not say 'how do we believe?' for this ought not to be questioned among the faithful; but if there is any way by which we can see by our understanding what we believe, what would this manner of seeing be?"[12] This is the question, stated absolutely clearly, to which the economy would have to respond.

The difference between theology and economy is the difference between believing without seeing and believing while seeing. To talk about the Trinity would only be possible using the economy of speech, which is to say, in the mastery of the remove that will always separate the speaker from the essence of his object—he will only ever be able to reach it relatively. The economy is therefore involved in a sort of semantic doublet. In effect, it will be both the science of the internal structure of its object, that is, the science of the relations between the Persons of the Trinity themselves (understanding and seeing), and the science of the doctrinal statement of those relations (speaking).

The Trinitarian Economy

In order to understand the trinitarian doctrine of relations as one upon which the doctrine of the image and the icon would come to be structured, let us now turn to a few significant textual examples. The first is from Hippolytos in his treatise against Noetos. Starting, as do all the church fathers, from the usage that Paul makes of the term *economy*,[13] Hippolytos understands by it the mystery of the divine plan from creation to redemption. This is also the most common meaning that it has in Ireneaus, where one finds it in both the singular and the plural to designate all the manifestations of divine activity. What is new in Hippolytos, however, is his effort to take into account the structure of the divine substance itself through its manifestations, and we find this in Tertullian as well.

It should be noted, however, that in using the term *structure* here, we risk pushing the economy toward an organicist or functionalist interpretation of divine substance; nevertheless, this is a risk that must be taken, because it is also necessary for us to investigate the form and foundation of the discourse that concerns the maintenance of unity in triplicity—how can the distinction between the Persons of the Trinity be formulated? "But if he desire to learn how it is shown still that there is one God, let him know that his power is One. As far as regards the power, therefore, God is one. But as far as regards the economy there is a threefold manifestation."[14] *Manifestation* here is the translation of *epideixis.* The economy thus determines a field proper to speech and to showing. This field does not put an end to the mystery of what determines it; it gives word and visibility access to it. If the concept of economy has anything to do with dialectic, it is therefore in an entirely Platonic sense. It does not produce reality by the productive resolution of oppositions; rather, it organizes the modalities of a line of reasoning in which the term is included in the definition of that very line of reasoning.

For Hippolytos, the economy really is the ensemble of the divine plan insofar as it reveals the triple organization of its substance. It is neither confusion of Persons nor division of divine unity; one is the will, and triple the action that shows it. Yet what becomes of the economy after Hippolytos, with Tertullian? Tertullian writes in Latin, and the concept of the economy appears there as *dispensatio.* J. Moingt[15] subtly analyzes Tertullian's use of the terms *dispositio* and *dispensatio* in order to show that the interpretation of the trinitarian economy should not be taken to a substantialist extreme, which he reproaches G. L. Prestige for doing.[16] By *dispositio*, we should understand the functional, triple arrangement of divine substance; disposition therefore still forms part of monarchical theology. *Dispensatio*, or economy, on the other hand, implies the fulfillment and historical unveiling of the divine plan. "To whom . . . does it belong to recapitulate all things in Christ, both which are in heaven and earth, but to him whose are all things from their beginning, including the beginning itself too; from whom issue the times and the dispensation of the fulness of times, according to which all things up to the very first are gathered up in Christ?"[17]

This temporal unfolding of God's design, through which his substance is distributed and revealed and that saves us, is the economy. Without Trinity, nothing is revealed. "We, however, as we indeed have always done (and more especially since we have been better instructed by the Paraclete, who leads men indeed into all truth), believe that there is only one God, but under the following dispensation, or *economia*, as it is called."[18]

Tertullian therefore needs the two notions of *dispositio* and *dispensatio* to account for triple unity. *Dispositio* is the internal organization considered according to its formal distinctions. *Dispensatio* is the historic organization of salvific actions. The divinity that exteriorizes its providential plan in the triple operation of the Persons of the Trinity is said to do so according to the economy.

Tertullian keeps the term *economy* transliterated from the Greek next to its synonym—*dispensatio*—in order to designate God's will to make manifest the plurality of his names, a plurality that is in him for all eternity but that becomes a manifest form starting at the incarnation. Moingt concludes in an elegantly metaphorical way: "The economy is what emerges from God's secret room [*sacramentum*] in order to take form in history. As well as being his plan, the economy is therefore also all those who execute it, and consequently also the plurality that was hidden in him and that is made manifest by the missions of the Son and the Spirit, when the secret will of the economy 'organizes unity into trinity,' as its implementation begins."[19] The economy presupposes the *dispositio* to be an immanent procession of the Persons of the Trinity, but distinguishes between them by the designation of their historical appearance.

Here, however, Moingt encounters a difficulty that he does not resolve and that leads him into contradiction. Refusing to give any philosophical status to the economy, in order to accord it only to *dispositio*, he maintains that it is synonymous with historical organization (*dispensatio*) and that the mystery of the economy "does not refer to the mystery of the divine being distributing himself in the plurality of Persons of the Trinity, neither in eternity nor in time." Yet he finally asserts that the economy "is above all else what is signified *in nominibus*," which is to say, "God's secret will to dispense salvation and administer his power by his Word and his Spirit, according to the economy that he gave notice of in the Scriptures."[20] Perhaps, rather than being a contradiction, however, this concerns a difficulty in delimiting the historical organization of the missions within the will to appear, without this forming a foundational unity of the Persons of the Trinity. The issue of the natural invisible image and the visible image has not yet formed the nucleus of economic thought, however. Trinitarian thought will only clarify itself when the economy subsumes the properly imaginal character of the Person of the Son and his redemptive iconicity. Once similitude has then become the substantial figure of the Second Person of the Trinity, the Holy Ghost will become the source of the incarnational operation by which the image of the Father will emerge from invisibility, thus opening the iconic field of history to the natural image.

An entirely new level is reached in St. Augustine's *The Trinity*, which comprises a long meditation on the image. From book 8 on, Augustine poses not the theological question of the revealed organization of divine substance, but one about the specific relation that man, made in the image of God, has with the trinitarian nature of his creator. The Trinity, therefore, is in man. Augustine looks for the images of the Trinity proper to man that will permit him to participate directly in the mystery of God.

> For God said: "Let us make man in our image and likeness," and a little later it was said: "And God made man in the image of God." It would certainly be incorrect to say "our," because it is a plural number, if man were made in the image of one Person, whether of the Father, or the Son, or the Holy Spirit; but because he was made to the image of the Trinity it was, therefore, said: "in our image." But again, in order that we might not think that we are to believe in three gods in the Trinity, since the same Trinity is the one God, it was said: "And God made man in the image of God."[21]

The term *economy* does not appear here, but what is interesting is the way in which the relationship of similitude is so intimately linked to trinitarian thought, which in turn will lead to the magnificent meditation on the Pauline formula in the first Epistle to the Corinthians: "For now we see in a mirror, in an enigma, but then we will see face to face."[22]

Further along, Augustine cites the second Epistle: "And all of us, with unveiled faces, seeing the glory of the Lord as though reflected in a mirror, are being transformed into the same image from one degree of glory to another, for this comes from the Lord, the Spirit."[23] He comments on this in the following way: "He uses the word 'beholding,' that is, beholding through a mirror, not looking from a watch-tower. . . . 'are being transformed,' that is, changed from one form into another, and we pass from an obscure form to a bright form. Because the obscure form is yet the image of God; and if the image, then certainly also the glory."[24]

However, to explain the term *enigma*, he returns to rhetorical tropes and concludes that Paul meant by this a sort of obscure similitude: *quamvis similitudinem tamen obscuram et ad perspiciendum difficilem.* He continues: "For the word enigma would not be used here if this seeing were something easy. And this is a greater enigma, that we do not see what we cannot not see."[25]

This enigmatic formula that attempts to deliver up to us the "great enigma" of the image accounts fully for what will constitute the essence of the economy and its theoretical difficulty. It is a vertiginous trope of spirituality that links the science of God with the science that humanity should have of itself. Once the temptations of sacrilegious curiosity have passed, the divine economy allows itself to be approached by a discourse about discourse that is itself transformed by announcing that the highest summit of the science of man is the science of the image that he carries within himself and that he can contemplate as an enigma of divinity. Of course, this does not concern the artificial image, but one can clearly see the effectiveness of the concept of relations that governs the trinitarian economy. Thanks to that concept, the inevitably apophatic character of theology arrives at the possibility of relative modes of speaking, in a linkage of the relations of the Persons of the Trinity with the image of that Trinity in man. *The science of the image is the science of humanity*; this is what will make the debate about the science of the icon so important. It will be the science of thought itself. And iconic doctrine will also be given a trinitarian foundation, under the three headings of homonymy, mimesis, and the line, which refer, respectively, to the Holy Ghost, the Son, and the Father.

In order for the visible to be transfigured, it is necessary to discover the term that will effect the transition from the gaze carried by our bodily eyes to the gaze of the spirit. One approaches an understanding of divinity by means of a doctrine of an obscure similitude, which progressively becomes enigmatic; this is exactly what the iconophiles will call a relative similitude (*katà skhésin*). Thought about relations will take over from thought about obscurity, just as the icon will take over from speech: what rhetoric only says obscurely the icon will make manifest silently, by means of formal resemblance (*homoïosis*).

Another fundamental account comes to us from Basil of Caesarea. In order to refute the heretics who made of the Holy Spirit a being inferior to the Father and the Son and different to them in nature, Basil replies:

If then in baptism the separation of the Spirit from the Father and the Son is perilous to the baptizer and of no advantage to the baptized, how can the rending asunder of the Spirit from Father and from Son be safe for us? . . . As we believe in the Father and the Son and the Holy Ghost, so are we also baptized in the name of the Father and of the Son, and of the Holy Ghost.[26]

This coordination of the three Persons of the Trinity refers to the usage that Athanasios makes of the verb *suntassein* in the third letter to Serapion: "If the Spirit were a being, [God] would not have set it in a specific order in relation to the Father."[27] Basil insists therefore on defining the relation of "community and continuity" between the Persons of the Trinity. He uses a synonym for *skhésis* (relation), *oikéïôsis*, as it refers to the relations of intimacy between the Persons:

As there is one Father and one Son, so is there one Holy Ghost.

And it is not only from there that proofs of its community of nature arise, but also from the fact that one says it of God. Not in the manner in which all things come from God, but in the sense of proceeding out of God . . . like breath from his mouth. But in no way is the mouth a member, nor the Spirit breath that is dissolved.[28]

In Basil, trinitarian doctrine does not have imaginal power comparable to Augustine's, but there is a close linkage between the breath of the Spirit and the incarnation, which brings to mind again Athanasios's third letter to Serapion: "This unction, in effect, is the breath of the Son, so that whoever possesses the Spirit might say: 'We are the fragrance of Christ.'"[29] In fact, all fourteen occurrences of the word *economy* in *On the Holy Spirit* deal with Christ's providential and redemptive plan of the incarnation, except when the issue involves the responsibility for souls. "All those who have been entrusted with the economy of souls provide witnesses . . . so as to produce them at some future day."[30] However, reference to the imaginal economy is found in a passage that precedes the one cited above, which concerns the consubstantiality of the Father and the Son. He then passes to the Trinity on the basis of the theme of intimate unity. This is a famous passage that will endlessly be included in iconophile anthologies:

How, therefore, if they are one and one, are there not two gods? Because we speak of a king, and of the king's image, and not of two kings. . . . In the same way that the sovereignty and power over us is one, so the glory that we render to it is not plural but one; because the honor rendered to the image passes on to the prototype. What the image is there by imitation, the Son is here by nature. And in the same way that in works of art resemblance is dependent on the form, so for divine nature, which is single, it is in the community of the deity that the principle of unity resides.

One also is the Holy Spirit . . . [31]

It is of great importance here that the "in the same way . . . so" that intervenes between the hypostatic image and the artificial image follows the homonymic remark concerning the king and the image of the king. This argument will be widely featured in iconophile anthologies in support of the "ascent" of the image to the prototype. The community of name (*koinonia*) will be supported by the economic relation (*skhésis*) that links the word, the thing signified, and the image. The image creates a bond that is neither natural nor artificial between the signifier and the signified. This bond is economic, that is, of a relative similitude.

When one worships one God of God, one confesses to the proper character of the hypostases and one remains faithful to the model of divine monarchy, without therefore scattering the mystery of God in several pieces. Because in God the Father and in God the only begotten one contemplates only, so to speak, a single form reflected in the mirror at no remove from the deity.[32]

Consequently, the trinitarian economy is both the principle of the organization of the three Persons interior to an indivisible unity, and an essential equality where the economy is the historical manifestation of the deity; but it is also the possibility of the power to express it and tell of it. Thus the discourse on the relations of the Persons of the Trinity inaugurates the discourse on the similitude between divinity and humanity, which, being in the image of what it speaks about, can for that reason, and under certain spiritual conditions, produce in turn an image "as a mirror" and "as an enigma." Let us not forget that it is in the writings of Paul that the term *economy* appears to designate the plan of God for the salvation of humanity, and that it is also in Paul that we find the foundational principles of the imaginal doctrine that will itself nourish thinking about the prototype.

The Christological Economy

The Christological economy finds its rightful place in a line proceeding directly from the trinitarian economy. In order to explore this, let us now turn to the *Two Christological Dialogues* of Cyril on the incarnation and on the unity of the Second Person of the Trinity. In the first dialogue, the term *economy* recurs nine times, and it is made clear that the christic economy cannot be separated from the virginal womb that bore it and to which it owes its visibility.[33]

Concerning the generation of the Emmanuel by the Virgin, they laugh loudly, those wretched ones, they criticize that economy, so wonderful, so worthy of God, for being dishonest. (679b)

This childbirth by a virgin and this manifestation [*phanérôsis*] in the flesh, how could it not be a futile effort, how could it not be madness and rambling talk, to describe it as mere appearance [*dokéseôs*], this economy that is so divine, so consistent and so evident? (681b)

As for maintaining . . . that the Word born of God scorned childbirth by the Holy Virgin . . . this is done by people who blaspheme the economy and who give themselves permission to criticize divine plans [*skémmasin*]. (682d)

The Only-begotten became like us, that is to say, a man in full, in order to rid our terrestrial body of the corruption that had entered it, by condescending to a life governed by the same laws, owing to the economy of union. (691c)

The mystery of the economy was harmoniously fulfilled in two ways: the Word made use of its flesh, on the one hand, as an instrument [*organon*] in relation to the workings of the flesh, physical weaknesses, and in everything that was not blameworthy; of its soul, on the other hand, for all the perturbations proper to humans for which they are not guilty. (692b–c)

Will we expel the Word born of God . . . from exact similitude with the Father . . . because of the humbled situation that his economy created for him? I will only say that it is dangerous and mistaken to cut in two and separate the man and the Word; the economy does not allow it. . . . For it is the Word born of God, united to humanity by an ineffable union in relation to the economy, that one understands by Christ. (698a–c)

Thus when the only Son, co-eternal with the Father and prior to all the ages of the world, when he was born of a woman and was established as Son . . . then he who was his Father by nature chose him a name, using, if I may say so, his paternal rights. You will make us very happy if you have perfectly understood the mode [*tropon*] of this economy. (699e–700a)

He indeed absolves of sin he who attaches himself to him, then annoints him with his spirit, the spirit that he sends in person and in its capacity as the Word of God the Father, and that he makes well-up in us, of its own nature, but [also] placing it together with the economy of the flesh, owing to its union with it. (706d)

The economy thus cannot be separated from the virgin gestation of the human flesh of the Word. The carnal economy of Christ's birth is the manifestation of the being who needed an instrument. This instrument relates to the redemption and cannot itself be conceived outside of similitude. The Virgin's flesh brought God's imaginal manifestation into the world, his perfect resemblance, with no discrepancies. The Virgin gives birth to the image, and the Father gives it its name. All these aspects of the incarnational economy will be found in full again in the iconic economy.

The economy is the assumption of the totality of human specifications except for that of sin. The true (not ghostly or illusory) visibility of the Son is part of the enigma of that economy, which is thus once again presented as the best response to the objections of Docetism.

The incarnation is economic in two ways: the first is kenosis, or the assumption of the form of a slave as an empty shape; the second is visible manifestation. Both are essentially mimetic.

To these initial points, we can add those that arise from a second series of quotations taken from a work dedicated to the unity of Christ. Cyril's economic battle is crucial for the icon's subsequent fate because it wrestles with heresies that divide or confuse the two natures of hypostatic unity: several centuries later, it would again become necessary to refute by means of the iconic economy those who would accuse the icon of dividing and confusing those two natures. Here are several passages from the second *Christological Dialogue*:

The ingenious economy in the flesh of the Only-begotten: they decree that it was of no use for the inhabitants of the earth. (721d)

If, therefore, instead of properly examining the idea of economy in the flesh, we were to look to the Word, the only Son of God, no longer engaged in the limits of his annihilation . . . (727d)

For everything that is human has also been made his. Therefore, to say that he took the form of a slave expresses in its entirety the mystery of the economy in the flesh. (734d)

For he no more ceased to be God any longer in becoming man than he refused the economy out of contempt for the limits of annihilation [*kenôseôs*]. (735c)

Why do they refuse him what would make him be considered to be annihilated? It is to reduce to nothing, in as foolish a way as possible, the ingenuity [*eutekhnès*] of his economy in the flesh. (753a)

We say that owing to an appropriation [*oikeiôsin oikonomikèn*] conforming to the economy, everything that is human is his, and, along with the flesh, everything that belongs to the flesh. (761a)

He has made a gift of his economy of incarnation to the whole world. (777b)

These few extracts allow us to round out the preceding discussion of the economy by bringing kenosis, or annihilation, into a closer connection with the "instrumental" nature of the incarnation. The term *organon* (instrument) had already been used frequently by Athanasios in his treatise *On the Incarnation* to refer to Christ's body, as in the following passage: "For being himself mighty and, and Artificer of everything, he prepares the body in the Virgin as a temple unto himself, and makes it his very own as an instrument [*organon*], in it manifested and in it dwelling."[34]

Athanasios, however, does not use the term *economy* and only refers to the body by the term *instrument.* In Cyril, on the other hand, it is the whole economy as a modality of the union of the Word and the flesh in its humiliated and perceivable manifestation that is subsumed by economic instrumentality. He even adds a touch of the ingenuity that prepares the way for all subsequent instrumental uses of the economy, and that will carry great weight in the defense of the practical and politically effective uses of the icon. Despite all this, however, the economic use of the term *instrument* should not lead to an instrumentalist heresy that would reduce Christ's body to a simple medium. The organon here cannot be separated from the salvational end that transfigures and saves the instrument in the resurrection of the flesh. As in the case of Docetism, one must always be on guard against any reductive interpretation when the flesh and the body are concerned.

The designation of Christ by the term *economy* covers the totality of the plan of salvation as Paul formulated it in the Epistle to the Ephesians, and it is used by Irenaeus in this way as well, in both the singular and the plural. This makes its rendering in italics or parentheses by the most experienced translators all the more surprising, as though the term's Aristotelian background or political fate makes its use without oratorical or scriptural precautions embarrassing. However, it is exactly on the economic interpretation of Christology that the whole philosophical, juridical, and political fate of the concept depended. For the majority of the most distinguished scholars in the patristic field, a not always conscious adherence to religious forms of thought has made them fear undermining divinity by using the concept of economy too freely. Yet the term is the very means by which something living and human comes to be spoken in Christian thought, even in its failings. How can the story of Christ's temptations be understood without recourse to the economy? Is it not more compelling to link them to an existential meditation on the question of the relation of evil to the image than to see them merely as a moment of edification? The church fathers were doubtless more courageous and realistic than our modern interpreters because they felt no shame, no contradiction or inconsistency in the polysemy of its uses and the diversity of its consequences.

Christ is therefore economy par excellence, in all senses of the term: he intrinsically forms a part of the arrangement of the Trinity, he made manifest the union of the Word and the flesh, and he condescended to annihilation and became the instrument of the Father in the plan of salvation. He is image, relation, and organ. And he is these things naturally, which is to say that he is by nature what his icon will be by technique and convention. Whatever is by nature and essence, is so *absolutely*; whatever is by artifice and convention, is so *relatively*. The economy, however, will take on two orders of similitude: natural, absolute similitude, and relative similitude, or formal resemblance. It takes on these two orders because it is an organ, the agent that relates them to each other. By means of Christology, the economy becomes the dominant concept of every possible kind of thought concerning similitude; by means of trinitarian doctrine, it remains faithful to thought concerning the organization and management of divine operations throughout the world and history. Alternatively stated, the economy only exists because there is an organization, administration, and management of the visibility of which the incarnation is the prototype, and from which the organization, administration, and management of all visibilities derive, as though from their model. In this context, however, it is important to recall once again that the visibility of the revelation is not in any way synonymous with an enlightenment that will put an end to mystery. We are dealing, rather, with its fulfillment, which is always and everywhere enigmatic and specular. Such is the economy that opens to us at present the double field of nature (body and cosmos) and symbolic operations (speech, jurisdiction, and strategy).

*Economy as Providence (*pronoïa*)*

In order to trace the development of the concept further, it is necessary to link the Christological economy to its corollary, the providential plan of God, which concerns the whole universe, and within that universe, the history of humanity. Only then does the passage from providence to nature appear clearly.

As in Aristotelian thought, the church fathers believed that the principles of organization, management, and administration should be drawn from a natural model, which is in this instance a divine model. This is because God is the *oikonomos*, the supreme administrator and manager, and the ensemble of his creation in the universe is *oikonomia.* However, because the concept of providence clashes with the existence of evil and suffering in the world, the *oikonomia* was split in two according to whether it was God's will and its effect that was being considered, or the free will of humans. John Chrysostom's work *On Providence* clearly shows this double meaning of the term as it relates either to the cosmological manifestation of the creator or to the granting of liberty to humans. The economy would thus have to find a solution linking universal providence to human liberty. For John, great orator that he was, this is first of all an occasion to display his eloquence before the beauty and complexity of the world:

This is why, when the whole of creation came into existence and received its own beauty, when that completely harmonious, extraordinary work, which strikes one with such great astonishment, was exposed to sight, . . . the lawgiver restrained any impudent words, saying: "God saw all the things that he made, and saw that they were perfectly good . . . there was not only light but shadow, not only fruit but thorns, not only cultivated trees but wild trees, not only level plains but mountains, valleys and chasms, not only humans but even venomous reptiles."[35]

Chapter 7 of the work is a long descriptive poem on the beauties of the world and nature, particularly in the long passage that sings the glory of the creator. It ends in the following way:

By the life and labor that fell to our share, by the food and drink that have been given to us, by the customs and arts, by the stone, by the mountain that harbors the metals, by the navigable sea, by the one that is unnavigable, by the islands and ports, . . . by sickness and health, by our limbs, by the constitution of our soul. . . . [There follows an evocation of the earth, the sky, and the depths of the oceans.] And all of this, man, for you! The arts for you, customs, cities, small towns; sleep for you and death for you.[36]

Thus, it is only if God's economies encompass everything that the incarnational economy will redeem the whole universe. If this economy disappears, everything disappears. Nikephoros will later take up this theme in relation to the image, and it will prove impossible to understand without reference to the cosmic implication of the economic plan of providence. Economic thought ensures the cohesion of the divine plan for the whole of the universe from its beginning until the end of time. Yet it is evident as well that this ineffable cohesion is not content to record only preestablished harmony; it also encompasses suffering, evil, and death because it assumes our liberty as well. There is no economy without the *spectacle of the world*, with all its complexity and contradictions. The economy is not in place to resolve apparent contradictions but to keep the route open between the visible spectacle and the spectacle of mystery, which, once again, will make of that creation an enigmatic mirror of its creator.

After having seen a great ocean opening up, and after having wanted to explore the abyss of this providence, gripped by a sort of vertigo when faced with the impossibility of explaining his economy, struck with admiration and astonishment before the ineffable, the infinite, the unutterable, and the incomprehensible [nature] of God's wisdom, he drew back, having allowed these words to escape, under the blow of astonishment: "O the depth of the riches and wisdom and knowledge of God!"[37]

Then, showing that he really has seen its depths, but was not able to measure them, he adds:

How unsearchable are his judgements and inscrutable his ways . . . so much so that not only is it impossible to reach their end, but the origin of their economies [*oikonomôn*] cannot even be discovered.[38]

The chosen vessel [Paul], having come to speak of the economy of God and making allusion to all the secrets that he learned, in the way in which he knew them, expressed himself in these terms: "I speak God's hidden wisdom, his secret purpose framed from the very beginning to bring us to our destined glory."[39]

What is more beautiful in your opinion than the sun? And yet, that luminous, sweet star, night to ill eyes, chars the earth by darting its burning rays, causes fevers, often dries out the harvest making it unusable, makes the trees sterile and transforms part of the earth into an area that we cannot inhabit. . . . But by leaving aside such reasonings and the troubles that they cause, we attach ourselves to that rock that is the word we have quoted: "And God saw all the things that he made, and saw that they were perfectly good . . . " Therefore do not say: "Why this? For what purpose is this?" But when the economies [*oikonomôn*] and creations of God are concerned, that silence of the clay before the potter, you too [remain silent] before God who created you.[40]

What is interesting in this work is the passage visible from an account of the providential economy to a providential justification of suffering, and from there to the management of evil in general, when this management is nothing but an instrument to reach a spiritual end. Without doubt inspired by Stoic thought, as were many church fathers before him, John easily expresses his wonder before the cosmological order in accepting human suffering. Nonetheless, this submission concerns neither an intellectual decision nor a cognitive process. If the providence that watches over the world (which is economy) remains an "ineffable and incomprehensible mystery" that we must refrain from questioning and explaining, it is nevertheless true that the instrumental explanation that targets evil and suffering as economy of liberty and *organon* of salvation makes the mystery intelligible on an entirely different level. *The economy makes us pass from a regime of mystery to one of enigma*, and it was Paul, as we have seen, who forever tied the status of the image to an enigma. The economy opens to humans the field of their own free will, beyond even the judgment that they will pass on their choices, or the means put in place to save themselves and others over whom they have responsibility. The economy refers to the exercise of our freedom. As for the responsibility that is incumbent on some to be the ministers and servants of providence, that will necessarily form part of the remit of the economy, and those who are responsible for being the instruments of providence for others will be the *oikonomoi*. . . . The pastoral economy is the *mimēsis* of the providential economy.

Chapter 12 of John's work, entitled "Why are the actions of malicious men, demons, and the devil allowed in this world," will consequently take up the theme of the integration of evil with the plan of salvation. Once he has reminded us of the silence required from us, clay that we are in the hands of the potter, he continues:

We say that these offences are allowed in order that the rewards of the just not be diminished . . . Paul also said: "Indeed, there must be factions among you, for only so will it become clear who among you are genuine."[41]

Moreover, the wicked have been left free for another reason: in order that they not be deprived of the usefulness that results from their conversion. . . . Concerning the Antichrist, Paul gives another reason. What, exactly? It is in order to suppress all the Jews' possible means of defense. The former would have been wronged if they had not had the opportunity to fight, but the latter, having suffered harm, should not be reasonably allowed to blame their fall on anyone other than themselves.[42]

The experience of evil and of suffering must encounter its economic solution in the free intelligence of whatever is most profitable for the salvation of Christians, and consequently, the greatness of the church. Thus the providential economy does not blindly put back in our hands some incomprehensible power that will only demand from us blind passivity or renunciation; rather, it leads us to administrate and manage for ourselves, to the best of our ability, what it is given to us to endure in the full exercise of our judgment. "Do you see what obedience he demands, what silence? It is certainly not to suppress our free will [*autoexiousion*] that he says this."[43]

Once the outrage of evil and death has been assumed by the incarnational economy, that economy is commented on in astonishing terms concerning a brilliant spectacle and revelation:

> He wanted the resurrection to take place in private and in secret. . . . But the cross, it was in the middle of the city, in the middle of a festival, in the midst of the Jewish people, when the law-courts were in session, those of the Romans and the Jews, when the festival brought everyone together . . . before the assembled world, that he was tortured; and as only those present could see what happened, he ordered the sun to announce it to the whole world by hiding itself, which it boldly did.[44]

We see here again the spectacular dimension of the economy, in all its fullness. It is directed at the gaze, it searches for it, provokes it, and makes it a means for the proof of salvation, by accepting the providential outrage of the suffering and death of the Word of God. In the words of Moingt, cited above in connection with the Trinity, the issue is one of leaving "the secret room" while still remaining hidden. Wherever the enigma of the economy is, there too is the enigma of the image, perhaps even still now, today.

John continues his rousing meditation on "providential" evil before finishing his work by recalling the gains and rewards that are made possible by it. True, only spiritual and salvational benefits will reward the victims of suffering, injustice, and evil, but sometimes even Chrysostom will plead for an enlightened sharing out of bitter remedies and guile in a better service of the truth, and this all still in the name of that same economy. The essence of revelation in the economy never stops linking together the incessant coming and going between the visible and the hidden, enigma and mystery. Every good Christian will have to be an "economist."

Economy of the Flesh

As a proper consequence of the providential economy that informs the whole of creation, the economy can only be found in the gaze focused on our own incarnation, that is, on our own bodies, which are completely implicated in the plan of redemption. The transfiguration of the flesh and its redemption presupposes that this, our body, which Christ assumed in totality (except for its sinfulness) carries the mark of the creator. The human body is in the image of God: it forms part of his economy. The mystery of eucharistic transubstantiation would make no sense if the flesh and blood of which we are constituted were not in the image of and did not resemble the one who desired to redeem that *mimésis* itself. Following is a quote from Irenaeus, who used the full force of his words to fight the Docetists, the heretics who made Christ a ghost and our body a straitjacket of sinful gloom that separates us from God:

In vain, anyway, do those who reject the whole economy [Adelin Rousseau (the French translator) still puts the word in quotation marks!] of God deny the salvation of the flesh, scorning its regeneration. As the blessed Apostle said in his Epistle to the Ephesians: "We are the limbs of his body, formed of his flesh and his bones"; it is not of just any pneumatic and invisible man that he says this, for the spirit has neither bones nor flesh, but he speaks of the true human organism, composed of flesh, of nerves, and of bones. For it is this very organism that is nourished by the cup that is the blood of Christ and strengthened by the bread that is his body.[45]

A little further on, he insists:

The flesh will be capable of receiving and containing the power of God, because in the beginning it received God's art and thus a part of it became the eye that sees, another the ear that hears, another the hand that feels and works, another the nerves that are stretched out all over and that hold the limbs together, another the arteries and the veins through which the blood and breath travel, another the different viscera, another the blood that ties the soul and body together, and more besides. For it is impossible to enumerate all the constituent elements of the human organism that were not created without the great wisdom of God.[46]

We have quoted Irenaeus at length because his argument is important for an understanding of icon doctrine in its powerful appeal to flesh and matter. The organic and physiological economy has its roots in the divinity of our primitive incarnation. Through its carnal economy, the Virgin's body, which was the true physiological receptacle of the Word in the course of an entirely human pregnancy, participated in the economic plan of redemption by agreeing to bring the image of the Father, that is, his economy, into the world. Alternatively stated, far from concerning a concept that, wanting to say everything, no longer means anything at all, we encounter a term that can, for the first time among the Greeks, give voice to something that can provide the foundation for both organic life and freedom of thought. This something, we might say, presents itself as a "to suffer," a *pashkein*, which will subsume both the affectivity and power of suffering by declaring it to be in the mode of a paschal joy. The body's economy for suffering is inseparable from the body's economy for resurrection. In *Peri tou anthropou kataskeuès* (On the making, or constitution, of Man), translated as *De natura hominis*, by the monk Meletios, a contemporary of Chrysostom, economic thought appears only in the form of a verb, never as a noun.[47] We encounter no instance of *oikonomia,* but *oikonomein* occurs several times with respect to the following topics:

—In relation to the liver, which nourishes all the parts of the body with blood. Here, the economy is referred to as providence.[48]

—Elsewhere, the phrase *arkousa dioikèsis* amounts to the same thing as *oikonomia* and means "the administration of expenses in sufficient quantity" within the interior of the body (referring as well to the beating of the heart).[49]

—In relation to the feet, the creator acted by giving each element its own place.[50]

Oikonomia therefore implies the science and technique of order and the subordination of parts to a whole. It refers to the principle of life (the mysterious, obscure aspect) and the principle of order (the clear aspect of wondrousness). . . . [51] Meletios marvels at the order of the organon that is the body, where the means implemented are perfectly adapted to the function that is their end. Only man is capable of walking, smiling, of having an "economic" nature here and a transformed nature in the beyond. In effect, what interests and fascinates Meletios is the internal, living administration of bodies that move, that breathe, that suffer and die. For the economic order also implies mortality.

To sum up, then, Meletios uses *oikonomein* as a verb to refer to the living, functional, and humoral effect of divinity within the human creature: the heart, for example, by its beating, economizes all things ("*oikonomoûsa tà sumpanta*"). The economic effect is therefore both vitalist and functionalist, as the body's providential economy gives each limb and each organ its proper place and the most perfectly adapted form for its function.

In the same fashion, the flow of mother's milk is a providential law whose very existence puts an end to the exposure of infants. Thus writes Clement on the subject of the *oikonomia tou galaktos* [the economy of milk]. Evidently, the economy therefore was also the primary concept concerning adaptation to circumstances, stressing the formulas most favorable to life and eliminating those that were not suitable to it. Thus monsters are excluded from it, just as illness eliminates them naturally, as was the case with Constantine V for Nikephoros. This is the same idea that will later make it possible for us to see a saint's body transform itself into an iconic mummy, provoking wonder at the whole corporeal mechanism. The economy can thus also lead to the closing of all orifices and the halt of all the elementary functions of life, even while it remains the principle of the organization and harmonious functioning of the body's organs.

A first explanation of these features might appeal precisely to the economic principle of adaptation: what is most fitting and desirable for all is not necessarily suitable to the saint whose body is also adapted to the mission that he gives himself or the goal he sets for himself, which is to be in the image of the image. But it appears that we must search further for what unifies the economy here, and examine other testimony as well. In the story that Eusebios tells of the martyr Polycarp, one reads that when the saint undergoes his final tortures, the onlookers are "struck at the sight of the economy of his flesh, seeing even the interior of the circulatory system of his blood and his arteries."[52] The same characteristics are also to be found in relation to the martyrdom of St. Artemios, who appeared absolutely clearly as an *écorché*, as reported by John of Damascus: "It is as though his human form has disappeared. He is naked, the bones crushed, the parts of the body broken, and one can see the economy of his human nature [*tèn oikonmian tès anthropinès phuseôs*]."[53]

Thus the saint, thanks to his martyrdom, shows us what he is made of, as we would say. The story of the sufferings of Christ's passion, the increasing complaisance in describing those sufferings and wounds, the vision of his sweat and his blood, are just so many proofs of his internal and true carnal economy. They are the tortures that deliver up to the eyes of all the body's naturally invisible economy. The unveiling of the viscera and the secrets of the flesh make manifest the path of incarnation and resurrection, just as the womb of the Virgin did. The Virginal body of Mary therefore participates in this plan in respect of everything that is physiologically necessary for a natural pregnancy, except for the seed of the father. The Virgin's body was not used by God as a canal but as a fertile womb, occupied by the bubbling up of blood and its supposed transformation into milk.[54] The economy of the flesh is the body's invisible interior suddenly become visible in order to deliver up the true economic message of the redemption. It is the organon, the organ, and the epiphany. It refers simultaneously to the bringing of the spiritual mysteries into the light of day and the coming into visibility of the organic interiority of the body. Thus medical discourse and theological discourse respond to each other and share among each other both the good and the bad. This unveiling of the primordial invisibility of the body's interior is essential for the plan of salvation, where the flesh must be revived; to phrase the same issue in a different way, the passage from darkness to light does not function as a simple dissection, but rather as a transfiguration. It is the mystery of the interior that offers itself enigmatically to the gaze in order to be deciphered, on the same model as he who seals the passage from the Old Covenant to the New. Thus, much later even, in the eleventh century, Garnerius of Saint-Victor would in the same way still enumerate the physiological and spiritual meaning of each part of the body in his treatise on man.[55]

In counterpoint to that flesh that fails us and is lost to us, the body also provides a full range of metaphors and portents of salvation. Thus, the bones are the framework of the body, the church, and Christ. As for the skin, it is the female saints who stick to the bones of Christ when the flesh (the disciples) fails him. In other instances, marrow is the food of bones, and therefore, by economic prefiguration, divine royalty, subtlety of spirit, hidden riches, and intentions. It is a highly economic part of the body because it participates in the things that are configured within a system in order to ensure its living power and its durability. These subtleties and intentions allow us to understand this marrow of speech as the very fat that feeds sacred eloquence and ensures its unctuousness.

From the point of view of the redemptive economy, it is interesting as well to note the unusual status of the viscera, which are that intimate part of the body that escapes the condemnation of the flesh. For the Marian womb as much as for the open body of the martyrs, the viscera are the shape of the ecclesial body. "The word viscera refers to those in the church who are worthy of the spiritual sacraments. . . . What should we understand by the viscera of the church other than the souls of those who contain within themselves some of its mysteries?"[56] Thus the viscera in our body are in the image of our sacramental incorporation in the ecclesiastic institution.

Visceral interiority itself prepares the way for the enigma of the inscription of the uncircumscribable, and we will later see the degree to which Constantine V's body will incarnate the monstrous invisibility of a depraved interior. Everything that concerns the devil is revealed under the sign of rejection, not of appearance. Excrement, the fetus, vomit, eructations are so many irruptions of diabolic invisibility. Conversely, Christ's body and those of the saints and martyrs allow the delightful mystery of the natural economy and sacramental organization to appear in full daylight. Whatever is inside (*tà eisô*) reaches the eyes by means of the economy. There is no contradiction, therefore, in physiological discourse rubbing shoulders with the two-sided sanctification of the saints' transfigured body. Consequently, demons maliciously attack precisely their victims' economy, as do the sorcerers of whom John of Damascus speaks with astonishment in his brief *On Female Vampires.* He reports: "Some say that women pass through the walls of their houses and grab hold of newborns in order to devour them, to eat their liver and even their whole *oikonomia.*"[57] In his edition of that work, Migne notes that John is referring there to *humor,* which is defined as "*omne ex quo habitudo corporis illorum constat,*" that is, whatever their mode of being corporeal consists in. Monsters are, contrary to nature, vampires who feed on the blood of others; this is the converse of Christ, who makes a gift of his flesh and blood in order to provide life for others. The economy thus participates in this way in the general move away from the Old Testament holocausts that had been necessary to achieve a true sacrifice.

Discourse about the body is closely linked to two themes: the eucharist and the resurrection of the flesh thanks to the womb of the Virgin, which is henceforth that of the church. The sacramental economy of flesh and blood and the "economy of wood" (the cross) uphold the whole physiological edifice that allows us to speak of the body of believers, of sinners, and of martyrs. The description of the atrocities perpetrated by female vampires is the reverse image of the appearances of the christic body; like it, female vampires pass through walls, but conversely, this is to spread death. Hélène Sorlin, in an article examining female vampires and goblins, lists several examples where sorcery myths were used for theological refutation,[58] as John of Damascus does. Although Sorlin stresses the question of the real and immaterial nature of the christic body after the resurrection in these stories, I would here like to highlight the destruction of the internal parts of the body, which are called economy. The aim of these stories always remains the same in the discourse of the church fathers: opposing pairs are established, with the economy always remaining on the same side: that of the sacred, the divine, and the natural order. Our created flesh is configured in the image of our redeemed flesh. The economic studies of human nature concern not the body inhabited by the devil, but only the one created in the image of the creator, and which will be redeemed by the image of that creator through redemptive iconicity and ecclesial incorporation. We will soon see the consequences of this in the spread of the iconic economy and in the inverted image of the emperor's body.

The Economy of Speech and God's Guile

Let us now turn our attention to the final facet of economic thought. Having dealt with the sacred and nature, we now come to speech and reason, which are the discursive, educational, and strategic aspects of the economy. In this context, let us examine the article "Économie" in Migne's *Encyclopédie théologique.* Noteworthy here is the fact that the section concerning what is generally considered to be the principle or most current meaning of the term, its Christological and providential senses, is very brief. On the other hand, the rhetorical and circumstantial aspects of the term are discussed at length, as though to answer urgently weighing Protestant accusations concerning Roman Catholic laxity and strategizing. Below are a few extracts:

> Economy: government. This term is sometimes used to refer to the manner in which it pleased God to govern men in the matter of salvation; in this sense, the old economy, which took place under the law of Moses, is distinguished from the new, which was established by Jesus Christ; this is the sense in which it is used by St. Paul.[59] More commonly, however, he uses it to refer to the leading of the church as it is entrusted to pastors.[60] It is usually rendered in the Vulgate as *dispensatio.* Simply experiencing its energy is sufficient to make one understand that the pastors' ministry is not restricted only to teaching or preaching, and that no one is permitted to exercise it without a special mission from God.
>
> Sometimes, the early church fathers used the term economy with a very different meaning, or at least, so the Protestants claim. They say that the Platonists and Pythagoreans had a maxim that deception, even lies, were allowed as long as they were beneficial to piety and truth, that the Jews in Egypt learned this maxim from them, and the Christians in turn adopted it. . . . In the third [century], the Christian doctors who had been raised in the schools of the orators and Sophists brazenly used the art of subterfuge that they had learned from their masters for the

benefit of Christianity; solely concerned with defeating their enemies, they hardly cared what means they used to win victory: this method is called "speaking with economy"[61] and it was generally adopted because of the taste for rhetoric and false subtlety.

After this introduction, Migne continues by quoting St. Jerome's thirtieth letter to Pammachius, which is a true topos on the matter of the economy. He cites the following passage:

It is one thing to argue, and another to teach. In argument, speech is vague; he who responds to an adversary says first one thing, then another; he argues as he pleases. He puts forward one proposition and proves another; as the saying goes, he shows a piece of bread, but holds a stone. In dogmatic discourse, on the contrary, one must show oneself forthrightly and act with the greatest candor; but it is one thing to search, and another to decide; and in the one case it is a question of fighting, and in the other, of teaching.

He then gives this commentary:

Does it follow from this that, following St. Jerome's sentiment, these church fathers cheated and used lies, affected equivocations, and mental qualifications to deceive their adversaries? *Aliud loqui, aliud agere: loqui quod non sentiunt, sed quod necesse est,* a much abused expression, means to not say what one is thinking; it does not mean to say the opposite of what one is thinking. However, we maintain that the church fathers, in disputing the pagans, were able to not say what they were thinking, that is, they were able to not expose their Christian belief, because that was not the place to do it. . . . This is what the church fathers did, and that is all that St. Jerome meant.

Also in the *Encyclopédie* is the following definition under the entry "Pious Fraud": "a lie, a deception, or a piece of trickery perpetrated on the grounds of religion, and with the aim of serving it." Such behavior, however, is completely condemned on principle: "It is a sin that purity of motive cannot excuse and that the religion itself condemns." The article then continues: "Jesus Christ ordered his disciples to join the innocence of the dove to the wariness of the serpent."[62] St. Paul did not want anyone to be able to even so much as suspect him of lying: "But if, through my falsehood, God's truthfulness abounds to his glory, why am I still being condemned as a sinner and why not say, 'Let us do evil so that good may come?'"[63]

The article also analyzes the exemplary cases of Origen and John Chrysostom, to whom we will return shortly, and whom the article's author places in direct relation with the text of Plato's *Republic* in which lies are distinguished according to their usefulness: "Any idea admitted by a person of [a young] age tends to become almost ineradicable and permanent. All things considered, then, that is why a very great deal of importance should be placed upon ensuring that the first stories they hear are best adapted for their moral improvement."[64] The article then ends with these words:

> Much fun has been made of the word economy, by which St. John Chrysostom and other church fathers referred to the innocent guile that they made efforts to justify. Mosheim's translator observed correctly that the economic method of argument consisted in adapting oneself as much as possible to the tastes and prejudices of those one was trying to convince. St. Paul himself said that he acted in this way, and that he became a Jew with the Jews, and so forth.[65] The nonbelievers, however, turned this into a crime.

These lines are sufficient to show the confusion and relative contradictions of those who, today as much as yesterday, cannot concede to accept the economy in its most profound, conceptual coherence. The theologian of the Trinity, the jurist, the preacher, the teacher—all are confronted by the problem of the adaptation of the law to real life, of means to ends, of transcendence to history, and cannot concede to admit that, for Byzantine thought, the totality of the incarnational plan and the redemption falls under the effects of the same principle that resolves the conflictual aporias between the spiritual and temporal world. Hence the notes, the italics, the parentheses, the comments in the form of pleas or excuses. Yet for the church fathers of the first centuries, economic thought functioned with all its resolvent effectiveness and responded with increasing subtlety to the requirements and needs of the times, and it did this with the most profound dogmatic coherence. It is also evident that its foundational principle becomes more specific with time and takes on extraordinary philosophical density, until at one particular moment, the image arrives and seals its conceptual unity. If God found it useful to employ guile with those who believe only in what they see by agreeing to promote the economic figure of his filial visibility in the visible world, then those who in turn are responsible (*oikonomos*) on earth for serving him can remain silent about the truth or use guile with the enemy, on the condition that they practice a nontransgressive accommodation (*oikonomia*) that has a salvational goal in view, for souls as well as institutions.

God's victory has its price and demands sacrifices. The expenditure (*dispensatio*) made in this respect resembles an investment because the benefits are redemption and divine victory. The sacrifice of the filial image saved him who, made in the image of his creator, had fallen. But that is not the only benefit of the economy. If it were only that, and if it reserved the field of measures that were effective in terms of strategy and accommodation only for itself, it would hardly be of interest to philosophy. There is more: the economy, as we will see, is only in the service of victory because it never stops defining itself as being in the service of life. This organic ambivalence between a tool and a vital organ is at the heart of a system of thought concerning *tekhné* that will assume a natural model in order to raise artifice to the level of an ontological manifestation. This will become yet another new way of defining the economy.

It is necessary, then, for us to return to the juridical nature of the concept, which is the aspect that has been best studied, having unfortunately been so often accused of total misalignment with its Christological meaning. Dagron's article, which we looked at earlier, concludes that the economy is totally inconsistent with respect to the issue of the rule and the exception. In fact, however, the saying according to which the exception confirms the rule probably has a grammatical and not juridical origin. *The patristic economy confronts the long shadow of the law*, from which it distances itself, the better to fulfill it, and by this means shows the complex relation of the law to history. An appropriate level must be found for the process of interpreting the law in an elastic, accommodating manner, for indulgence and tolerance toward its contravenors, and the conditions of application of these practices must be formulated in order for the economy to be able to negotiate with reality without thereby contravening the law sensu stricto. Dagron makes quite clear that the economy is neither casuistic nor jurisprudential. The issue here rather concerns the relation that the economy maintains with the law in canon law and in the historical circumstances that led the church fathers to take measures that strict *akribeia* (the rigorous application of the law) may have required, but that thereby may have rendered it ineffective. The economy concerns the relation of life to the law, a law that no exception could ever confirm. The exception is much more than a convention of communication and custom that keeps it in statistical isolation. The exception can only occur once, or a limited number of times, and yet not modify the rule that prevails in all other cases. The economy, however, is entirely different: its christic model could never be thought of in terms of the exception! It incarnates the new definition of the law, and its condescension still continues to fulfill a plan that is exceptional in its mystery and perfectly natural in its internal configuration. To not understand the way in which this incarnational development generates law would amount to considering, as do the heretics, that the Son (and therefore the manifestation of the Father's economy) was only a circumstantial remedy to our spiritual maladies. Dagron cites in this respect Eulogios, Patriarch of Alexandria, whose polemical work is noted by Photios, and who is undoubtedly the first Christian author to devote himself to the concept of the economy in a systematic manner in order to question the conditions and limits of its effectiveness and legitimacy. He distinguishes three sorts of economy: the first is temporary and circumstantial; the second concerns the choosing of words or, if necessary, silence; and the last concerns the suspension of the application of a decree. His Christological model is clear as well; it concerns time, words, silence, and the law. Thus Christ's economy is historical, it is made manifest by preaching and the silence of the passion, and it modified the meaning of the law. Yet Eulogios is also careful to link this economy to ecclesiastic responsibility by reminding us that only those who are already servants of Christ and invested with episcopal authority can judge and act with economy.

The economy is always put into practice by a mediator who in a critical or conflictual situation must find a formula for legitimizing and justifying a decision that would not, even occasionally, reduce the law to the rule by means of an exception. As the science of compromise that must never compromise anything or encourage any future repetition by setting a precedent, the economy, far from being an exception, in reality lessens all circumstantial exceptions and is similar to an exercise in prudence, which is to say, in existential wisdom. Let us call existential wisdom every act of interpretation and adaption to circumstances that chooses never to separate thought from life, or the concept from the flesh that makes it manifest. It is always exemplary in method, but never in the content of what it does or decides in each circumstance. Contrary to jurisprudence, the same case can involve economic measures that are completely contradictory (taking into account historical situations that are always individual), and contradictory attitudes can, at the same time, involve the same economy. What prevails in all cases is the end goal. Only the unity of ends allows one to admit the plurality of means.

The economy is thus a manifestation in history, but it is not limited by history. It exceeds all strictly historical circumstances in order to reveal the meaning of history itself. The economy is the historical modality of the configuration of truth for fallen souls, and that until the end of time. The model of every economy is God himself, who offers us the image of his Son and the model of his actions. Once we are saved, we will see God no longer in the economic enigma adapted to our weakness, but "face to face." It was, in fact, imperative that the economy be everything except a "blurred concept," "purely negative," or "empty." The economy is an operative concept that is defined by its living fertility. And this is all the more clear in that it takes for its historical model the fertility of the virginal womb. If there is any emptiness in the economy, it is only by the effect of kenosis, of the hollowing-out of the incarnation itself. How could it have been otherwise for a term that refers to divine providence and the incarnation of Christ in a single movement?

Dagron, however, convinced of the conceptual emptiness of the term, ends up defining the economy as "rhetorical." He is therefore only able to define its unity by referring it to a specific manipulation of speech that pleads, defends, or justifies. But this is once more to take the concept for what it is the condition of: the cause for the effect. In order for rhetorical power to exist, it is necessary that economic thought be able to serve as a model for the administration of the relations between truth and the living strategy destined to make it triumph. God's guile results from his freedom, a freedom that is immanent to reality itself.

In order to clarify the economy, whether holily strategic or simply tactical, let us now examine three key examples that continually served as references for the church fathers in their justification of their terrestrial and temporal practice of the truth. The texts are drawn from Origen's *Commentary on the Gospel According to Matthew*, in which the economy concerns the idea of accommodation; Basil of Caesarea's *On the Holy Spirit*, where the author explains his silence on the subject of the consubstantiality of the Third Person of the Trinity; and John Chrysostom's *On the Priesthood*, which deals directly with economic guile and deceit, and which leads us directly to the initial and fundamental question of the incarnation as the constitutive legislative "abeyance" of the law itself.

Adaptation

Origen's commentary appears in the French series "Sources chrétiennes," translated by Robert Girod, who apparently feels the need to put the word *economy* in parentheses: "The Gospel text is not only simple, as some think, but it was presented to simple people with economy as being simple. For those who want to understand it in a more penetrating manner and who are capable of it, realities full of wisdom and worthy of the Logos of God are hidden within it."[66]

Girod then cites St. Augustine's *Commentary on the Lord's Sermon on the Mount* in a note: "[God,] through his holy prophets and servants and in accordance with a most orderly economy of circumstances . . . gave the lower precepts to a people whom it behooved to be bound by fear; through his Son, he gave the higher precepts to a people whom it befitted to set free by charity. . . . [He] alone knows how to proffer to the human race a medicine adapted to its circumstances."[67] This association of the economy with medicine dispensed by a doctor more worried about health than truth is a topos of the same sort as the stories in Plato's *Republic* that are intended to make small children behave properly. Origen even goes so far as to say that the truth has a fatal effect on those who are not ready to receive it:

> Those who are still ill are not able to receive the blessed bread of Jesus. But if someone, instead of listening to the words: "Let everyone put himself to the test," and thus prepared, he "eats of this bread" and paying no attention to this warning, and in the state that he is in, takes part in the bread and chalice of the Lord, he becomes weak or ill, or even scatterbrained, so to speak, by the power of the bread, and he dies.[68]
>
> The Lord comes in the form of the Savior, as a good physician.[69]

The general precept that governs all these economic uses is the phrase taken from Matthew: "Do not give what is holy to dogs; and do not throw your pearls before swine."[70] Misfortune will come to those who obtain what they are they not worthy of. What characterizes Origen's conception of the economy and differentiates it largely from Basil's and Chrysostom's, however, is that it is tied to qualities of attentive listening and to the spiritual level of the person that it addresses. Like all medicine, it is adapted to the illness that it treats. In the words of Athanasios, "Just as the doctor has recourse to subterfuge in order to make one drink the medicine," so the church will make us swallow its message by employing formulations adapted to our respective illnesses and dispositions.

The fact that medicine is capable of returning one to health, however, does not mean that it must be continually employed in order to remain healthy, and even less that the medicine is the general cause of health—once cured, the patient can dispense with it. In this sense, the visible world is nothing but the medicine that our blindness calls for, and the future use of the concept will go beyond even this point by making the visible the very essence of our own relation to the truth. Thus the economy, having started out simply as a circumstantial cure, turns into a synonym for all thought incarnated in life.

Silence and Accommodation

In order to reach that point, however, the economy had to take a new philosophical and spiritual step. A century after Origen, the church's position had become critical because the emperor Valens had converted to Arianism. The first Nicene council had ruled on the consubstantiality of the Son, but it still remained for the church fathers to establish the consubstantiality of the Holy Spirit before trinitarian doctrine would be able to establish the identity of the hypostases in terms of their substance and their divine equality. At just that moment, just as the trinitarian question was proving to be a serious stumbling block with the Arians, Basil, then bishop of Caesarea, found himself divided between his doctrinal mission and the threat that hung over his episcopal seat as well as over the security of the Christians of Cappadocia, who the Arians were then preparing to persecute. He therefore adopted a median solution by speaking of *homotimie*, that is, of the equality of honor between the Persons of the Trinity, but mentioned nothing about the consubstantiality of the Holy Spirit. As a result, a debate arose concerning his silence, and it is exactly on that subject that Athanasios and Gregory of Nazianzos invoke his economy. Basil, it turns out, had used such shrewdness and taken so many precautions in setting out his doctrine that he even became suspect in the eyes of strict Nicene orthodoxy. Even here, then, at the very heart of the debate about the divine economy of the incarnation, we encounter a use of the economy in its sense of a strategic accommodation to circumstances in the form of silence. Yet, because the economy is itself a principle of continuity, we also discover its operational cohesion within the activities that constitute its own field, and it is for this reason that we cannot agree with Benoît Pruche, the editor of the Basil text in the "Sources chrétiennes" series. Speaking of the term *oikonomia*, Pruche notes: "The word was coined by Athanasios and Gregory of Nazianzos. It characterizes the fairly complex attitude of the Bishop of Caesarea before the explicit declaration of the divine consubstantiality of the Holy Spirit; it therefore has a special meaning here, *bearing no relation to what it normally signifies in patristics*: the mystery of the redemptive incarnation, in opposition to theology, which refers to the mystery of God."[71] To say that the word was invented by Athanasios and Gregory of Nazianzos when their use of it still conforms to its Classical meaning of the management of and enlightened adjustment to real, critical situations is already an astonishing statement, to say the least. To assert in the same breath, however, that this usage bears no relation to the patristic sense of the term when we are located at the very heart of the patristic oeuvre itself shows the degree to which conceptual confusion leads to the refusal of any theoretical efforts concerning the cohesion of the system of thought itself. The meaning of *oikonomia* in Basil corresponds entirely with Dagron's study concerning the relations between canon law and individual cases, and it is in full agreement with what canon law calls the ecclesiastic economy. There is nothing in this meaning of the term that has been made up; rather, it makes use of its classic sense within canon law, and more generally, in all circumstances of pastoral or political life where the person who is about to take action must keep in mind the ends that he is aiming for in order to adapt the best means possible for attaining them, all the while keeping alive the spirit of church doctrine and not losing sight of the interests of the moment. As in the previous case with Origen, what disturbs the commentators did not disturb the church fathers in the least: using the same word to refer to the mystery of the incarnation and the enlightened process of deliberately adapting to a given situation. Opportunism thus became a political and spiritual virtue that served the interests of the church better than an intransigent rigorism would have done in an unfavorable power struggle, where the victory of doctrine or the institution was not assured.

Consider in this connection Theodore of Stoudios, who on a different occasion demonstrated his demand for *akribeia* in relation to the adulterous marriage of Constantine VI, yet who also wrote the following:

> Question: how should Christians, who live amidst heretics and must maintain their desire for perfection, behave?
>
> Answer: no monk should share his meal with a heretic unless he has no choice: in doing this, he is adopting an economic attitude [*ei mè ti oikonomias tropoi*].[72]

Theodore in this instance is only following the example set by Basil in relation to the question of the baptism of the Asians—Basil believed that those baptisms should be recognized as valid without entering into the particulars of orthodoxy in an inadequate fashion, owing to the economy of many things ("*oikonomias eneka tôn pollôn*"), by which we should understand a managed organization of the truth that takes into account many circumstantial parameters. To be economic is to take into account, to reckon with, to calculate the advantages and disadvantages.

What, then, is this ongoing refusal to recognize the doctrinal coherence of the term *economy* other than an early disavowal of the links that bind the future of the doctrine concerning the Father's natural image to political stakes and temporal interests? In appearing to dissociate themselves from a highly metaphysical or religious integration of the concept of economy, historians and translators arrive at the same result as strictly religious souls do because both, in the same way, separate out what is structurally designed to communicate. In trying too hard to avoid the philosophical questioning of a world that continually integrated spiritual care with political decisions, however, one also loses whatever constituted the specific unity of that way of thinking, by setting it in contradiction with itself or even attributing to it inconsistencies that are groundless. Thus in the debate over Basil's silence, Athanasios and Gregory both defend him against accusations of cowardice or anti-Nicene treachery. In his letter to Palladios, Athanasios condemns "the audacity of those who dare to raise their voices against the beloved and true servant of God, Bishop Basil."[73] The monks must "consider his economy and render glory to God, who gave to Cappadocia this bishop, the like of whom all countries wish that they had." The struggle between the "pneumatomachs," or adversaries of the Holy Spirit, demands a response that is specifically tailored, at once both firm and prudent. Thus Basil writes in a letter, "Above all else, it is necessary to avoid renewing the battles over consusbstantiality in relation to the Holy Spirit. The situation of the Asian churches is too precarious to take such a risk,"[74] and the treatise *On the Holy Spirit* ends with this comment to Amphilochus: "For these reasons, I decided that it was better for me to remain silent than to talk. A human voice cannot make itself heard in such an uproar . . . ; your levelheaded and calm character was a guarantee against the untimely disclosure of what I would have said to you. Not that it was necessary to hide it, but to avoid throwing pearls before swine."[75]

If this debate foregrounds Basil's economy of silence, then, it is nonetheless also the case that he uses the term *economy* to refer to the plan of salvation and the message of the Gospels as well, even as he talks without any sense of inconsistency of the *oikonomia tôn psuchôn*, the economy of souls, when referring to his responsibility as a bishop. Here again, there is no contradiction or recent invention.

Guile

Questions of guile and lying are explicitly approached for the first time in John Chrysostom's *On the Priesthood.* In order to grasp fully the development of his thought in relation to the economy, it is necessary to recall the circumstances that brought him to make use of it, which concern his friend Basil, who Chrysostom loved and revered with all his heart: "Their union was sturdy and without flaws." At the moment when both were about to join the priesthood, the beloved Basil seemed to his friend to possess all the intellectual and spiritual qualities required for such an undertaking. But Chrysostom himself did not yet feel ready for that step, torn between his taste for pleasures and the world, an aging mother who did not want to see him distanced from her, and the love of his friend, who was trying to win him over to the religious life. Here are the words of the "Golden Mouth" himself, describing what happened on the appointed day of the two friends' ordination:

> For looking to myself, I found nothing worthy of such an honor. But that noble youth having come to me privately, and having conferred with me about these things as if with one who was ignorant of the rumor, begged that we might in this instance also as formerly shape our action and our counsels the same way: for he would readily follow me whichever course I might pursue. . . . But after a short time, when one was to ordain us arrived, I kept myself concealed, but Basil, ignorant of this, was taken away on another pretext, and made to take the yoke, hoping from the promises which I had made to him that I should certainly follow, or rather supposing that he was following me. For some of those who were present, seeing that he resented being seized, deceived him.

Then follows a description of Basil's grief and helplessness, and his feeling of betrayal by his friend, so that "Grief cut short his words before they could pass his lips." Then Chrysostom begins a long plea regarding his attitude:

> What is the wrong that I have done you? . . . Is it that I misled you and concealed my purpose? Yet I did it for the benefit of thyself who was deceived, and of those to whom I surrendered you by means of this deceit. . . . And if you investigate the history of generals who have enjoyed the highest reputation from the earliest ages, you will find that most of their triumphs were achieved by stratagem,[76] and that such are more highly commended than those who conquer in open fight.

Chrysostom then launches into an explication that is all too strategic for his unhappy friend, who says: "But none of these cases apply to me: for

I am not an enemy, nor one of those who are striving to injure you, but quite the contrary. For I entrusted all my interests to your judgement, and always followed it whenever you bid me." To which John responds sublimely: "But, my admirable and excellent sir, this is the very reason why I took the precaution of saying that it was a good thing to employ this kind of deceit, not only in war, and in dealing with enemies, but also in peace, and in dealing with our dearest friends. . . . Go to any of the physicians and ask them how they relieve their patients from disease."

Then follows a long detour that uses a medical example. Finally, John makes the following astonishing declaration: "For great is the value of deceit, provided it be not introduced with a mischievous intention. In fact action of this kind ought not to be called deceit, but economy, cleverness and skill, capable of finding out ways where resources fail, and making up for the defects of the mind."[77]

The French edition of A. M. Malingrey obviously does not retain the term *economy*; she uses the term *forethought*[78] instead, as she does for all three occurrences of the term in books 1 and 2. For John insists further:

That it is possible then to make use of deceit for a good purpose, or rather that in such a case it ought not to be called deceit [*apatē*], but economy worthy of admiration.[79]

Will you, then, still contend that you were not rightly deceived, when you were about to superintend the things which belong to God, and are doing that which when Peter did, the Lord said he should be able to surpass the rest of the apostles?[80]

John proclaims that the sole instrument of recovery and victory is speech: "This is the one instrument [*organon*], the only diet, the finest atmosphere. This takes the place of medicine, cautery and cutting, and if it be needful to sear and amputate, this is the means which we must use, and if this be of no avail, all else is wasted."[81] And despite this, a little further on, he uses an entirely different argument:

For it is not for one kind of battle only that we have to be prepared. This warfare is manifold, and is engaged with a great variety of enemies; neither do all these use the same weapons, nor do they practice the same method of attack and it is not possible for us to counter-attack using only one means. He who has to join battle with all, must needs know the artifices of all, and be at once both archer and slinger, captain and general, on foot and on horseback.[82]

In other words, for Chrysostom, incomparable orator that he was, the economy is the oratorical exercise of authority par excellence, one that surpasses all worldly exercise of power. It is to put oneself at the service of Christ's body, the model of every economy, by using all the weapons demanded by the attacks of the devil himself. The economy of speech seems to be the exemplary instance of the art, but the therapeutic and military models that support it leave open the door by which certain means other than the sole proclamation of the truth could be introduced in order to obtain results.

With this use of the concept of the incarnation, Chrysostom, more than anyone else, inaugurates what was to become the field of the image, although he had no reason to be interested in it in his own day, at the end of the fourth century. However, if we restrict ourselves to the economy of speech only, we see that it already closely associates the incarnation with the fields of strategy and pedagogy.

Pedagogy

It would be an injustice here to limit ourselves to citing only Chrysostom, considered one of the greatest models of sacred eloquence, in his use of deception and guile. Following, therefore, are several other examples concerning the issue of the pedagogical conception of the economy, which is the logical consequence of the interpretation of divine condescension (*sunkatabasis*), another name for the incarnation.

In his *Dogmatic History of Dionysios's Struggle Against the Arians*, Athanasios says that the apparent similarity that can be noted between the writings of Dionysios and Arius should not deceive us.[83] If Dionysios writes in the way that he does, it is by economy—as with the doctor whose cures can sometimes surprise the patient. When the goal is only health, however, then one may use whatever has been seen to be successful in the past. The apostles, according to Athanasios, cannot be criticized for having spoken of Christ in relation to his carnal reality and the criteria of humanity; on the contrary, in that respect they showed that their economy and pedagogy was well adapted to those who listened to them ("*tèn en kairo didaskalian kai oikonomian*"). In this connection, it is worth noting that most of the (sometimes overly sophisticated) pedagogical senses of the economy come to be justified on the basis of commentaries on Jeremiah: at one point, finding himself in conflict with God, Jeremiah asks him, "Why did you deceive me?" The Origenist commentary on this passage distinguishes three lines of reasoning that all function similarly to the story of the kettle with a hole in it:[84]

1. Jeremiah did indeed say those words to God, but that was only a manner of speaking: this is the economy of speech.
2. God appears to deceive us, but when we understand the truth, we too understand that we have not been deceived: this is the pedagogical economy.
3. Furthermore, if God does deceive us, it is because he has no other means to get from us what he wants: this is the strategic economy that considers only results.

Evident in this hermeneutic reasoning, then, is a summation of all levels of economic effectiveness: a manner of talking, a way of teaching in order to save, and a method of subduing.

The Listener's Emotion

The church fathers believed that truth only obtained its authority by means of its emotional power, its direct access to the heart. The speaker must touch his listeners in order to convince them and change their attitudes. Intelligence is not enough—it can even corrupt by the perverse manipulations of its arguments. Pathways must therefore be found that lead the intelligence directly to the enthusiastic passion for the truth. A flash of brilliance is not enough; ardor is necessary as well. As we have seen in *On the Providence of God*, John Chrysostom was endowed with a faculty of speech that could be called magical, with both poetic force and emotional power. He was an extraordinary sacred manipulator, practicing a shamanism of the word.

In order to fan the flames of love to the point of martyrdom, reason is powerless, and revelation is given only to those who are prepared for it. Moreover, the opening of the heart to revelation is tied to the suspension of critical reason and to the sole action of the fires of grace. Nothing is more enlightening on this subject than the fully developed expositions of the *Encyclopèdie thèologique*, which are thoroughly imbued with the teachings of the church fathers. Let us turn, then, to the entries "Emotional Arousal" and "Oratorical Precautions," which will give us a better understanding of the economy of speech and its future career in the church:

Emotional Arousal: the preacher does not know his own power. . . . He is unaware of the better part of it when he believes that he can only instruct and clarify. . . . He can still impress on the heart whatever feelings he wishes; he can and he must. . . .

The truly eloquent orator does not restrict himself to instruction and being well received; in order to reach perfection, it is also necessary to arouse hearts, stir passions, and influence the most rebellious wills. . . . The grace of pure light is the grace of the creator. It sufficed when man was innocent; but the grace of the redeemer, healing grace, contains still more delights, which sinful man needs. . . . I speak the truth when I say that if your words have brilliance about them, that pure and honest brilliance of the truth, they will still be nothing more than beautiful but cold ice [*glace*]. Light and warmth must appear in them, activity and force. They must be one of those mirrors [*glaces*][85] in which one appears as one is, and in which one can moreover see a flame forming that is capable of consuming and purifying. To expound Christian truths coldly is to do them wrong.

The displacement of meaning in this passage from ice that freezes to a mirror that reflects will be readily appreciated; here, indeed, is a homonymic play that honors the economy of speech! The author then proceeds to eulogize Chrysostom's eloquence, which is capable of representing both hell and salvation with fiery images that are unforgettably moving. The article concludes: "It is difficult not to surrender to speech of this character. One feels imperceptibly carried away by some sweet violence that he does to the heart and spirit. Waves follow one after the other, waves not blindly or timidly conceived, but ones that an enlightened reason leads and arranges as if by degrees and which form a passionate speech, wise and reasonable, which it is impossible to resist."

The article "Oratorical Precautions," on the other hand, specifies the necessary modulations of the true and the false, speech and silence, temerity and prudence—in brief, all the care "that the orator must take in order not to offend the delicacy of those before whom or of whom he speaks, as well as the studied devices, adroit and ingratiating, that he uses to say certain things that, without them, would appear harsh or shocking."

Our flesh and hearts must thus be reached by the evangelical message in the name of the redemption of the flesh, and because the regime of the flesh is that of pleasure and pain, a sermon that addressed itself only to the spirit would commit, in short, the same error that the monophysites fell into with respect to the incarnation. And because sight is quicker in this domain than hearing, the instructional image will touch people more surely and rapidly than speech. Did the Old Testament God not choose to reach us by allowing himself to be seen, he who was not obeyed when he used only the word? The visible signs of his anger did not have anything like the same effect as those of the carnal suffering of his image. No identification is possible when faced with a deluge of snakes, whereas a crucified and revived body, a body similar to our own, immediately arouses emotional and redemptive identification.

Emotion thus forms a part of the well-adapted, specifically targeted organization of good and evil. Seduction and terror are resources to be administered and managed, in order that they not be abandoned to the devil. The expenditure of holy eloquence and images that touch people is therefore part of the direct effect of the salvational economy. Here too, there is a principle of nonwastage: truths must not be dispensed through speech without art. Thus, the management of speech is an investment in emotional expenditure, aiming to gain time and force. This is the principle of all propaganda and publicity: how to spread the maximum information in the minimum time, and how to obtain agreement without reserve, conviction and obedience without objection. This is the strategy of seduction, the temptation of the flesh itself put at the service of salvation in a political doctrine where the means are justified by the ends. Beauty, like the lie, has the advantage of seduction and emotional arousal, and such weapons must only be used by the hand and mouth inspired by the grace of the Holy Spirit. The confessor, the preacher, as the painter, must allow themselves to be imbued with divine grace in order to be assured that all their negotiations with the perceptible world and the universe of sin are entirely guided and transformed by the divine spirit.

The eye and the ear are thus only the "meatuses," orifices that open the visceral body to discourse; speech and the image must speak to the gut. Rabanus Maurus, in his description of our body, would write: "*viscera mystice significant affectum pietatis et misericordiae*": the viscera, mystically speaking, refer to the affect of piety and mercy. This emotional economy joins together perfectly with the visceral character of the church institution and the sacrament, of which we have seen an example above.[86] Emotion is the trick of a God who forces a path to our soul through our body, who dispenses his grace within everything that carries the mark of life in order to lead us to the heart of institutional and salvational vitality. To arouse emotionally, to seduce, is to force a path not in the spirit but in the entire body of the listener or spectator, and in occupying it, to become the master of what it digests and rejects. Music, too, therefore has an important role to play in the emotional economy, and it is not by chance that in physiological texts, one encounters a belief that bodily cohesion can be maintained by musical, resonant harmony.

In relation to seduction, then, it appears as though God possesses ownership, and the devil usufruct. The economy is truly the commerce of God and the devil in a sort of life annuity based on the durability of both parties, but the eternity of only one. This is an extremely sensitive issue, of course, because it concerns the management of our feelings and desires. On the one hand, they are the chosen ground of the devil; on the other, because of this, they are the chief concern of the redemption. They are what must be taken back from the diabolical usurper. He who came to earth to preach the word of love became established as the supreme model of redeemed affect and desire. Emotion is therefore anagogical, as is the whole economic plan, which must always be understood with the nobility necessary to avoid complicity with the devil.

The image will pose the same problems in negotiating our weakness on the road that leads to salvation. It will not be content just to remind and instruct; it will have to stir. Upon seeing it, eyes brimming with tears will be illuminated by proof coming from the heart. As Grumel writes: "It would be impossible to deprive the church of so powerful a weapon in its fight against the devil," and it is sometimes necessary to fight him with his own weapons. Thus the *oikonomia* becomes the sublimation of the diabolical, with the forces of satanic ensnarement and menace diverted and put to the service of the good.

Temporal Management

The church has as its task the management of both our feelings and the temporal realities that the devil would be only too happy to appropriate exclusively for himself. Yet there again, its power was contested. Is that not, however, the scenario that is generally supposed to be at stake between the iconophiles and iconoclasts? Nonetheless, if those feelings and temporal realities are objects of dispute, it is to prevent the devil from occupying the terrain of life itself.

Returning to Chrysostom's *On the Priesthood*, we find that in the rest of the text, the term *economy* is used again without any sense of inconsistency to refer to the priestly office and responsibility for souls. Yet the French translator, without any warning, suddenly writes "governance"[87] to translate the word that she had rendered as "forethought"[88] in the preceding book. "Those who attain to this economy should be contented to be consecrated to the dignity or removed from it, as becomes Christians."[89] An additional note, however, states that "Here, the word *oikonomia* has a very broad meaning; it covers all the administrative responsibilities incumbent on the bishop, being used to talk of each one of them: the distribution of goods and the care of widows. Its general meaning[90] refers to the obligations that the ministry carries with it." Why, however, is this meaning described as being very broad? Has the reader been given the impression from the beginning that it has a narrow or restricted meaning? Moreover, it is evident that the "general meaning" invoked by the translator is not the one that Benoît Pruche cites in the case of Gregory and Athanasios. Similarly, there is no allusion to the use made of the same word earlier in books 1 and 2, where as we have just seen, it concerns lies and guile. Further, by translating the word as "governance," as the "Sources chrétiennes" edition does, one ends up with a somewhat contradictory statement by Chrysostom, because he explains precisely that one must be ready to abandon power if the situation requires it, and that "I do not think a word is needed to prove what great gain they [the sinners] procure from him [the virtuous man who renounces power] by their wickedness."

The economy, then, does not have as its goal the pure and simple seizure of power by all and any means; on the contrary, it is the result of a fair and wise evaluation of the profits and losses pertaining to a certain office. The idea of this office, however, is peculiar to the economy and not to government, specially when power is the effect of a violence or authority devoid of any salvational inspiration. The strength[91] of the economy should never be confused with a pure and simple appropriation of power.[92] It is neither the abandoning of thought to the profit of a short-sighted and ambitious realist pragmatism, nor blind service to immediate interests in a disregard of the truth. It is what thought must pass through to be alive, even as it maintains the authority of the law. Paradoxically, however, there are those who attempt to defend the church by bringing into play disjunctions at the heart of the economy that end up with the opposite result, because they turn the economy into a sort of perverse concept. Yet the economy is rather a philosophical and political concept that tries as hard as possible to escape the perverse effects of power by privileging strength and authority. The fact that the institution does not always succeed in this, however, is yet another problem that concerns the inevitable ambivalence of every iconic choice produced by the dynamics of the concept.

Remaining with Chrysostom's text a moment longer, we find that the term reappears in book 4, evoking this time the management and distribution of goods. In this instance, it concerns Judas, whom God had not only chosen as an apostle but to whom he had confided the economy of goods ("*oikonomian tôn chrématôn*"), and who was punished for having misused them.[93] Even more significant, however, is the use made of it in chapter 2 of the same book, where Chrysostom passes directly from the management of goods to the management of the christic body, by taking up the medical metaphor again:

> It is not the economy of corn and barley, oxen or sheep, that is now under consideration, nor any such like matters, but the very body of Jesus. For the church of Christ, according to St. Paul, is Christ's body, and he who is entrusted with its care ought to train it up to a state of healthiness and beauty unspeakable, and to look everywhere, lest any spot or wrinkle, or other like blemish should mar its vigor and comeliness. For what is this but to make it appear worthy, so far as human power can, of the incorruptible and ever-blessed Head which is set over it? If they who are ambitious of reaching an athletic condition of body need the help of physicians and trainers, and exact diet, and constant exercise, and a thousand other rules (for the omission of the merest trifle upsets and spoils the whole), how shall they to whose lot falls the care of the body, which has its conflict not against flesh and blood, but against powers unseen, be able to keep it sound and healthy, unless they far surpass ordinary human virtue, and are versed in all healing proper for the soul?[94]

As we have seen several times, *oikonomia* is regularly used to refer to the responsibilities and administrative offices of the clergy, this being an intrinsic effect of its conceptual unity; the corresponding term in Latin will frequently be rendered as *administratio.*[95] From this point, the transition is easily made to the management of goods and the distribution of charity, which necessarily form part of the ecclesiastic economy, for the enlightened exercise of charity and the administration of alms is similar to the administering of medicine or the teaching of truth. And because the concept of economy is indistinguishable from the notion of service and actions that are successful, the precepts of charitable economy thus come to be formulated in its name.[96]

Because the economy implies both the notions of organization and expenditure, it justifies all the expenses entailed in maintaining its authority or in making a convincing case for its necessity. Thus alms, which are charitable economy (which will designate all the forms of social and hospital assistance), cover all expenses, the receipts for which are always anticipated by the church, spiritual though these may be. In this way, a meaning concerning accountancy enters into the notion of economy in a direct line from the Classical economy. The creation was an expenditure; Christ was an expenditure; speech as well as the image figure in the program of necessary expenditures. This is the *dispensatio.* But in this notion of expenditure, nothing is arbitrary or free. All the sacred expenditures, all the divine expenditures, are methodical, purposeful, justified, balanced by material profits as well as by spiritual benefits. This is a tidy piece of accountancy whose principle is the optimization of investments in view of a particular result.

The economic thought of the church is thus a system of thinking that is both administrative and corrective. It is administrative in that *oikonomia* is at one with the organization, management, and development of each ministry. But it is also necessary to add to it a corrective function, because human initiatives that are not inspired by grace can only engender inequalities, injustices, or transgressions. The divine and ecclesiastic economy must therefore take charge of the wretched management of our history and regulate it in an enlightened and redemptive way. By compensatory management, it reestablishes a justice that human iniquity does not know how to, and cannot, avoid. In this sense, the church does nothing other than manage an ensemble of expenditures to maintain an equilibrium. One only has to refer to Martin-Doisy's *Dictionnaire d'économie charitable* to discover the balanced accounting of the ecclesiastic economy: in the article "Capital and Revenues," chapter 17 is entitled "Charity profits everyone."[97] It states: "Is it not better to lend [one's wealth] to the poor who can repay it . . . than to push them into bankruptcy or the sea that will swallow them, or set them to gambling, which consumes everything?"[98] In other words, charity, like any expenditure, must be an investment. This conception of expenditure and distribution also provides an entirely new way of thinking about a different subject: that of sacrifice. The economy can no longer be content to spill the blood of holocausts in a pure oblation to assuage the hunger and thirst of God. The New Covenant, under the sign of the economy, only sacrifices with a view to repurchase and resurrection.

Conclusion: Dangers and Precautions—A First Look at the Iconic Economy

It will be readily understood that on the historical level, which is where the concept plays out, there was a constant danger of lapses, and these did in fact take place, whether for reasons of cowardice, want of rigor, or a taste for profit. The same applies to the image: it was a fertile reality, but it was sufficiently ambivalent to lead to the excesses of idolatry and superstition. In other words, there is therefore no escape from the question, at first glance already eliminated, of perverse effects.

What makes this notion of the economy so fascinating is not its power in mediating between instances that without it would be unreconcilable and contradictory—human and divine, truth and lies, the visible and the invisible . . . ; if the doctrine of the image and icon had not produced the connective tissue that legitimates the pathways between disjunctive realities, the economy would have been able to stay in the vague terrain of adaptation and compromise. Rather, in the many-colored relational field that it deals with, the economy tried to resist the confusion that could have reduced its tidy, living dynamic to both a psychological and political opportunism. It is like a one-of-a-kind cloth woven from a medley of colors.

Yet how can respect for the truth and the liberty of others be guaranteed if, in the final analysis, the only criterion of the economy is the triumph of the cause that it defends? The decision to act with economy can only result from an internal deliberation that has no model other than the condescension of Christ himself and the grace of his own counsel. As far as the management of the iconic economy is concerned, we will see that only purity of intentions will serve as a guarantee of the good use of our carnal pleasures at the heart of the visible world.

When Basil decided cautiously, yet wisely, to remain silent on the subject of the consubstantiality of the Holy Spirit, Gregory of Nazianzos wrote him a letter making plain how difficult the situation was: "Some reproach us for impiety overtly, others for cowardice; impiety by those who are convinced that we do not profess to the holy doctrine; cowardice by those who accuse us of dissimulation."[99] Gregory then tells Basil how he was criticized for his position at a recent banquet with some monks: "He contents himself, they say, with causing things to be obscurely glimpsed, and so to speak, only skirts around the doctrine. With more politics than piety, he harps on, and by the power of his words masks his duplicity."

At this point, Gregory says that he attempted to defend Basil's economy, but "those present did not accept this economy, finding it vain and believing that it made fools of them, under the pretext that we were defending our cowardice rather than the doctrine." Gregory then makes a special appeal: "I dismissed them. . . . But as for you, divine and holy friend, teach us how far we should go in the theology of the Spirit, what terms must be used, how far it is necessary to be economic [*oikonométéon*], so that we may know these things when we face our opponents."

The crucial question thus remains one of the moral control of economic practice and its doctrinal limits. The only good steward[100] is the one who maintains Christ's condescension as a model and acts only when he is invested with spiritual authority, which alone guarantees sound judgment. Such a condition limits the practice of economy considerably because it requires that the church hierarchy and the sacrament stand guarantee for it. How, then, to generalize the economy—or rather, how to universalize it? Considering that in principle it manages thinking, life, and history, how to open it up to the whole world that the full breadth of its salvational plan concerns? This could only be accomplished if it were based on an ethics of *mimésis*, the exemplary object of which would be the icon.

In order for the economy to be applicable to everyone (that is to say, it should no longer need to be invested with the highest hierarchical authority in order to escape suspicion of transgression, laxity, or abusive opportunism), it would be necessary to find a solution that would combine all the effects of both pedagogical strategies and church doctrine. An instrument had to be found whose message was unambiguous and allowed no further contradictions, a universal instrument that ignored the barrier of languages and obstacles such as knowledge. This instrument would have to be a holy and divine ruse, taking into account our body, our elementary adherences, and our emotions. This rational and magical instrument, it will be clear, is the iconic image. . . . Inanimate matter undertaking the manuduction of matter toward spirit, something double that will respect the distinction between two natures, the icon will incarnate the word at the heart of its own silence, under the order of univocal revelation. It will supply a solution as efficient as it is elegant because the doctrine that constitutes it and legitimates it shelters it from falsehood, while endowing it with all the adaptive and seductive power of the economy. The image, we might say, is phenomenologically true. It is the visible manifestation of something that founds the truth of the gaze inasmuch as it arouses not only our eyes, but the ardor and passion that inhabit us in the production of truth. It addresses itself to the element in each one of us that founds our adherence to life and thought as though they were the same thing. The *tekhné* that Chrysostom defends concerning language is nothing other than the art of speaking in order to show, to incarnate the Word in the flesh of language that cannot be anything other than our own living flesh. It is for this reason that the same word speaks of the christic incarnation, the incarnation of speech and the incarnation of the image.

This brief presentation of the economy, then, comes back to rhetoric in the sense that we discussed at the beginning. The art of speaking, as will prove to be the case with painting, is in an immanent and existential relation with our incarnation; but the flesh that it is concerned with does not reduce to the fragile and mortal envelope that renders us visible to the eyes of others during our ephemeral passage through this life. That flesh is nothing but appearance that is deceitful and deceived. The true flesh, however, the one that lives in the word and the image, does not concern appearance, but a becoming visible, there, where the order of manifestation overcomes all the traps of illusion. This flesh participates in the Parousia of being by keeping itself at a remove from it; it is the reign of "resemblance." But if this remove is of the order of the sign in the case of the word, the operation is even more complex in the image, because the icon, in having the right to the name of symbol, is no longer at the same remove with regard to being. It *reflects it as an enigma*, thus becoming the index and living proof of the existence of what it "crosses over to" (*diabainein*). The icon will escape the function of reference; rather, it will itself become what is referred to. As we will see shortly, the order of reference remains peculiar to the word, and more specifically, to the voice. But at the tribunal where the innocence and legitimacy of the icon is pled, however, transfigured flesh will be found not guilty because it produces the proof of its own redemption.

PART II

THE ICONIC ECONOMY

You shall not make for yourself an idol, whether in the form of anything that is in heaven above, or that is in the earth beneath, or that is in the water under the earth. You shall not bow down to them or worship them.

—Exodus 20:4–5; Deuteronomy 5:8–9

You shall not make wrongful use of the name IHVH, your God, for IHVH will not acquit anyone who misuses his name.

—Deuteronomy 5:11

When you cross over the Jordan into the land of Canaan, you shall drive out all the inhabitants of the land from before you, destroy all their figured stones, destroy all their cast images, and demolish all their high places.

—Numbers 33:51–52

IHVH spoke to you out of the fire. You heard the sound of words but saw no form; there was only a voice.

—Deuteronomy 4:12

For those whom he foreknew he also predestined to be conformed to the image of his Son.

—St. Paul, Romans 8:29

He is the image of the invisible God, the firstborn of all creation.

—St. Paul, Colossians 1:15

3

The Doctrine of the Image and Icon

To those who consider Byzantine art in a cursory fashion, it can appear repetitive and monotonous, immovably confined in hieratic iconographic forms, congealed by scriptural demands, by their cultic function and their place in the liturgy. This is so to such a degree that if we ignore the pleasure that the brilliance of materials, the luster and the pomp of the pictorial ensemble, confers on us today, we may ask ourselves whether we are in fact dealing with an art at all, in that for several centuries now, artistic development has most often been identified with the successive (more or less abrupt) introductions of new formulas, of singular works, marked either by the avatars of psychosociological analysis or the fetishism of novelty. The problem is compounded in that the Orthodox themselves are repelled by any museographic, hence pagan, exploitation of something that is fundamentally linked to a path that for them is spiritual.

It so happens that iconic doctrine supplies a response to the question of whether it is necessary to differentiate sacred from profane art generically, and it does this by means of the relational economy. With astonishing modernity, this doctrine provides its own solution to the question of the essence of art.

The canonical appearance of unchanging forms in Byzantine art is based on an economic doctrine that takes charge of the circulation of different gazes involved, as well as the question of abstraction itself. The problems of formal resemblance, of essential similitude, and of imitation (*ho-*

moiôsis, homoousia, mimêsis) appear as so many openings to action, so many horizons for knowledge, directions for active contemplation or efficient evangelization, while the servitude of reproduction and representation, as well as the imagining of illusory forms and the production of fictions, are radically excluded. In truth, Byzantine art never stopped "moving"—exactly like Alice on the other side of the looking glass, who discovers that she must run continuously in order to stand still. In order to preserve (*diasôzein*) its mimetic place, which is a place of movement, the icon had to fight on all sides against the temptations of *homoiôma* as *eidôlon*, that is to say, against the idolatrous threat that the fabric of the copy, of the *artefact*, constituted for the nature of the gaze when they became substitute objects receiving sacrilegious cult, by which we should understand a deadly adoration of nothing. For the iconophile, the idol, not having an ontologically based model, can only show fallaciously what does not exist or what is only the inanimate sign of death within the world. Conversely, through the effect of its doctrine, the icon sought not to fall into the categories of representation, fiction, or illusion at all. It belongs no more to the reign of the animate than the inanimate. Such is the strange situation that leads for the first time to the formulation of what a picture is. To say that the icon wanted to be a picture and not an idol or representation is to say that it institutes a gaze and not an object. Participating entirely in the Pauline reign of similitude and enigma, it aims at no "resemblance" other than assimilation, the ad-similation of seeing and being seen.

The iconoclasts were Christian believers. The temptations of atheism and rationalism that some would have liked to detect in their thought in order to be able to claim to be their followers during other periods of iconoclastic upheavals are totally foreign to them. Iconoclastic thought in Byzantium was not meant to be in the least revolutionary, and the worst accusation aimed at one camp or the other concerned the suspicion of innovation. Nonetheless, something new would be expressed, and what makes the reading and recognition of that novelty difficult is that it is expressed in terms of loyalty to memory and tradition. The iconoclastic crisis was a period of theoretical creation in a world where all novelty was regarded as diabolical and consequently condemned. Let there be no doubt, in order to invent a new world in the name of conservativism, extreme ingenuity is required, but we should also recognize in the liberties taken with classical thought during the crisis a true movement of philosophical inventiveness rather than a reprehensible effect of bad faith. Besides which, economic effectivenes and adaptability would of course demand the abandoning of rigor (*akribeia*) in the philosophical domain if required by spiritual interests. If pagan thought proved to be useful at any one moment, it could be used without regard for its integrity, then dropped when it stopped presenting immediate advantages.

The first iconoclastic crisis, which ended with the accession to the throne of Irene (784), had led to the formulas of the second council of Nicaea, which defended the true faith in respect of the true religion. The second crisis, after Irene's death (802), however, encountered a more demanding audience. This was a renewed iconoclasm, which regarded the responses and refutations issued by the Nicene council (formulated against Constantine V) as being neither persuasive nor sufficiently definitive to end the debate. Thus when Nikephoros speaks out against iconoclast thought from his place of exile, it is as a well-read philosopher and academic as much as, if not more than, a theologian.

In the face of the invasive expansion of the icon in Byzantium that began in the sixth century, it can be easily understood why a group of theological intelligentsia and the holders of spiritual power became alarmed.[1] Superstitions, fetishism, and all the pagan perversions linked to the talismanic manipulation of the image were all feared, and all of these fears were grouped together in the global condemnation of Hellenism and idolatry. However, besides this spiritual concern, the fact that iconoclasm was initiated by imperial power indicates the degree to which both faith and power were entangled with each other in this issue. When the emperor Constantine V (741–75), spokesman for state iconoclasm during the first iconoclastic period, denounced the icon, he did so by setting forth the following objections:

1. If the icon is like the model, it must be of the same essence and nature as it. However the icon is material and the model is spiritual, therefore this is impossible.
2. If the icon claims to resemble only the physical and perceptible form of the model, it necessarily divides it by separating its perceptible form from its invisible essence. The icon is therefore impious because it divides the indivisible.
3. If the icon draws the figure of the divine, it encloses the infinite within its line, which is impossible; therefore it only encloses nothing or falsehood, which forces it to renounce all homonymy.

4. If the icon is only venerated in what it shows, it is therefore its matter that is venerated. It is therefore an idol, and the iconophiles are idolaters.

Conclusion: the only *mimêseis* (we should not translate this too hastily as imitation, but rather as an act that aims to make present, to make *manifest*) "in truth and spirit" will be the cross, the eucharist, the virtuous life, and good government. The cross, because it respects divine invisibility by renouncing resemblance; the eucharist, because, being of the same substance as God, it is pure similitude without relative resemblance; the virtuous life and good government, because they are active engagements that aim at rejoining their model without claiming to identify with its form or essence. The living imitator would never attribute to himself the name of God and would therefore never be homonymous with him. Every other image is a pseudonym.

These iconoclast grievances comprise several different issues that are all nonetheless closely connected to the problem of the relation between the image and icon. The first is *homoousia*, or consubstantiality, which concerns the nature of any resemblance possible between the natural image and the artificial image. Both camps reject the idea of identity in terms of substance; for the iconoclasts, however, consubstantiality is part of the definition of every image of whatever sort, which in turn makes any artificial image impossible without sacrilege. For the iconophiles, consubstantiality would never be part of the definition of the image except, on the one hand, in the case of the natural image, where there is similitude between Father and Son, and on the other, in the eucharist, where there is no icon. Consubstantiality, for them, is not of the same order as manifestation. In all other cases, therefore, a different definition is required, one of a relational type, which would maintain similitude through the aspect of formal resemblance, even though substances are heterogeneous.

The second and third points made by Constantine concern objections to two constituent elements of the icon that the iconophiles would still have to meet, the doctrine of the graph[2] and homonymy. His last grievance deals with a different issue, the cultic consequences that are implied by the difference between the image and the icon, on the one hand, and the difference that prevents the icon from being confused with the idol, on the other. Here the iconophiles would have to show that the icon respects the hypostatic unity of divinity and therefore, even though it does not have the right to adoration, it nonetheless has the right to respect (*timé*) and prostration (*proskynesis*). This distinction would in turn be made possible by an argument that would rigorously separate the holy from the sacred, not allowing them to become confused with each other.

Given the overabundance of publications on the topic of what an icon is, what might still be possible to add to the many glosses, knowledgeable, aesthetic, and religious, already in existence? My answer here is that I believe that the philosophical analysis of the concept of the economy allows us to grasp something in icon doctrine that touches on questions that are essentially modern concerning the issue of images in general. It is therefore from an economic point of view that I will consider the following issues: the natural consubstantial image; the artificial image (or the icon) in its heterosubstantiality and its relational economy; and the nature of the graphic line and homonymy. Finally, I will put forward some brief thoughts on the placement of the icon in sacred places and public spaces—in sacred places, in order to examine the vocabulary of its sacredness in the profane world, and in public places, in an attempt to understand the pedagogical and political issues at stake in its constituent elements.

The Natural Image and Consubstantiality

Greek philosophy never neglected the image, but it also never left the site of an ontological questioning of *mimésis*. Rather, it almost appears as though the image had been summoned before a noetic or eidetic tribunal that made it renounce all dignity as a product of *tekhné*. During the early centuries of Christianity, discourse about the image was much more indebted to Platonic and Neoplatonic thought than Aristotelian. It concerned two things: the similitude of God's human creations in Genesis, and the interpretation of the Pauline expression of the Son as image of the Father. In what sense, however, do we resemble our creator? The reply is in the first instance spiritual and does not lead in any way to the possibility of making artificial images. In fact, the earliest Christian thinkers were mostly hostile to portrayal of any kind, in order to emphasize the distance that separated them from any form of Greek paganism and idolatry (bearing in mind that all non-Christian cults, including Jews, were called idolatrous!), and it was this aniconic tradition of proto-Christianity that was then passed on, in its anthology and references, to the later iconoclast thinkers.

The more the doctrine of the incarnation became a direct auxiliary to the establishment of the church's temporal power, however, the more the resemblance between the Father and the Son and between the Son and his mother posed problems that were extremely important yet delicate. It soon became necessary, therefore, to establish the relative unity of foundational similitude and historical resemblance, without making of the latter a purely transitory accident; as we have seen before in trinitarian theology and in the management of historical visibility, this is the crucial point where all economic thought hangs in the balance. In this connection, Gerhart Ladner, in his study retracing the development of iconic thought, notes that "The transfer of the image concept from the sensible to the intellectual realm [is] a long process traceable in Hellenistic and Early Christian thought from Plato to Philo and St. Paul, and from Plotinus and Proclus to Pseudo-Dionysios the Areopagite and St. John of Damascus."[3] It appears, then, that this trajectory permitted the legitimation of the perceptible world's spiritual participation in the intelligible world, and that this inspiration was anagogical in nature.

When the iconophile fathers, however, confronted iconoclast thought, the issue of the incarnation meant that they had to answer two separate questions: how did the natural, invisible image take on flesh, and how does the flesh of our visible images lead us back to that invisible image? With the arguments of the first iconoclastic period being so strongly Christological in nature, however, it was not until Nikephoros and the second iconoclastic period that icon doctrine became a philosophical doctrine based on the relational economy concerning images in general. This meant, therefore, that when Nikephoros came to formulate his arguments, he had to cast about for some theoretical assistance for them, some model for reasoning, and in the end, it was Aristotle who was invoked. Yet although it was true that evangelical doctrine could no longer do without a philosophical framework, it is also the case that the predicament could only be worsened by an attempt to use Aristotle to resolve theologico-political questions that originated in the social, political, and doctrinal history of Byzantium alone. This predicament, it is worth adding, is in itself fascinating to observe, as Nikephoros can be seen wrestling with a Classical vocabulary that he has trouble adapting to the new conceptual situation, and we should note in this context as well that the apparent lack of rigor evident in his writings is simply an effect of a system of thought searching for the language of its own formulations.

Nikephoros's knowledge of the Aristotelian texts is in all likelihood second hand, derived from commentators who were studied as part of the

Trivium and *Quadrivium*. Yet although several passages of the *Antirrhetics* show an ambiguous relation to Aristotle, the appeal that Nikephoros makes to him is never a mere token, either when he is not named or cited explicitly, or in quotations that are faithfully retranscribed. Was Nikephoros, then, so far from his sources at the end of his life that he no longer felt capable of accounting for them? Or again, did this great Christian thinker have to adopt either a universally apodictic tone or one of unshakable confidence to avoid making himself too explicitly dependent on a pagan thinker? In any case, his appeal to Aristotle is an appeal to natural reason, because from this point forward, the iconic cause becomes a natural, logical one, and the icon a question whose stakes are universal.

For the well-read Byzantine, Aristotle was first and foremost the author of the *Organon*, a work whose goal was taken to be solely the formulation of the logical rules of rigorous discourse. This "instrumental" use of the book resembles certain school exercises in the medieval universities, which is a far cry from the way in which references to the *Metaphysics* were made. The instrumental use, rather, reduced Aristotelianism to the mere learning of formal exercises for the foundation of propositional logic. Yet what still emerges clearly in the church fathers in respect of this is the idea that theological discourse ultimately amounts to choosing a theoretical and practical *manner of speaking* about something that had previously been regarded as having a character that was fundamentally unknowable and incapable of being formulated in words. This question of how to speak of the ineffable, which is central to theology, is of course a major concern of the economy as well. Relational thought as applied to both image and speech allows a purely nominalist discursivity to be avoided by proposing the existence of a specific kind of intimate relation between speech, the image, and their divine object. Image and icon doctrine is economic because it administers the possibilities of access to the manifestation of the divine and to its *relative* comprehension. It is thus effective in a way that is entirely at odds with the interpretation of the economy as a mere formal exercise of rhetoric.

In relation to these issues, several different problems arise: What is the link between the science of speaking and the legitimacy of the icon? What are the implications of the graphic constituents of inscription and writing? What is the relationship between a message borne by speech and one by icon? In order to deal with these, Nikephoros makes liberal use of the *Organon*, although he is not in the least hesitant to clash with Aristotelian opinion when doctrinal necessities require it. We should add in this connection that this philosophical pragmatism, which could also simply be called a tactical instrumentalism, was not difficult to arrive at because the *Metaphysics* was not taught in the cleric's or theologian's curriculum.

Image doctrine was thus born and developed under the pressure of a political crisis. That said, the fact that it was necessary to turn to the *Organon* in order to mount a defense against iconoclasm demonstrates clearly that the enemy had already reached a certain level of philosophical sophistication. The icon's defense was clearly no longer a simple defense of religion alone; rather, it had become a broader plea concerning the conditions and modalities of thought itself, and the future of that thought in a culture that was preparing a royal place within it for the image.

As the final word on Nikephoros's sources in Aristotle, we should note that since the incarnational economy necessarily engages the economy of speech, he occasionally has recourse to the *Categories* as well. Definitions, distinctions, and syllogisms based on a logic of inclusion appear, with quantifiers and operators that are characteristic of, or authorized by, Greek and a somewhat motley respect for Aristotle's text.

The initial step of Nikephoros's refutation of Constantine V concerns the essential and therefore consubstantial identity of image and model. The text begins by citing what was doubtless one of Constantine's questions (*Peusis*), although, as is fair enough under the circumstances, it is taken out of context: "That is why Mammon[4] adds immediately: 'If the icon is good, it is consubstantial with what it is the icon of.'" Nikephoros responds to this as follows:

> Therefore, you do not simply object that an image is made of Christ, but [you object] that the iconic copy is heterogenous to him, because Christ is one thing and the material out of which his icon is made is another. . . . If his intention were the natural image, which is absolutely opposed to the artificial image, and I mean the Son who is the image of the Father, his argument might have been tenable. He has failed, though, by using the copy here in an unintelligent way, since there is no need here for copies nor for objects to be aimed at [*stokhasma*] by our sight.[5]

Further on, he continues:

> Art imitates nature without the former being identical with the latter. On the contrary, having taken the natural, visible form [*eidos phusikon*] as a model and as a prototype, art makes something similar and alike. . . . It would be necessary then, according to this argument, that the man and his icon share the same definition and be related to each other as consubstantial things.[6]

What, however, is a *relation* of consubstantiality? The first question here concerns what a natural image is and in what sense one can still speak of a relation when there is an identity of substance, that is to say, when the image and the prototype are one. As we have seen, it fell to trinitarian theology to turn this original relation into the very essence of relations, and thus to raise the question of the image to the theoretical heights that it later reached. Nikephoros, however, does not pose the question of the nature of divine essence, but of what it is in the essence of our nature that depends on its imaginal nature, and that makes it participate in the natural image, which is to say, in the deity. *Similitude is in God; he is the Same without division.* The origin of the image is divine because the original image is divine. It is an invisible image, but the supreme image, the model of every image. The image is at the beginning, because in the beginning was the Word, and the Word is the image of God.

Within the domain of iconic thought, the Trinity can be expressed as *the Father, the Image, and the Voice.*

The nature of plurality, while it excludes alterity, is both imaginal and pneumatic. This relation is neither a relation of pure logical identity nor a homonymic relation because it does not refer to an equivalence of signs in the unity of the signified or a simple relative participation of the Son in the name of God. Rather, there is a plural unity of meaning itself that will come to form the basis for the legitimation, by derivation, of the icon's own duality. Whether situated on the level of the natural image or the artificial image, the image is underpinned by a system of thought that does not concern the sign, but rather concerns meaning. The foundational model of the consubstantial relation makes the image into a figure of meaning forever, not into a referential sign cut off from signification, and it is this that the church fathers call a symbol. Additionally, *figure* here must be understood as having nothing to do with rhetoric; rather, it concerns the figural character of the incarnation. The incarnation is not an in-corporation but an in-imagination, as we will see shortly. The image is everywhere a figure of immanence, absolute in the one case, relative in the other. In one it concerns a presence, in the other an absence. It is what Nikephoros calls *symbol,* in opposition to the sign privileged by the iconoclasts.

In what sense, then, is the relation of essential similitude still a relation? We have already encountered this point in our analysis of the trinitarian economy, and the answer is that the relationship in question oscillates between the rigor of the Aristotelian *pros ti* and the relational—that is, economic—mystery of the procession of divine uniplurality. Édouard

Hugon summarizes the formula in the following way: "The Son, because he originates from the Father, must have a real relation with him; the Holy Spirit, because it originates from both the Father and the Son, must have a real relation with both of them. In turn, the Father, because he has a nature that is identical with the Son, cannot not have a real relation with him."[7] This means that apart from the problems specific to the terrestrial incarnation (the problem of circumscribability), the Son and the Father have, for all eternity, a natural and real relation, through which the idea of a natural image is defined. This relation is called *skhésis*, not *pros ti*, and the term is attested in the trinitarian works of Gregory of Nazianzos, Athanasios, and Gregory of Nyssa. *Skhésis* has an advantage over *pros ti* in that it can absorb the *pros*, that is, the differential specificity of the relation, because its objective is intimacy. *Skhésis* has an emotional tone, keyed here not in a psychological or physiological mode, as sometimes happens, but referring rather to the relation of love or grace that ties the image to its model. *Skhésis* is the relation as it is comprised economically and no longer only logically; it is the mark of things that live, the mark of life itself. To be "the image of" is to be in a living relation. This is why the model of every relation is that of father and son: it is a donation of life (this implication is foreign to the Aristotelian *pros ti*), and it leads to the emotional power of each and every imaginal, and consequently iconic, relation. The grace of this imaginal relation will soon come to be rediscovered in the charismatic intimacy that supports the iconic relation, and Nikephoros himself will play on the two terms of *skhésis* and *pros ti* in order to pass more easily from the theological level (the natural image) to the economic level (the icon).

Skhésis does not originate in the vocabulary of logic. According to H. Bonitz, it occurs only twice in Aristotle, in *On the Movements of Animals* and the *Fragments*, where the phrase "*skhésis andros pros gunaika*," that is, "the relation of the man to the woman," appears.[8] In this case, the term has a heightened psychophysiological connotation with an emotional meaning, referring to familiarity and intimacy in the contact between people. A later use of the term is also found in Chrysostom, as noted by G. W. H. Lampe in the *Patristic Greek Lexicon*, associated with *oikéiôsis* and referring to the relations of proximity and intimacy that tie God to the angels.

Returning to the question of father and son, we find that they are in fact ordered in relation to each other; in this sense, paternity and filiation are relatives, and their relation is symmetrical, reciprocal, and simultaneous. This relation, however, does not refer to the essence of the terms, but only to the means by which they are related to each other. On the one hand, there is essential identity between them, yet on the other a verbal distinction (*secundum dici*) between individuals. Thus Gregory of Nazianzos writes: "Father is not a noun that refers to an essence or action; it is a noun that indicates the father's manner of being in relation to the son and the son's in relation to the father [*onoma skhéséôs*]."[9] Akakios of Berroia too speaks of a "*modus substantiae seu nomen est habitus*," *habitus* here being translatable by *skhésis*,[10] and Cyril of Alexandria writes in his *Dialogue on the Holy and Consubstantial Trinity* that "Father is a relative noun, and son also. . . . Whoever denies the father denies the son."[11]

The same insistence is found in John of Damascus, who reminds us in *The Orthodox Faith* that "Nouns of this sort do not refer to essence, but to a reciprocal relation and a mode of existence."[12] There is therefore one case, and one only, where *skhésis* refers to a relation of identity in order to maintain a distinction without confusion, and that concerns the Son of God, image of the Father, when both are referred to not in their essence but in their relation. Interestingly enough, if we return momentarily to the *Categories*, we find that there is nothing there that contradicts this, because within the father-son relation, it is not essences that are under discussion;[13] rather, the relation is simultaneous and reciprocal, as the *Categories* provides for.[14]

However, although it is not as essences that the father and son are relative, Aristotle does tell us, on the other hand, that whatever is similar is relative to what it resembles ("*to te gar homoion tini homoion legetai*").[15] In what sense, then, is the son the image of the father? Certainly not in the same way that an image is related to its model, as we will find in the case of the *homoiôsis* of the icon. Rather, the essence of the image "as itself" is in divinity. Everything that proceeds from the Father is his form and his voice.

Recourse to Plato is both tempting and embarrassing where Christian thought is concerned. Although Aristotle is only invoked methodologically, Plato was able to serve both iconoclast and iconophile causes, according to whether it was his condemnation of all images as copies of a model already untrustworthy because sensorial that was under consideration, or the *Timaeus*, where he takes the temporal display of the natural world to be the perfect and harmonious image of the eternal paradigm, the manifestation of the divine.[16] The Plato of the iconoclasts, however, is rather more the one who inspired Origen and Eusebios.[17] Is Christ not, in some way, the "mobile image" of the Father, he who the icon would have to represent with respect to a canonical, metrical system, the proportions of which are mathematically fixed? It is only through this that the "celestial image" of which Paul talks will become capable of being visibly and canonically portrayed, rejoining the harmony of the created cosmos that is the joy of the creator.

In order for the artificial image to rejoin the natural image, several conditions that are closely connected to each other, yet of different orders, will have to be united. The Holy Spirit will have to breathe upon the heart and soul of the person who is drawing and painting; the iconography will have to respect the canons of cosmological harmony, arithmetic canons that rule over the beauty of the world and the body. And last, and most importantly, it will be necessary to have an unimpeachable doctrine of the infinity of line and homonymy.

On the first two conditions, here is the painter's prayer: "Direct the hands [of thy servant] for the irreproachable and excellent depiction of the form of thy person." And here is the voice of the master:

Learn, O pupil, that in the whole figure of a man there are nine faces, that is to say nine measures, from the forehead to the soles of the feet. First make the first face, which you divide into three, making the first division the forehead, the second the nose and the third the beard. Draw the hair above the face to the height of one nose-length; again measure into thirds the distance between the beard and the nose; the chin takes up two of the divisions and the mouth one, while the throat is one nose-length. Next divide from the chin to the middle of the body into three measures, and from there to the knees two more; for each knee you take one nose-length. Take again two more measures to the ankle-bones, and from them to the soles of the feet one more nose-length, and from there to the toe-nails one more measure. From the pit of the throat to the shoulder is one measure, and likewise to the other shoulder. For the thickness of the upper arm take one nose-length and measure to the elbow from above one measure, and again one more to the base of the hand; from there to the fingertips is one more measure. Both the eyes are equal, and the distance separating them is equal to one eye. . . . When a man is naked his waist should be four nose-lengths across.[18]

The numerical obsession evident here clearly has Pythagorean origins and attests to the secret hope of finding a material itinerary worthy of essential similitude, by the use of a canon of proportions.

To sum up, then, the natural image allows a fundamental definition of the image radically *independent of visibility.* To be seen is not its aim, and visibility does not belong within its essential definition. The remove that necessarily separates every model from its expression in signs is outside its remit, because neither expressiveness nor the sign are part of its definition.

Being one only with the economic figure of the divine procession, it is its manifestation and configuration, first in the invisible figure of similitude, then in the display of carnal visibility. Thus the icon, made in the image of this image, will no longer be expressive, signifying, or referential. It will not be inscribed within the space of a gap, but will rather incarnate withdrawal itself. It is in the withdrawal of the figure that the *transfiguration of the flesh that is made into the body of the natural image* is effected. *It is the natural image that refers to the icon and not the reverse.*

The theme of contempt for the flesh does not in the least contradict the glorification of the body. The body must once again become glorious. It is for this reason that two contradictory interpretations arose from the theme of the transfiguration. For the iconoclasts, it concerned a victory of spirit over matter, thus rendering the portrayal of that triumphant and radiant immateriality useless and impious. For their adversaries, it was on the contrary the triumph of the flesh over sin, suffering, and death. Portrayal is therefore the *portrayal of life* itself, of which the economy was the condition of possibility and manifestation, organic as well as spiritual.

The status of the natural image's relation to its own essence finds a new application when the visibility of the Word maintains a specific relation of intimacy with its essential similitude in the incarnation, and the transfiguration then makes manifest the imaginal identity of this essential similitude. In rejecting this relation, however, it was difficult for the iconoclasts to avoid the temptation of Docetism, which made of the living flesh a phantomlike or transitory appearance, no longer maintaining any intimacy with the natural image. Rather, the image as Word remains invisible and consubstantial, but Christ, because he took human form, will go to the ends of dissimilarity in order to finally recover his foundational identity and at the same time make us participate in that recovery. It is this participation that is at stake in the icon.

What links the economy of the natural and consubstantial image to the artificial icon and prevents them from being confused with each other is the question of *absence* or *emptiness*, which is also the mark of the historical economy. This is no doubt the reason that, instead of appearing to be a philosophical meditation, the economy is thought of as an "empty concept" by those who refuse to understand that what is at issue is the specification of something in the foundation of the imaginal gaze that always necessarily involves a problematic of withdrawal and vacuity.

It is this that is also undoubtedly the "secret" of the image, by which

I mean that which it both secretes and hides, and which Paul gave voice to in his formulation of the specular enigma. What is an enigma? The providing of meaning to hidden words, a cryptic word that suddenly exposes what was until then a pure mystery. An enigma is opposed to a mystery not in its negation, but as a figure of its hidden manifestation. The icon does not fall within a theological mystery, but within an economic enigma. There, the Word marries the flesh, the voice fertilizes the body. Whoever understands this accepts the power of the gaze and renounces the naive declaration that he only believes what he sees or that he only sees what is visible. Thus the first way of thinking about looking at the icon is established, inasmuch as it is the first way of thinking about an invisible gaze coming from the image itself and *dispensed* by it. The constituents of the icon summon the gaze and challenge vision without, for all that, trying to take advantage of it.

The Artificial Image, or the Icon

> He believes that copies do not differ in anything at all from the models that they are the copies of, and that the identity of nature and substance between elements that share only resemblance is purely maintained. But how could someone distinguish the image from the copy if there is no difference between them, resulting from their different natures?
>
> —Nikephoros, *Antirrhetics*, I, 228 B. [trans. V.D.]

The question raised by icononphilia concerns the icon's legitimacy and faithfulness to the image that is its original, foundational model. The economic relation of the artificial icon to the natural image concerns precisely the organization and function of visibility in its relation to the invisible image, which remains the only true image. In other words, the question ceases to be whether the icon is either by nature or definition true or false, or good or bad, because its truth is derived not from itself but from its founding cause. *The essence of the image is not visibility; it is its economy, and that alone, that is visible in its iconicity.* Visibility belongs to the definition of the icon and not the image. This is why the icon is nothing other than the economy of the image, and its task is to be faithful to the prototype of each and every economy. The question, then, is how the artificial image will resemble the Word. For if God's Word chose the visible and the flesh in order to distribute the salvation of the image by means of the image, it is up to us to take into account this choice of the flesh in order to render forever present and visible the memorial of our redemption. Whoever rejects the icon refuses to arise from the dead.

How must an icon be if its goal is to be recognized in its similitude and legitimacy by the gaze that the Image directs at it?

The icon aims at resemblance to its prototype without trying to maintain with it the relation of similitude that the prototype maintains with its own substance. What relation of resemblance, therefore, would be possible between the icon and the essence of similitude? This is the question internal to each and every *tekhné*, which, being authorized by the use of the term *stokhasma* ("the object aimed at" or "target"), must carry out an act of *mimésis* that is not only purely formal, but as one might say, deliberate and abstract as well.

The Iconic Economy and the Mimetic Relation (Mimésis-Skhésis)

Once Nikephoros has departed the terrain of consubstantiality, he rethinks the category of relations in order to establish the foundations of the icon. He thus switches registers and resituates himself, which he does because the question of the icon can only be broached from within the economic order—which is exactly the one that controls the switching of registers.

In constructing his arguments, Nikephoros turns to the *Organon*, because it deals with definitions, homonymy, synonymy, and the category of relations. Aristotle thus becomes the instrument through which the aporias of theological discourse will be reduced to a pure problem of language. Returning momentarily to the *Categories*, we read there that essences can never be relative ("*oudémia ousia tôn pros ti estin*").[19] Playing on *pros ti* and *skhésis* in turn, Nikephoros gives them a technical sense that is closely linked to the question of the icon. Thus the Son has a double relation: one with the Father, which is pure, essential intimacy, and the other with humanity, which is a relation of relative identity because it is subjugated to the visible and perceptible conditions of our world. Thus, if the carnal Christ continues to be an image of the Father, and therefore a natural image at the time that he assumes the human *morphé*, then it must be the case that an economic relation of similitude ("*homoiôsis kat' oikonomian*") occurs between God and his Son, an effect of purposive organization in the temporal world.

The statement that Jesus continually remained an image of the Father may be taken to mean that Christ was necessarily the most beautiful and intelligent of men possible, spared from suffering and mortality, the natural image conferring on the visible the whole organized manifestation of his perfection. Yet this is also a dead-end solution that can only lead to Christ's sacrifice being a useless act, because he would in that case no longer resemble us. Additionally, if that were so, the redemption would constitute an impasse that would extinguish all hope for the salvation of our own weakness and mortality. Christ must therefore share our imperfection; it is only through his being similar to us that he saves us. In other words, the natural image of the Father must have agreed to imitate us. He made himself similar to us, with the exception of sin. Christ is thus twice an image, being both the image of the Father and in the image of man. The steward (*oikonomos*) of the paternal image, he teaches us to imitate by submitting himself to imitation. The christic mimetic is therefore not the imitation of a model, no matter how one considers it, because neither God nor man is a model for him. *Mimésis* is the act by which the image rejoins the image, because it is the image that is the prototype. The image is made flesh. And if that is so, what will the flesh of our own images be?

All this raises yet another question: how can our imperfect hands and our gaze, blurred by sin, produce an image of such perfection, all the more so now that the transitory flesh that assumed the Word is no longer here to inspire our eyes? Undoubtedly, it was this melancholic observation that partially inspired the tradition of acheiropoietic images, those not made by human hands, but rather produced miraculously by divine grace. These images made it possible for an artist to be highly faithful to the real model because they were its direct, immediate, unstained imprint. As we have already seen, however, the artists' canons tell us that the true solution lies elsewhere; it is of a doctrinal order and can only arise at the end of the debate regarding the real meaning of mimesis and grace. Of course, the issue of the imprint and the trace, called by some an index, often finds an echo in icon doctrine. However, the question then becomes one of justifying the resemblance of the figure to an absent original, rather than being about submission to a real model. Passed on by the metaphor of the seal and the wax, the indexical trace is as inseparable from the history of our images as the stain and blood, for the image is fundamentally tied to the question of absence and death. Here, however, rather than considering the icon in its mythical or imaginary aspects (which Ewa Kuryluk has already done in a thorough and stimulating study),[20] we will examine it in terms of its doctrinal constituents only.

Within this context, then, let us now turn to questions concerning the graph and iconic inscription. Here, the icon is categorially separated off from the indices of the acheiropoietic tradition, despite the iconographic imagination being broadly nourished by the legendary existence of those images not made by human hand, and the fact that the theme of the veronica also bore a close connection with the history of relics and the founding myths of iconicity. These issues, however, we will return to later.[21]

The icon sets the visible and the invisible into a relation with each other without any concessions to realism, yet without contempt for matter. This relation would then make it possible to begin considering the meaning of the icon's abstraction, and the economy would in turn become able to implement that "abstract" relation that characterizes the formal, deliberate resemblance of the icon to its model. This is the question of iconic *homoiôsis*, or the formal resemblance that cannot be reduced to the material constituents of *homoiôma*, that is, of the facsimile, of the material copy. The model is called the hypostasis, by which it is to be understood that the historical Christ is the existential manifestation of God in a synthetic unity that mysteriously links the two natures, human and divine, to each other without mixing them together or altering them. The chosen moment when this hypostatic unity appeared in the visible world of history is the incarnation. By the time the question of the icon arose, of course, this event already dated back more than eight centuries, but the nature of its actual presence, its remembrance, and its cult became a topic of active debate.

The general question of the image always concerns the term *eikon*. For the artificial icon, the term *homoiôsis* is the one that recurs everywhere as the general concept of similitude, even though constant attempts are made to diversify it through analysis—if not in kind, then at least in aspect. In order to grasp the specificity of *homoiôsis*, then, we need to return to the definitions that give the vocabulary of the icon its chief characteristics.

In terms of its materiality, the icon is called *apeikasma*, *eikonisma*, and finally *homoiôma*, which is associated with *ektypôma*, which itself refers again to the copy and the ectype. The inanimate object itself is neutral, and this can only be fully grasped by linking it immediately to *stokhasma*: the object with which one aims to deviate from the similar (*paragôge toû proseikotos*). Here is Nikephoros on the subject:

The archetype is the principle and the model underlying the visible form that is made from it, as well as the cause from which the resemblance derives. This is the definition of the icon such that one could use it for all artificial icons: an icon is a likeness of the archetype, and on it is stamped, by means of its resemblance, the whole of the visible form of what it is a likeness of, and it is distinct from its model only in terms of a different essence because of its material. Or [another definition]: an icon is an imitation of the archetype and a copy differing [from the model] in its essence and in its underlying substance. Or [it is] a product of art portraying the visible form of the archetype by imitating it, but it differs from the model in its essence and its underlying substance. Indeed, if the icon does not differ in anything [from the archetype], then it is not an icon, but nothing other than the archetype itself. Thus, the icon is a likeness and a replica of beings who have their own existence.[22]

The vocabulary that refers to the model, on the other hand, is not as broad in scope. Even when it implies an irreducible duality in what it refers to, it is far from being as ambiguous. It is called *hypostasis, hypokeiménon,* that is, the formal, not the material substrate of the icon, and also *archétypon* and *prototypon.* And when Christ is referred to in his carnal economy, he appears as *eidos,* that is, a visible form, *morphé,* a perceptible form, *skhéma,* a figure, *charactèr,* a line of the face or the silhouette, *tupos,* an image as a sign or imprint, and therefore less strictly iconic than a symbol.[23]

How, then, does Nikephoros deal with the question of relations?

It is not inopportune now, I think, to add to my speech that the icon is related to [*skhésis*] the archetype and that it is the effect of a cause. Therefore, it is necessary that the icon both be one of these relatives [*pros ti*] and be called such. The relatives, these very same things, depend upon things other than themselves, and change their relationships reciprocally [*antistréphi te skhési pros allèla*].

For example, the father is called the father of his son and inversely, the son is called the son of his father. In a similar way we can talk about the friend of a friend, and about the right of the left and, inversely, about the left of the right. Similarly, the master is the master of the slave and inversely, and the same can be applied to all similar cases.[24]

In this section, Nikephoros is following chapter 7 of the *Categories* fairly closely: "We call relatives all such things as are said to be just what they are, *of* or *than* other things."[25] Although Aristotle is not speaking of images here, what he does say is still of great importance for us: similarity is a relative, and he adds to this the point that all relatives have their correlative, as the master and the slave ("*panta dè tá pros ti pros antistréphonta légetai*"). Nikephoros, however, continues as follows: "So, in this way, the archetype is the archetype of the icon, and the icon is the image of the archetype. Anyone who asserts that the icon does not concern a relation could not assert that it is an icon of something."[26] Earlier, he had already provided some additional information:

As if, for example, when talking about a man, it were said not that his icon resembles him but that he resembles his icon. It is as though even if the existing relationship between the icon and the archetype were reversed, their relationship would remain the same and unchangeable, and it could be said that not only is there an icon of a man but also that there is a man of an icon. On this premise, from this point on, one could wonder which of the two is the cause of the other and antecedent to the other.[27]

These passages are entirely imbued with Aristotelian concerns that warn us against the inadequate conversion of correlatives. Aristotle states clearly that there is a natural simultaneity of the terms of a relation, but that certain relatives have a necessary anteriority over their correlates,[28] and he gives the example of the object of a science, which has a de facto anteriority over that science. Nikephoros, it is true, does insist on the anteriority of the prototype, but because *homoiôsis* is a knowledge (*gnôsis*), the model cannot therefore participate in the same type of anteriority as the object of science itself. The concept that he is wary of analyzing more rigorously, however, is the notion of cause. In the case of the natural image, the relation of the Father to the Son had already smoothly absorbed the problem of the causal relation; here again, in the domain of the artificial image, the prototype becomes the objective cause of the icon thanks to the *oikonomia.* Materially, Christ can no longer be the cause of his icon, but formally, he continues to inform the perceptible world, to the degree that this world aims toward him, offers him that empty (*kénon*) zone that was once the site of his incarnation and which remains henceforth the site of his manifestation. There is, indeed, a relation between the icon and the prototype that is nothing other than the one that ties science to its object, for *mimésis* is a relative gnosis.

The Aristotelian *homôion*, taken from the outset as a relative, is first of all defined as a copy (*homoiôma*), which is to say, as a fabricated image (*apeikasma katá tekhnèn*). This is the dimension of the *périgraphè* (outline) in the strict sense, which Nikephoros calls again *apotélesma tès tèkhnès katà mimèsin*: the fulfillment of the art according to *mimésis*, and therefore different to *mimésis* itself. Its primary characteristic is that it is essentially graphic; it is the visibility of the visible, in the same way that the copy aims at that visibility as *stokhasma.* All the aspects of the *homoiôma* inscribe Christ's body in matter as his impression (*typos*). In this way, the Aristotelian demand regarding the correct attribution of correlatives is respected: it is not essences that are relatives, but only the correctly attributed relative and correlative. Here, that means circumscribed, circumscribable, and circumscription. *Homoiôma* is a relative.

To be an image is to aim toward a model, it is to be toward it, as St. Thomas clearly reminds us: "A relation, by its essential logic, is not something, but to something [*non habet quod ponat aliquid, sed ad aliquid*]."[29]

The specific feature of *homoiôsis* (which refers to similitude in the iconic relation) is to mediate between extreme terms (*mésiteuei toîs akroîs*), so much so that "it is the hypostasis itself that one can see in the icon of the one who is painted." The icon *mimeitai,* which is to say that it renders the relation to the Word (*pros logon*) present and visible, that it is *ad-verbum,* to paraphrase Meister Eckhart, who speaks of both man and the image as an adverb. Additionally, if the icon is mimetic, hence "adverbial," the earlier images, such as the lamb, had no status other than "pro-verbial." *Mimésis* refers therefore to *homoiôma* as a directed emptiness. Ladner writes in this connection: "For the church fathers and for the Byzantines, identity between image and original does not exist with respect to the former's matter or the latter's nature. . . . The identity is only a formal ideal, a relational one (according to *skhésis* or *pros ti*)."[30] This is what allows us to use the phrase "formal resemblance" to translate iconic *homoiôsis* in all its senses, with the proviso, however, that the concept of form falls entirely within the category of relations, and that relations itself refers not to dependence, but to orientation.

From this perspective, the icon is perhaps the best historical introduction to the development of abstraction. Within it, form has a nonobjective reality very close to Mondrian's admonition to "no longer be concerned with form as form." It is as indifferent to empirical reality as it is to an ideal or fictive beauty that would bring *mimésis* and the icon into the orders of reference and representation respectively. Difficult though this may be to accept, it must be admitted that the icon attempts to present the grace of an absence within a system of graphic inscription. Christ is not in the icon; the icon is toward Christ, who never stops withdrawing. And in his withdrawal, he confounds the gaze by making himself both eye and gaze.

The nature of this withdrawal can only be understood by thinking of it within the framework of the double register that constitutes it. The first bears the mark of the absence of the model. The anagogical property of the icon leads us through a site of which it is the itinerary, the path. The limit of iconic vision is the gaze of the icon in the uninterrupted volt of the face-to-face encounter. Because the function of the *homoiotic* icon is to relate the human form to the divine Word, it is *mimésis* of the incarnation itself. "Whoever rejects the image rejects the incarnation," "Whoever rejects the image rejects the economy," is how the existential role of the icon must be understood. The relation that ties *tekhné* to *mimésis* is the same as the one that links *morphé* to *logos*. Thus in the third apology of *On the Divine Images*,[31] John of Damascus writes: "For each thing, that which is according to nature comes first, and only afterwards, what is according to convention [*thésin*] and according to *mimésis*." *Mimésis* is therefore no closer to essence than a simple material copy. It is its iconic correlate.

That the Aristotelian notion of *mimésis* should become slowly contaminated by *kharis*, as Kantorowicz argues in "Deus per Naturam, Deus per Gratiam," should not surprise us at all.[32] This contamination demonstrates again, although it is hardly necessary to do so, that by way of imitation, *mimésis* aims for nothing other than the actualization of the incarnation, that is, the uninterrupted propagation of the *oikonomia* as a relation. In this way, the ancient privilege of vision over speech is reconfirmed, as Theodore of Stoudios recalls once more: "*opsis protêra akouei.*" Kantorowicz cites a considerable number of examples drawn from Greek and Latin patristics where the pairs *phusis-mimésis* or *natura-imitatio* and then *phusis-kharis*, or *natura-gratia*, refer to a relation that moves from theology to economy, then more specifically, from God to humans. He also notes that these pairs correspond naturally to the opposition "*possidere aut consequi*"; thus, for example, St. Jerome writes in the *Tractaeus in Librum Psalmorum*: "*Quod dii sumus non sumus natura sed gratia.*"

This famous distinction has its origins in Psalm 82:6, which was constantly reinterpreted with reference to the significance of our divinity: "You are gods, children of the Most High, all of you." Yet is there really a substitution of imitation by grace, as Kantorowicz claims? He considers the terms to be interchangeable, and that the former tended to be abandoned because it was too anthropocentric in character. Additionally, grace, on his reading, would confer on God alone the centrifugal power of radiating even the possibility of a contemplative relationship. Personally, I do not believe this, at least not in relation to Nikephoros's text. *Homoiôsis* appears to retain there, in its considerable density, all the relational properties of *ho-*

moiôma and *mimêsis*. Equally, the claim would appear to neglect the whole side of the economy that ensures the ongoing, endless exchanges between perceptible matter and essences. Above all, however, it would prevent the notion of knowledge (*gnôsis*) that Nikephoros speaks of from being given its true value. Perhaps for him, still under the influence of the Aristotelian model, a relation remains a specific aim, not only of gesture and look, but of human intelligence as well, because it makes the hypostasis known to us without "representing" its object, even as it still respects its anteriority and activity. What does not constitute grace, however, and yet produces *mimêsis* is the sensitive contemplation of a glittering absence, made by the hand of man. *Homoiôsis* does indeed play a role in the human tasks of seeing and knowing. The icon was willing to wager that a man-made image would be able to renounce the representation of reality and attract instead the gaze of truth. Kandinsky once said that there were some people who, departing for Berlin, would get off the train at Ratisbonne, by which he meant that they considered themselves to have arrived safe and sound when they had completed only half the journey.[33] In this sense, Orthodox painters and thinkers refuse to get off at Ratisbonne. To us, this is not only due to grace, but also to the rigor with which mimetic doctrine was briefly cast. To identify *homoiôsis* too actively with grace would be to betray this ardent, polemical, and theoretical will to establish the only view possible of the visibility of the invisible. That, in effect, is the iconoclast perspective. Nonetheless, there can be no doubt that the chance of ending up in Berlin arises only because the correlate of *mimêsis* is grace. Otherwise stated, it is because the relation between the natural image and the icon is a function of the charismatic economy established on the model of the incarnation that the iconic shadow takes on a colored hue, that the copy (*homoiôma*) becomes mimetic. The knowledge that the mimetic icon makes possible concerning the hypostasis is in turn supported by the acquaintance that the hypostasis has with us. Thus, seeing implies being seen. The icon contemplates us. In its turn, it becomes God's gaze at the contemplator's flesh, which gets caught in an informational and transformational circuit of relationships. The flesh transfigured by the icon transfigures the gaze turned upon it. The icon acts; it is an effective instrument and not the object of a passive fascination. Perhaps it is in this way that we should understand the story, endlessly repeated, of a viewer who is gripped with emotion and then converts at the mere sight of an icon. Unfortunately, we cannot enter here into the problem of miraculous images from a sociological, psychological, or magical standpoint. In terms of *mimêsis* and *kharis*, however, the issue concerns the iconic body's effective power as a transfigurative agent. It functions within the evidence of the *manifestatio*. Whoever sees it sees himself or herself. Whoever sees it is seen. The icon derives a particular power from its relational and theoretical status that explains the role that it was then able to play in Byzantium in civic, administrative, and juridical life. It functioned as an effective presence, the presence of a gaze that provides guarantees and cannot deceive. Born under the sign of relations, it presides over all contracts. However, the presence of the iconic gaze cannot be described as a real presence. In the artificial image, it is the pressure of absence that bears all the weight of authority. The icon teaches us that the economy of gazes never substitutes for the people in whom those gazes found their physical flesh. As we have already said, the issue here is not one of representation. What becomes law in the icon is what it portrays the lack of for us. It is the effective and efficient form of the lack that the divine model of each and every economy assumed in the "kenosis" of its annihilation.

The icon perhaps never had any model other its own end goal, that is, the visible experience of a truth whose imprint it makes present on its own flesh and whose grace it makes present on its own horizon. Thus the contemplative gaze produces the truth of the icon, the truth as an existential relation. Consequently, form becomes inobjective and settles upon its own emptiness. The icon's obvious disinterest in both realism and Classical-style aesthetic idealization bears witness to its bitter struggle against the simulacra of the *morphê*. The prototype is interior to the desert heart of the icon. In "Byzantine Art in the Period Between Justinian and Iconoclasm," Kitzinger, having performed a subtle analysis of the stylistic influences operating on the icon, is surprised to discover that on the eve of the iconoclast crisis the tendency that prevailed was what he calls *abstract*, believing rather that it should have been the development of Hellenistic realism that would have had to have been responsible for the iconophobe reaction.[34] However, the argument that we have been making about economic thought and its graphic, doctrinal, and political unity leads directly to the conclusion that it is precisely the abstraction of the icon that is in question in the debate with iconoclasm. Moreover, it is striking that a half-century before Kitzinger, Wilhelm Worringer had used Byzantine art as an example illustrating a tendency toward abstraction against *Einfühlung*.[35] Will scholars never stop talking only about iconoclasm in relation to abstraction?

The oriental doctrine of the icon, then, should no longer be categorically opposed to the image relation as it is found in the West. We turn now to an investigation that will demonstrate, on the contrary, that the greatest western pictorial works of art also necessarily concern an existential relation to the presence of an emptiness, although in a place where this is not always perceived. By this we mean that in their secret emptiness, they remain faithfully indifferent to representation, in order to maintain a *skhésis*, a *pros ti*, where mimetic polarities are linked together, between the spectator and their invisible center. All great art is kenotic.

*The Line, the Void, and the Virgin's Body (*Graphè-Périgraphè*)*

What does it mean, in terms of principles and consequences, to portray a face captured in iconic space, and constituted by a setting of closed forms? For the iconophile, the pictorial inscription of the body is not in any way a circumscription that might imprison or limit that body. The iconoclast, however, claims loudly that such a gesture encloses and limits divine infinity, the unenclosability of the Word.

In this respect, one must be wary of taking the incarnation as a corporeal weightiness of the Word that will be filled with flesh. The infinite cannot be filled. The Word illuminated flesh. The incarnation, called *sarkosis*, is also referred to in Pauline and subsequent texts by the term *kenosis*. When the word was made flesh, *it emptied itself*.[36] This hollowing out of the incarnation is found again in the defense of the icon itself. The icon is not in any way filled with Christ. Its graphic limits do not in any way contain or keep captive the essence of the Word. The iconic line, as much as the Virgin's womb, is therefore a threshold always overflowing with the existence of the Word, for a gaze that resigns itself to doing without circumscription. In Paul, the kenosis of the Son definitely refers to Christ's agreeing to take on the form of a slave ("*labôn morphèn doulou*"), which means that the Son's epiphany in the visible world was carried out under the sign of dereliction and death. Christ's anthropomorphism even went so far as to cause the Father to be left behind, the sacrificial rupture between the image and the model. Kenosis therefore really signifies abandoning divinity, leaving it outside the world. By his sacrifice, the divine imitator filled in the distance that separated the image torn from the model, assuming its decay. In rising from the dead, he carried along with him the carnal image that he had agreed to identify himself with for a time, opening for it a heaven of promises in which the human image and the natural image would be reconciled. This is a true saga of the image, which is nothing other than the saga of the incarnation itself, where the salvation of the body, expressed as the salvation of the soul, is nothing other than the salvation of the body expiated by a God who reveals himself as the essence of the image. Once God is hidden, the God of all mysteries emerges in the light of his enigma.

It must be understood in what way the line, this incision or marking of the medium that separates the plane in two, that cuts it, subjugates us to the artifices of form, without (for all that) undermining the essence of its model. The line is an edge where being begins, an embankment where something ends. Inscription (*graphé*) allows nouns to be declined. Thus form is that roll[37] of the world that encircles masses, or rather, conceptualizable zones, in an homogenous space, but that encloses nothing. Does whatever exists within the line, ringed by it, therefore have meaning, or a hollowed-out meaning? Does the line engender a full and differentiated space, or with its raw wound, its graphic fissure, does it mark the visible limits of the void itself? Form in the icon is exceeded by its function. The iconic line, the one that forms a contour, will never be a perimeter, a limit for the being that it shows. Christ's face, which allows itself to be seen in the form of *morphé, eidos, skhéma, tupos, charactèr*, resembles him according to a mimetic that must be firmly distinguished from circumscription (*périgraphè*), even if this limitation was his lot during his terrestrial life. To imprint is not to encircle. To draw is not to delimit. Christ is not the prisoner of the icon; *the iconic graph is neither a prison nor a tomb*, as it was for the Platonic soul and body. It is crucial to understood that the duality that inhabits the icon has nothing to do with the duality of body and soul, but with that of the Word and humanity.

The invisibility of the Word is different in nature to the invisibility of the soul. This is why the iconoclast reproach concerning the inanimate character of the icon is unacceptable to the iconophile, who can only see in it an Apollinarist confusion. The iconic graph must be understood as a triumph of the flesh, which is transfigured by the spirit of the Word, not the *psykhe*. This, at least, is the doctrine that underpins the graph. The fact that the iconic object is inanimate establishes a relative similitude with the humanity of its model, and the fact that it is visible creates another relative similitude with the divinity of that same model. The icon is no more similar to man than it is to God. But it maintains with both natures a relationship of which line and color are the sole vectors of the manifestation of a relationship between them. There is no pretense, therefore, to a summoning or evocation of the prototype, as is the case with the idol, to which the effigy *appeals.* In iconophile thought, the idol tries to take possession of and retain the occult force that it dreads or invokes. The idol, as we will see, is on the side of the double.[38] The iconic mimetic, however, is alien to duplication. The icon claims to show the liberty of the omnipresent God by not seizing it anywhere, by not calling to it, but rather allowing its voice to be raised and to act causatively. To not circumscribe is to make manifest infinity and liberty.

As an effect of line, the incarnation operates in withdrawal. *The mimetic of the line is its withdrawal.* The absence of God at the heart of the icon is to be understood in Christ's double mimetic articulation: the emptiness of the kenosis (*kenósis,* the annihilation assumed by the Son in radical exile, far from the Father) became the emptiness of a perceptible form, and then a luminous radiation of the maternal flesh transfigured by the *Father's voice.* It is within the remit of the iconic economy to make itself similar to this double hollowing out. The icon speaks of mourning and the resurrection by turns. The icon's flesh strives toward what was the flesh of the resurrection that it commemorates and of which it maintains the promise. Christ's icon is empty of his carnal and real presence—in this it differs radically from the eucharist—but is full of its absence, which by the trace that it leaves and the lack that it incarnates, produces the very essence of the visible. *To incarnate oneself is to empty oneself, or what amounts to the same thing, to become similar to one's own image.*

When the Word became flesh, divinity did not fill up with matter, no more than matter with divinity. The icon, as a memorial to the incarnation, is therefore really a memorial to the hollowing out that is brought about by the infinity of the line. In order to understand Christian doctrine as being no more or less than a doctrine of the image, it is crucial to avoid the fundamental error of confusing the incarnation with materialization. The incarnation is not a materialization: the icon as a memorial of the incarnational economy makes use of a flesh that is not matter. This is what the iconophiles accuse the iconoclasts of having missed in reproaching the icon for its materiality, as is supposed to be the case for the object labeled "idol." Idol, in fact, is the word with which one denounces the supposed "materialism" of one's enemy.

It is because "became flesh" is not equivalent to "became matter" that the question of what it is that constitutes the flesh of our images and the body of our institutions arises in a completely new way. Economic thinking about the flesh is even more complex and subtle than it might first appear in that it demands that another error, as weighty as the first, be avoided. This is the claim that the incarnation is a dematerialization, or alternatively, constitutes the idealization of matter. But transfiguration is not idealization. The light that forms Christ's flesh is real and natural, similar in every way to the flesh of our similitude before the fall, and to what that flesh will once again become by means of the redemptive economy.

The meaning of this cannot be understood without further examination of the doctrine of kenosis, which I take to be a system of thought concerning an emptiness that makes place for the light of real, natural, and transfigured matter. Only then does it become possible to glimpse that element that has the ability to become imaginal flesh rendered visible in iconic flesh. Kenosis has often been interpreted solely from the aspect of divine condescension as referring only to the humility, poverty, and nudity of the Messiah. The "form of the slave" of which Paul speaks would in this sense be nothing but terrestrial exile, far from the Father's glory. But in the debate over the image, the question of the incarnational emptiness takes on a whole new amplitude, because it perpetuates the emptiness of the Parousia in the very form of the iconic memorial.

The line produces a partition of space, as the coming of Christ produced the partition of time between the Old and New Covenant. Henceforth, the representation of the Messiah in the symbolic form of the lamb can be abandoned; henceforth, Christians have the right to the face, a sign of the new law. Christ is risen, his face, his person (*prosôpon*) triumphs over the cross, and the transfiguration of his body continues in the icon. Transfiguration, *métamorphôsis*: this is the word that refers both to the glory of the risen body and the workings of the gaze upon the icon. Iconoclasm claimed that Christ's body could only be portrayed before the resurrection, before he had reencountered the luminous immateriality of his divine nature. Nonsense, exclaimed the iconophiles; the icon is a memorial to both natures, and therefore to his arisen nature as well. The line on the panel can no more imprison than the cross could annihilate. The icon of Christ's face rims Christ, just as his absent grace rims the gaze of the contemplator. The face in the icon rims an essence whose incarnation and resurrection the icon reiterates, *but never represents.*

Faced with the iconoclast's leitmotif concerning divine uncircumscribability, Nikephoros, in a veritable theoretical tour de force, convinces his audience that there is a radical difference between iconic spatiality and the spatiality of natural perception. This is his one truly novel contribution to the philosophy of the image. The law of the icon, which I will call its *ico-nomia*, is its topical singularity, its phenomenological specificity. The visible is not the perceptible. What is unduly attributed to aesthetics has nothing to do with perception. And despite everything, the icon looms up before our eyes to manifest a body whose light it welcomes, without ever appropriating. This is what graphic inscription can do: it relates a visible periphery to an invisible and transfigured content. It has no existence other than the preliminary, and the threshold that it marks is the threshold of infinity. Idolatry is averted because the gaze finds nothing to graze upon (to take up again Paul Klee's word) in this delightfully empty object that respects the uncircumscribability of its prototype. The iconic line is a flaw that refers to Christ's body as a passing weakness of God, both willing and salvational. Kenosis situates the icon definitively beyond any metaphorical or indexical sign; it owes its status as a symbol only to the combined operation of the gaze and the voice. The invisible similitude that haunts the visible image does not concern any category of material signs. Rather, it is the gaze that constitutes an index.

The line is a kenotic practice that the history of images will never go back on, and the doctrine of the iconic graph is the earliest formulation of pictorial abstraction. Iconic anthropomorphism should never be taken for representative realism: the figure is only there in order to show the emptiness and absence of what it indicates to the gaze constitutes its horizon.

Line and Color

As Dionysios of Fourna tells us, in the making of an icon, the graph concerns copying and drawing.[39] Note, however, that the question of colors has not yet arisen. At this level, Christ's icon, which is nothing other than an icon of the image, is called *apomagma*, that is, an imprint, Christ being the seal (*sphragis*), like the intaglio (*antibola*) image engraved on coins and seals. The vocabulary of sigillography and numismatics is significant here, for it aims at establishing an ever-closer relation between doctrinal and political choices, as the *reddere Caesari* had already implied. In the third *Antirrhetic*, Theodore of Stoudios also stresses this characteristic: "*allo sphragis kai héteron apomagma.*"[40] Whatever in the visible universe touches Christ's body closely becomes his graphic trace. A tenth-century text recounts an episode from the life of St. Nikon that bears some significance in relation to this. After Nikon dies, a fervent admirer of his desires to possess his portrait. The artist given the task of painting the icon, however, still experiences great difficulty with it, even after obtaining the description of the saint by hearsay. Then one night, Nikon appears and refers to himself by name (homonymy). The text then tells us that on waking, the painter found that the panel on which the painting was to be done already bore an imprint. Everything was there; all that was left to do was to add the colors: "*ta loipa tôn chromatôn prosagagôn kai tèn eikona téléôn.*"[41] This legend confirms both the links as well as the distance that exist between the icon and the acheiropoeietic image. The imprint not made by human hand transmits a contour, a homonymic graph, but it will only be brought to completion as an icon by the luminous grace of color. Thus John Chrysostom writes: "For however long somebody traces the lines of his drawing [*charagmata*], there will only result a type of shadow [*skia ti eétin*]. But when one paints over the top of the shading and puts on the colors [*chrômata*], then there is an icon [*tote eikôn ginetai*]."[42] The same echo is found in John of Damascus: "When the painters trace their lines [*grammas*] on wood and draw the shadow, they then add the truth of colors [*alêtheian tôn chrômatôn*]; Christ himself did it in this way."[43] And Cyril of Alexandria, addressing himself to Akakios of Melitene, should be understood in the same way: "We say that the old law is the shadow and graph for the contemplation of those who see reality. The graphic shadows on the wood of art are the first lines [*charagmata*] to which are added the luster and brilliance of the colors [*anthé tôn chrômatôn*]."[44]

Many more such examples could be given. What always emerges from them is that the relation between shadow and color, contour and brilliance, confirms the relation that links the Old Testament to the New. In Nikephoros this amounts to an understanding that when covered with brilliant colors, the *périgraphè* of the *homoiôma*, the circumscribed copy, "presentifies" the new law. Thus it was for the above-mentioned painter of St. Nikon, to whom fell, upon waking, the mimetic task of color, which alone could link his work as a painter to his faith as a Christian. The term concerning color that flows constantly from the pens of the church fathers is *anthos* or *anthê*, which refers simultaneously to flowers and to brilliance. Color, chromatic richness, the use of brilliant materials like gold, precious stones, and pearls,[45] should not be understood on a mimetic level as a naive investment of riches where the church displayed its power. It concerns something else entirely. These materials act in their *skhésis*, that is to say, in a relation of specific intimacy that maintains the gaze and the absence. A site of brilliance and light, matter becomes a mirror for the Word, aiming in its orientation for the blind spot in the eye that catches only the divine *vestigium* in the icon's flesh.

There is therefore at the heart of the icon a whole mimetic that continuously forms an obstacle to the repose of any gaze that might happen to alight on some object capable of satisfying it, and above all, of fulfilling it. The *homoiôma*, or facsimile, simultaneously bears the language of technique and incarnation, to which the grace of color lends a vertiginous quality. This attribute of the icon necessarily implies that the *mimétès*, who is both a painter and a believer, is himself already touched by his desire for truth. In other words, painter is a relative term, a *pros tí*, a *stokhasma*. The only definition it has is that of a vector, always active. The contemplator is no more a subject than the icon is an object. It is a magnetic pole, both an aiming and the object aimed.

No portrait of Christ, therefore, is possible, and the anthropomorphic resemblance of the facsimile always remains within mimetic ambitions concerning knowledge of uncircumscribability. When the painter paints, says Pseudo-Dionysios, "He looks continuously at the form [*eidos*] of the archetype, without being distracted by any other visible thing, paying no attention to anything else. . . . He will show the truth in the copy, and the archetype in the image."[46] This human "similitude" is specially important in that it is differentiated completely from the simulacrum, even if it is symbolic. Nikephoros cites in this connection the councils, particularly canon 82 of the Quinisext synod, that demanded that the lamb henceforth be replaced by Christ's human face.[47] This theme, which opposes Old Testament symbolism to the new economy, is of the greatest importance. It allows the iconophiles not to be satisfied with nothing but the cross or the lamb, both of which make use of the relation of sign and symbol.[48] In the same way, Melchisedek is not a true image, insists John of Damascus, but a premonitory shadow (*proskiasma*) whose truth is Christ. In other words, the similitude of Christ in the icon is greater than that of the lamb in previous symbols, not in terms of the reproduction of a human model, but as the production, the visible institution, of the New Covenant (*oikonomia*). In this sense, whoever rejects the *homoiôma* rejects the incarnation and continues to place him or herself in the expectant situation of the Old Testament; such people are henceforth impious and know only shadow and simulacrum. They confine themselves to symbolic representation. To accept the *homoiôma* is to leave behind the old prophetism in order to approach the field of *mimésis* and grace. It is because the relation between *oikonomia* and *homoiôma* exists in truth (*en alèthèiai*) that *homoiôsis* bears witness to a mimetic relation opening up at the heart of the icon.

Just as drawing is the inscription of a body that has disappeared, the chromatic surface that graces it is the indexical trace of the pressure of its light-producing gaze. Color then follows and perfects the transfiguration of the line. The graph is prefigurative, as was the prophets' shadow-writing (*skiagraphè*). It is also completely identified with the field of writing. When color arrives, however, one enters the field of light-writing, which may already be called "photography." The analogy will certainly be made many centuries later, as we will see below.[49]

In the icon, color is laid on in successive coats, starting with the darkest and ending with the lightest, which is transparent. The painter's gestures thus become a memorial to the redemption of the flesh, by the ascent from darkness to light.

The iconic graph and its chromatic treatment is truly an unprecedented philosophical invention because it marks the first appearance of a question concerning the life of the image. There was no doubt for the protagonists of both camps that life belonged to the model itself, that is, to the imaginal prototype, but the iconoclasts then reproached the icon for being an inanimate figure of that life. Iconophile thought therefore had to deal with and resolve a problem that had never before been posed on the subject of the image in Classical philosophy. What the concept of the economy allowed is precisely the linkage of the filial relation to the idea of a living image. In the Old Covenant, life is breath; in the economy of the New Covenant, life is light. Its opposite is therefore not death but darkness, and it maintains with death neither a productive nor (above all) a dialectical relation, but a prefigurative one. Darkness is the enigmatic mirror of life, and through the transfiguration, the organic life of the flesh receives the light that raises it beyond its status as prefigurative.

The Icon and Virginity

In order to open us to his "relative" visibility, God chose the flesh in which the Word assumed a body, so that he could shoulder the fate of the figure completely. The instrument that served to redeem the body was none other than the womb of the Virgin, within which "the Word was made flesh." It would therefore be incorrect to claim that the Virgin was a simple material cause, in the Aristotelian sense of the term, because in order for flesh to be capable of being fertilized by the Father's voice, it must already occupy a special place in the economic plan of the redemption. That body must already be in the image of what fertilizes it. It is also pure, virginal, and open to grace. In other words, the Virgin is already inscribed in the economy of the natural image; the new Eve, her virginity is imaginal in its essence.

The issue at stake therefore does not concern the comical, organic monstrosity of being simultaneously both virgin and mother. On the contrary, that state is a totally natural, internal effect caused by the nature of the image itself. It is the imaginal life in the icon that produces the economic concept of the virginal womb. For the icon is nothing other than that when it carries the image within itself. Fertilized by the grace that speaks to it in the primary voice of the *épigraphè* that was the annunciation, it becomes the fertile womb from which all future images will be born.[50] What is at stake in the virginity of the Virgin is the purity of the image. Henceforth, the rest of us women will have to choose between the redeemed visibility of our virginal, maternal image, and the diabolical darkness of our unimaginable matter, impure and deflowered.

Such useless sniggering over this virginity! At this very site, through her flesh, woman becomes the place of choice for the body of the whole imaginal economy. In this way, the immaculate womb of the invisible is opened to iconic life: panel, canvas, blank page, veil, vaults, unknown lands; in a word, endless space, no stain of inscription whatsoever, the body with no border of jurisdiction, the mirror empty of specularity. For the rest of us women, this is what is henceforth offered as the flesh of our sovereignty! Even today, the fate of the image of women cannot be thought through without an initial, fundamental consideration of what *the woman in the image* is. The virginal body both keeps and sustains every cloth and every shroud that collects the traces and stains of life, death, and resurrection.

And what if this were the foundation of painting of every sort?

That said, however, let us now return to the icon. In order to condescend to human form, that is to say, in order to pass from the state of the natural, invisible image to icon for the gaze, it is necessary to have a womb. And this human mediator was pregnant with this son, imaginal and virginal like her, to whom she transmitted her traits, her form, her temporal and spatial definitions. She was the circumscribed envelope of a circumscribable son without suffocating the uncircumscribability of his imaginal nature. A virginal, uterine space was thus defined by the economy. This womb, which is of value only for its borders and to which the visible owes its form, is really the body of the mother. The dawn of the first icon appears with the announcement of a voice saying to a woman that she is henceforth the dwelling place of the infinite. The icon reiterates and perpetuates in turn the implantation of the Word within the virginal border, a uterine *khôra* traversed by divine breath, sustained by the voice of the herald.

It will be readily understood, therefore, just how philosophically important it was to anathematize those who claimed that Christ was preformed, and that he only passed through his mother as though through a canal. Thus Gregory of Nazianzos, for example, insists vigorously on the absolute naturalness of the phenomenon of the Virgin's pregnancy.[51]

Christ's unimagination in the maternal and virginal body means that his image cannot be dissociated from the *femininity of the temporal institution* that makes his economy visible, the church itself. The Old Testament images are inverted. First, fallen Eve had taken her form from Adam's body; now the virginal institution becomes the space from which the new Adam arises, and within which it will be possible to register the full power of temporal conquests.

Thus, as a result of the image being saved, she who caused the loss of our pure similitude in the Old Testament story is redeemed as well. In order for this to happen, however, a woman exempt from original sin would be required, and this in turn became a necessary dogma. The point to be made here is that Christian discourse, taken as a whole, is nothing other than an immense ordering and management of the question of the image, whether it is flesh, sin, women, nature, or art that are concerned.

Within the institutional universe, one enters a peaceful belly that, in its analogical fertility, will be able to pass easily from one image to another: "Listen, my Son, to the words of your Father, and do not dismiss the institutions [*thésmos*] of your Mother. . . . Our Mother, the church, carries within it institutions that cannot be dissolved."[52] *Thesmos* has taken the place of the teachings of the Torah.

*The Voice and Homonymy (*Épigraphè*)*

The epigraph is the written name that always accompanies the person or people portrayed in the icon. If the icon is neither an expressive convention nor a referential sign, however, what is the phenomenological meaning of this practice? What does the graph of the name do?

The scriptural foundation of the economic link between the graph and both the written name and the voice that sustains it allows us to understand the close link that connects the prohibition on the portrayal of the face with the ban on pronouncing the name in the Old Testament. This is the same prohibition that banishes the image and its homonymy. *By means of the epigraph's voice, the image pronounces itself.* In Deuteronomy, he who makes his voice heard prohibits his name from being taken in vain. Henceforth, the voice will no longer be raised against the image; it forms one with it, it registers itself in its flesh. This is the meaning of the homonymic economy.

If economy and incarnation cannot be separated from kenosis, the voice too unfolds in an empty place that only the icon has the right to fill, although without ever filling it up. Thus is raised that strong voice that knew how to refer to the Incarnate one in order to announce him, the voice of St. John Prodrome, representing itself perfectly: "I am the voice of one crying out in the wilderness."[53] Such is the voice in the iconic wilderness, where the kenotic figure of removal[54] is the condition of acceptance of the natural image and the divine gaze.

The incarnation is nothing other than the redemption of the image by the image. The imaginal contract of the God of Genesis with his human creations had remained without issue since the fall in the Old Testament. *Being of a God without an image, the people had no sense of hearing.* Yet God did not stop calling out to his people, talking to them, inscribing his law in writing. But would that writing not remain as if dead, with the image not sustaining it? Thus God, through his providential will, set in motion the economic power of his iconic nature and decided to renew the only covenant possible with humans, the inherent covenant of the creation, similitude.

In Aristotle, who was not concerned with the image as such, *homoion*, resemblance, is nevertheless cited as a *pros ti*, a relative. The problem of the image is thus present, although only indirectly: it arises not from the viewpoint of relations, but from homonymy, and it is from that angle that Nikephoros, following the church fathers of the second council of Nicaea, makes use of it. Here is his text: "Moreover, the resemblance confers homonymy. The name is one and the same for both [the icon and the model]. The icon of the king is called 'the king.' The icon could say:

'the king and I are one thing,' despite the evident fact that they are different in essence."[55]

Nikephoros thus asserts that a relation exists here because there is a sharing of the name, that is to say, homonymy. The example of the king is a topos of patristic literature, but it comes to be used in a completely new way by the iconophiles. Previously, the king's voice had allowed for the explanation that just as there were not two kings as a consequence of his image, a fortiori, there were not two gods as a result of the duality of the Persons of the Trinity. Thus, in Athanasios we see: "The king and I are one [*égô kai ho basileus hèn ésmén*],[56] which is modeled on the voice of the Logos in St. John: "My Father and I are one," which in turn echoes the demonstrative voice of the Father during the baptism in the Jordan: "This is my Son, the Beloved."[57] With the iconic crisis, however, the king's voice, invoked afresh, takes on a different weight as the iconophiles see the rediscovered splendors of imperial iconoclast art being unfurled before their eyes. The theological meaning carried by the example of the king's image is therefore intensified by political allusion. For the emperors, always careful of ensuring that the sacred character of the Savior be respected by means of aniconicity, for their own part never stopped seeking to derive the maximum benefit possible from the spread of their own "icons."

But how will the question of iconic homonymy be dealt with when it becomes necessary to justify it not theologically or politically, but philosophically? In the first place, it is interesting to discover the following quote at the beginning of Aristotle's *Categories*: "When things have only a name in common and the definition of being which corresponds to the name is different, they are called *homonymous*. Thus, for example, a man according to whether he is alive or in a picture."[58] And at line six: "One will give a definition specific to either one or the other [*idion ekatéron logon apodôsei*]." In effect the definition is given according to essence (*ousia*) and not according to name (*onoma*). Homonymy in Aristotle does not form part of the relatives. It is Nikephoros who asserts simply of this homonymy that "it is in relation [*tèn skhèsin ékhei*]."

This point can only be understood by returning to the example itself and Nikephoros's follow-up to it, on what we might call the voice of homonymy. Whoever worships the icon worships the prototype, because homonyms have no de facto identity. As a result of the economy's jurisdiction, however, they do have an identity by right than can only be understood from the point of view of *mimêsis.* The name is not an abstract, isolated, or arbitrary convention. Rather, it is sustained by the authority of the voice that refers to the project of similitude and on which it rests. I refer here to the analysis of E. Martineau, who suggests that the sign is a "deictic, demonstrative *sémeion.*"[59] The claim being made is thus that the word stops being purely conventional when a thing refers to itself in its image. A *homoiôsis* then takes effect that is neither nature nor convention, but the voice of reference as the foundation and guarantee of identity. The gap that separates the model from its icon is thus transformed into an intimacy that is relational (*skhésis*) in the voice that says: "I am this one." What must be stressed here is the imperative character of the homonymic voice, the index of its jurisdiction. The homonymic icon gives an order: in the case of the king, it commands respect and obedience; in Christ's case, it decrees the direction of the gaze. The fact that the model and the icon share the same name functions as a contract for a response by rights: it is the spiritual contract of the visible and invisible guaranteed by the voice. It is not Christ in person, but a voice in this place (the icon) that designates it as a place of a relation that is contemplative. Homonymy draws the icon out of the silence of the idols in order to make it enter into that demonstrative silence where the Father will name his Word. Within the homonymic relation, Nikephoros insists on the alterity of definitions that imply the alterity of essences. There again we find the topos of hypostatic thought. There is no *allos kai allos* but *allo kai allo*,[60] which is to say that there is no alterity of two things, but a distinction between two modes. This argument is set out with some rapidity, but it is no less important from the point of view of the *homoiôma*: even as the material copy of the physical model, the icon does not in any way share the definition of the material elements that comprise the archetype. This material alterity is also imposed by homonymy. Between Christ's flesh and the matter that constitutes the material of icons there is a distance as large as between heterogenous essences, an essential heterogeneity that leads the iconoclasts to describe the icons, precisely, as pseudonyms.

The icon is either deceitful or a homonym. The most original feature of iconophile thought is to make of homonymy a relation of intimacy that is both essential and relative. In other words, it consists in an economic ordering and administration of the identity of the name. But, Nikephoros reminds us, Christ's flesh is animate, liable, mortal, which are all so many properties that the icon's "flesh" does not share. Homonymy therefore does not institute a metonymic relation any more than a metaphoric one. The icon is neither part of nor substitute for its model. This is essential in order to answer the iconoclast argument concerning the division of hypostatic unity. From the moment that homonymy comes into being, there is an alterity of definitions and natures. The icon shares nothing with the model in the way of conjunction, reproduction, or even allusion or participation. It shares nothing of the appearance of an intelligible reality. *Eidos* is the mode by which the prototype allows itself to be seen in the icon. This is the immanence of sense and not of essence. It resembles similitude without ever being confused with it. This resemblance is of the order of the gaze of the flesh and not of the matter of bodies. The matter of which it is made has no pretensions to resemble what was its living flesh. It cannot be concerned with the double reproach of being inanimate like an idol or animate like a magical object. It is the site of an autonomous, singular relation that does not compete in any way with historical or tangible reality, but which, as has been said, will refer to it, as the arrow refers to the target. The graph is not a part of Christ; it is only a mark of formal unity that inscribes in the flesh the union of the gaze and the voice because it is the same word that refers to the iconic graph and the graph of writing.

The voice operates at the junction of the visible and the readable, or the audible, we should rather say, because the epigraph is often a cryptogram that does not really lend itself to reading. The epigraph takes over from the voice that had long (since the time of the prophets) announced the incarnation of the Father's Word. The voice speaks the name. The finger points to the body that has the right to that name. And we know that this voice and this finger refer to nothing. They do not make a sign, they make meaning. Once again the iconophile differentiates himself from his adversary in not generating any distance between the named-shown and the operations that name and show. Just as the Persons are one and not removed from each other in the Trinity, so the Father, his image, and his voice are united in the icon, in the iconic manifestation. The voice of the epigraph is the voice of invisible similitude that is united with resemblance.

What proof do we have of Christ's royalty and divinity when he came to earth? We have nothing other than Speech, the word of the Old Testament that announces both him and that his coming finally brings enlightenment, the word of the angel Gabriel whose voice left Mary in no doubt, the words of St. John the Baptist. And finally and most importantly, the voice of the Father heard at the Jordan, saying, "This is my dearly beloved Son," which is often illustrated iconographically by a forefinger suspended over Christ's head. Thus a most perfect image advances toward humanity in the annihilation of its flesh, saying, "I am here," and always accompanied, preceded, overcome by the voices that say, "He is here, it is Him. *Ecce Homo.*"

This vocal reference is of the utmost importance. How is one to know that the image fits the model? By what is expressed by the voice, which gives them the same name. This is a constant theme in the icon's defense, and it can be summarized by saying that the icon is a homonym. It is for this reason alone that a name must be inscribed (*épigraphè*) on the icon; it has nothing to do with providing information about its contents. The epigraph, the hand of the Virgin Hodegetria (which shows while referring), the forefinger of the Father, St. John the Baptist, or the apostles, which refer everywhere to the Son, are so many signs that allow the image in the icon to be identified. The choir of voices that murmur unanimously around Christ's body in order to attest to the homonymy of his portrayal only has to stop for the figurative illusion to be undone, for the mechanism by which he is presented to us to be made clear. As soon as it is named, however, the kenotic body shines in its absence "with a sparkling radiation."[61] Only two sorts of lines remain before us: those that form a corporeal envelope, intensified by the icon of the mother who holds her son in her arms, and those that form the signs of the epigraph and that refer back to the Father's voice. The position of Christ's fingers, which form the first letters of his name, intensify this homonymic coming together of the graphs that inscribe flesh and name.

The child born of the union between the flesh and the voice: that is what the icon is. The fruit of the womb to which these lines refer is the icon itself. It is there, he is not there; he is no longer there, but it (the icon) is. Thanks to it, he is there "in some way"—that is to say, relatively there and relatively not there. Thus it is as though the Word enters a mise-en-abime in the icon, coiled in his mother's body, resting in his Father's voice, promised to this world, a completely imaginary iconic object that confers universal royalty on him.

How not to reproach the voice of the iconic epigraph with the pictorial game of Magritte: "This is not a pipe," as though he wanted to untangle the economy of the homonymic incarnation in the painting, and only succeeded at the price of a play on the signifier? What is the voice that sustains this ludic space if not that of a forger of a theological parody? This is a poetic but extremely naive game. The iconophile is less naive and certainly less poetic. He shows the iconoclast a graph and says clearly: "This is not Christ, but you, you remain deaf to the voice that calls your gaze, you remain blind to the graph that inscribes the presence of that voice."

Christ's icon does not refer to a higher reality, one that is more authentic; that would be the reality of an exterior model, invisible and distant. The distance is rather inside the icon itself, and it allows us to hear the echo of a voice within it.

It is clear that the iconophiles were duty bound to attempt to escape the threat and accusation of idolatry. But they found in it a linkage that mediated between the presence of the divine image and the presence of the material icon. It is the voice that provides that linkage.

Mention may be made in this regard of Byzantine music, which with its chants fills the sacred places filled with icons. Monodic music, or the human voice, exclusive of all instruments, turns its back on narrative, anecdotal melody, and functions instead on two planes simultaneously that are closely related to each other: the recitative and the drone.[62] The sustained note of the drone is conducive to prayer in that it rests only on the rhythms of breathing (*pneuma*). This pneumatic character of the drone makes it the privileged instrument of the breath of the Holy Spirit. It is the Spirit of the Word that breathes and that underpins all attempts at expression. As for singers, they develop their threnodies and prayers on the basis of the sacred texts. In song, the voice sets up a decomposition of sense, which functions by rhythmic effects that completely distend the semantic units to such a degree that the vocalizations end up forsaking all meaning. This happens in the chant dedicated to the fruit of the Virgin's womb ("*to karpos tès koilias soû*"), which ends in a stressed "*terirem-terere rirem*" that sounds highly significant but means absolutely nothing. The Byzantine voice is thus faithful here to the iconic voice, in the sense that it brings the spiritual actors face to face with each other in a meeting based on the grace of the breath whose operation is transfigurative (*métamorphôsis*).

The Anti-icon of the Iconoclast Emperor's Body

Let us now turn to Nikephoros's description of the iconoclast emperor's body. On the basis of the foregoing material, we are now in a position to read this passage in an entirely new way, one that will allow us to decipher it as a discursive performance that molds the emperor into the antitype of the iconic economy.

What Nikephoros chose to cite or to have his iconoclast adversary say is of no less value for us than an original iconoclast speech would be. It is a sort of hollow mold meant to make us understand again, but in a negative way, what is at stake in the icon itself. This portrait by an iconophile of someone who, by rejecting the icon foregoes by the same stroke all visibility, cannot fail to affect us.

If God, on the one hand, can no longer manage without the image and icon in order to reveal himself and to reign over the world, then he who turns himself, on the other, into the occasional iconographer of the devil has recourse only to words, which form a tight weave of logical arguments, ruses, and insults. This "anti-icon," which is highly significant, is specifically tailored, meant to show us just what an enemy of the economy of the gaze and speech is made of. This man no longer has any place to be because he has no place to appear, and Nikephoros's description is of a body of whom no icon is possible. In it we recognize as well the constituent materials of the rhetorical structure representing the savage and the barbarian, a structure destined for a great and terrible future. The enemy of culture distinguishes himself by the characteristics of his body and the unacceptable nature of its space. The "ideological" power of such a description can only be grasped if it is compared to the essence of the Christian body and the iconic space within which that body constitutes the paradigm of its own visibility and power.

The catalog of insults directed at Constantine V can be seen as one of the many "breviaries of hatred" in which the history of Christianity was so abundantly fertile. There again, it is the concept of *oikonomia* that determines how the model of abjection will be developed. It is because the concept recoups the idea of nature, which the very definition of the image is associated with, that Constantine was relegated to the camp of monstrosity and unnaturalness. To reject the image is a teratological act that only an already unnatural and perverse being could commit. *It is therefore extremely important to understand the sense in which the image is first of all a natural reality, because it is in the nature of the image to show what it itself is, namely, nature itself.*

The list of insults leveled at Mammon is highly systematic. The enemy of the economy incarnates an inverted model of the economy of the incarnation, and through that, of the iconic economy. Repeatedly making his point, Nikephoros states that the icon's enemy is a triple enemy: he is an enemy of the sacred, of nature, and finally, of reason. These three charges are expressed in a specific triple lexicon that covers the whole field of the economy, of which he is the antitype.

Let us begin by looking at the terms in which exclusion from the field of the sacred and order are expressed.[63] The iconoclast is an atheist, Christ's accuser, an apostate, unbelieving, a blasphemer, a Christomach, a criminal, reckless, destructive, defamatory, idolatrous, heretical, an outlaw, impure, impious, merciless, intractable, unbelieving, infamous, ungrateful, unstable, iniquitous, Jewish at heart, wicked, disloyal, perverse, a plunderer, a polytheist, rotten, profaning, sacrilegious, villainous, dirtied and dirtying, a theomach, a desecrator, violent. . . . All these words function to describe the enemy of the theological and Christological economy, that is, the economy that is constitutive of Christian doctrine and the true religion. This concerns as much his opposition to the doctrinal order as to the ecclesial order, both of which define the order of sacredness. It is because he is an idolater that he considers the icon through idolatrous eyes. This is the same argument that was used to justify the ban on making images in Deuteronomy: it is because Jews are by nature idolaters that they were ordered not to make graven images. Such an order, however, no longer has any raison d'être when one is dealing with an enlightened, faithful people who will no longer confuse the icon with the idol, or render to the one the honor that is due only to the other. Thus the enemy of the icon is placed in the camp of those he is denouncing. This hypocrite, this deceiver, to no one's surprise, thus conceals an entirely pagan allegiance to the figures of diabolical polytheism behind the mask of fundamentalism. This aspect of the accusation meets up with the theme of a break with tradition, both evangelical and patristic. He who is faithful to the letter of Scripture transgresses it. Constantine thus stands accused of rejecting Christ through blind faithfulness to Old Testament injunctions: the ban on images is addressed only to idolaters, and therefore to Jews. To respect the letter is to transgress the spirit. Constantine has understood nothing of the idea of fulfillment. The sacred Scriptures and the words of the church fathers, inspired by the Holy Spirit, cannot but legitimize the sacredness of the image as the fulfillment of the messianic prophecy. The whole of Scripture is nothing but an anticipatory and annunciatory sketch of the Father's uncreated image coming into the world, which reconciles and saves the created image. He who desacralizes the image can therefore only desacralize and profane Scripture and Tradition. A darkened spirit who knows only the writing of shadows, Constantine and his friends err lamentably in the Sheol of their sins and errors.

By this means, too, Constantine becomes an enemy of history and therefore of any type of memory and commemoration. The icon, however, is both a tradition and a memorial. Because the economy is the very concept through which theology enters historicity, the concept that deals with the fulfillment of prophecy in human temporality, iconoclasm cannot grasp what is fulfilled in the production of the iconic gaze. This inability to understand the difference between what constitutes a product and what constitutes a reproduction in large measure supplies the material for the catalog of insults aimed at this enemy of nature.

The second charge against Constantine concerns the claim that he is excluded from nature. Here is the vocabulary describing him in this way: he is an animal from the breed of wild beasts, of snakes, and all others concerning depravity, excrement, and the pigsty. Familiar with the horrors of hunting and the hippodrome, he loves blood, manure, mud, and feces. He delights in smells and only appreciates the unction of refuse. A cavalier enamored of his coachman, he maintains relations with him worthy of Sodom and Gomorrah. A ferocious beast who loves combat and cloacas, he slithers, grunts, eructates; his stomach rumbles, and he cannot hold in his stool or his vomit. A gaping gullet, an insatiable stomach, a fetid drunkard wallowing in the dregs, he ferments until his viscera explode. Irascible and melancholic by turns, he knows only states of excess; he is a being without form and reserves. Incapable of speaking, of understanding, unfit for any limit or regulation, he is nothing but pride, vanity, and dissoluteness. A theatrical ham wearing makeup who parodies Christians, he offers a sadly ridiculous spectacle that he is the only one to applaud. A monstrous runt, he in turn gives birth to a fetus even more monstrous than himself. A stinking, ruminant ventriloquist, he wallows in manure, where he likes to assuage his degrading passions.

And so the list of infamy goes on; what it amounts to in the end is an impossible portrait of a body without a soul and without speech, an open body whose orifices are nothing but uncontrolled sphincters. This incontinence, however, must be understood in the light of the iconic economy, underpinned by a doctrine of the line that closes without enclosing, of the complete equivalence of the icon and speech. The man with the gaping incontinence is the one who invented the concept of circumscribability, which implies the Word's confinement in its flesh and in the flesh of the icon. Being a pervert of unlimited openings, he has understood nothing of the written graph, and above all, of the iconic graph, which is the enigmatic closing of infinity. What can a debaucher understand of the mystery of the virginal body, and therefore of the icon? Behind all the insults, then, there is rigorous doctrinal intent. The theoretical aim of this anti-icon in a debate that is centered on the visibility of the incarnational memorial is to make the enemy's body into the emblem and symptom of his own heresy. He who has not understood the distance that separates inscription from circumscription is himself a body excluded from symbols and limits. Whereas iconic thought is based on the fertility of the virginal belly that offers the Word a womb capable of receiving the grace of its infinity, the iconoclast's belly is a diabolical cloaca that can only produce wind and feces. Was Constantine not named Kopronymos to remind us that on the day of his baptism, he dirtied the holy water that made him a Christian?[64] A profaner in the cradle, he already exhibited there all the signs of his Satanic incontinence. Dilated by evil, he must therefore also be a homosexual, in exile from the Father's power and the Mother's fertility. Nothing is lacking from this paradigm of sterility.

What Constantine lacks, however, is the subject of the third slate of insults that the portrait paints to perfection in its anti-iconic systematicity. In the last place, the enemy of the sacred, of order, and of nature is also the enemy of reason, of every form of logos: he is a madman. A whole new vocabulary is now deployed to condemn the alogos concerning his incapacity for speech and theoretical speculation, as well as his brazen manipulation of lies, calumny, and falsification. The gaping, mute mouth of a moment ago is suddenly long-winded, spouting gibberish. It gushes idiocies, nonsense, and childishness worthy of a young child or an old woman. Nikephoros turns to the Epistles of Timothy as the basis for this description of the scandalous absurdities that emerge from Constantine's dreams and fantasies, at least when they are not the delirium of the excessive drinker driven to fury and distraction. Constantine divides things that are one and confuses those that are separate. As with his Monophysite or even Nestorian friends, everything with him is nothing but disorder and confusion. Ignoring the elementary principles of logic, he flounders in contradiction. A liar and a sophist, he teeters on the abyss of incoherence and stupor. There is no need, incidentally, to be wise in order to notice his stupidity; simple good sense will suffice. This loathsome character, devoid of intelligence, gives complete license to his unbridled tongue and is ensnared by his own stupidity. Once again, no limit is in evidence: quarrelsome, a driveling old fool, humming twaddle, his talk is hollow, his speech empty. Pettifogging, a quibbler, a logomach, an onomatomach, he is a past master of false subtleties and possesses as well the pervert's dexterity. He deceives, he falsifies, he feigns, and he knows only one *mimésis*: he apes the devil. He is to be found everywhere from the bottom of the most gloom-laden insanity to the most consciously diabolical premeditation.

This aspect of the attack on Constantine brings us closest to what is at stake philosophically with the question of the icon. He is devoid of intellect, yet the icon is entirely a question of intellectual thought; the icon is not only a matter of faith, but concerns what is at stake generally in terms of thought itself. Icon doctrine, in fact, attempts to establish its legitimacy in the name of reason and the foundation of symbolic production in general. It is madness to deprive oneself of the image if one wants to rule, and it is perverse to deprive the church of it in order to appropriate it. One senses from the violence of the accusations that the eructations and stomach rumblings of this supposed drunkard must truly have had considerable theoretical power, putting the temporal power of the church at serious risk. The devil lacked neither force nor persuasion, and it proved necessary to formulate a solid doctrine in order to refute him.

The formulation of this doctrine was a secular procedure and it never stopped serving its purpose: to produce its monster, to make him an unnamable *ekphrasis.* The hatred present in that discourse is always in direct proportion to the fear of the power that is being fought against. The entire rhetoric of the ideological battle constantly reminds us that the enemy must be an enemy of sacred values, of the natural order, and of the most elementary good sense. But it is undoubtedly when he is exiled from the world of thought that the most dangerously perverse scenario arises, because the unthinkability of someone who does not think authorizes anyone who rejects him to no longer be accountable, in relation to his own thought, for what he will do or say against that unthinkability. The history of hatred for the other's body lies at the core of the abdication of thought itself.

In the case that we are concerned with here, the iconoclast's body is opposed not only to the iconic model, but also to the body of the holy man, which was itself constituted as a paradigm within the system of thinking about the iconic body. The holy man's body was often already transformed into iconic flesh during his own lifetime. Anyone who, in imitation of Jesus Christ, departs this world without being limited by the temptations of the flesh and spirit ends up with a body closed to the devil's penetrations. For, as we have come to understand, evil acts by penetration, intrusion, occupation. It lays siege to the body's openings, and salvation cannot occur other than by closing them. Little by little, the holy man's orifices no longer function. Nothing more enters or leaves. In the closed gravity of his silence, in the enclosure of his retreat, the immobile saint dries up, and his flesh becomes as flat and thin as a piece of parchment on which could be written any letter of his choosing. Transfigured matter, transformed by grace, it accedes of itself to the sort of two-dimensionality that makes it a living image. Thus it was for Daniel the Stylite, whose body was fixed to a board after his death to be shown "in the manner of an icon and exposed to the view of all."[65] At the end of the third *Antirrhetic*, Nikephoros puts on display these two bodies, the iconoclast's and the saint's, when recounting the last days of Constantine and bitterly recalling his cruelty to saints.

> He lived an extremely sad and harrowing life, assailed by those unspeakable pains and sufferings that those who have ulcers know. His limbs were disabled by the effect of wounds and in places he was losing his skin. Endlessly terrorized by evil spirits, he spent horrifying, miserable nights going over his decisions when the faith that he had pursued turned back on him. . . . He could not swallow any food placed in his mouth and he vomited constantly. What shamelessness and bestiality he showed to those close to him, what abominations he demanded! Who can say what these people endured? Lacerating backs and arms with innumerable blows of the whip, he was no more human than a wild carnivorous beast.[66]
>
> Laugh, therefore, at the lives of the saints and ascetics whose bodies show angelic, not carnal, nature. Denounce continence, humility, sweetness, tranquility, courage, magnanimity, criticize the straw mattress on the bare ground . . . crow against the angelic and apostolic habit.[67]

Thus the body of circumscription, doomed to death, is the opposite of the body of iconic inscription, whose earthly transfiguration already shines with the fires of eternity, the full display of which we will witness shortly. The art of describing these bodies *is* the very deployment of the mimetic operation. The body resembles the soul; even more, it is its epiphany. But for anyone who is haunted by the devil, there is no image other than the symptom, the sign of dissimilarity with the one and only image of divine similitude. The devil is not an ulcer, but the ulcer signifies the devil's presence. In opposition to this, the sanctified body of the saint and the icon manifest an essential similitude, and an image of it is therefore possible, taking, as it does, the natural image of the Son as a model. The wounds that tear at the holy man's body show his economy. *Transfiguration is neither a symptom nor a sign, but a relative participation in the manifestation of the economy itself.*

The Docetists, who rejected the idea of the carnal reality of the incarnation, could have placed themselves either in the iconophile camp by supporting the idea of the icon as the redoubling of an illusion, or in the camp of the iconoclasts by defending the one and only natural, invisible image. Their heresy is undoubtedly the richest in its teachings on the modern question of the image and "semblance." During the Byzantine crisis, however, they were disavowed by both, for they took up the idea of the economy in all its radicalness and unity. Iconoclasts and iconophiles both, however, officially make use of only one inconsistent, partial interpretation of it.

The iconoclast economy is the economy of the incarnation that accepts no imitation other than the *mimêsis* of the virtuous life and good government—actions, therefore, and not symbols. They recognize only the eucharist and the cross as the true image and *sign* of Christ's economy. The cross and the eucharist imitate nothing. By means of the sacrament, the eucharist is consubstantial with its model and therefore acts by the effect of real presence. However, it requires consecration and consequently can only spread its charisma within the sacred precinct and by institutional means; there is never any question of its becoming a profane and universal instrument that would be able to appropriate space and authority.

As for the cross, it is by definition a memorial to torture that can only act by the indirect voice of negativity. It is the site of the separation of the Father from his own substantial emanation, and is therefore what separates him from his own image. It is what the Son's death has vanquished and is consequently the active, sacred antitype of the resurrection. The symbol of the dissimilar, it is not able to inscribe itself in a doctrine of mimetic relations. It is therefore a sign rather than a symbol, because it refers to something other than itself. It is a site rather than a space, and this by virtue of its very form that does not contain anything, as with the *Khôra* of the virginal womb and the icon. It is a *tupos*, that is, an incision that marks, that crosses out, and that orients. It crosses out our mimetic hopes by proposing the sign of the crossroads over any illusion of presence, even though it be administered by the economy of symbols.

Conclusion

Given that the voice of the image makes itself heard on several occasions, we should not be in the least surprised to find Nikephoros putting words into its mouth and making it speak in a prosopopoeia that is, in itself, nothing short of astonishing.[68] Let us pause here specifically at what might be called the discourse of the throne. In the third *Antirrhetic*, Nikephoros develops the theme "My kingdom is not of this world" and attempts to demonstrate that the anthropomorphic image of Christ is not in any way the anthropomorphic image of the kingdom. In order to make himself better understood, he evokes the spectacle of royalty, there at the very place where royalty is itself a spectacle, implicitly referring to those rulers so familiar to the whole of the East, particularly during the Byzantine period, who were simultaneously dazzling and terrifying. At this time, the Christian empire and the nearby Caliphate rivaled each other in pomp and magnificence, and the iconoclast emperors, whose reign was marked by a particular upsurge of the imperial cult, formed an obvious target for the iconophile patriarch. In his text, Nikephoros means to show that Christ's icon is not in any way a luxury art intended to dazzle with its luxury and gems the people who the church wished to subjugate. It is not the icon that is an art, but the economy. What he is defending is therefore really a doctrinal position on the icon, not a particular category of objects that happen to have been marked either by the seal of wealth, a sumptuous spectacle, or a sequence of aesthetic choices.

For a prince, to present oneself to one's people is a whole art. Nikephoros's prosopopoeia leads the reader to think of royal power in terms of images underpinned by the voice. This is the foundation that I call the "ico-nomics" of power, which is the source of its legitimacy, its force, and its fertility. Power is drawn not from things themselves, but from relations between things. It is relations that are power, it is circulation that is fertile, and it is the voice that is their guarantee. Some princes seek to impress with ostentatiously scintillating displays that are meant to be inimitable. Others show a Spartan austerity that make them models of virtue, and that one would balk at imitating. None seems capable of escaping choosing an image, and it is God who sets the example.

Ecclesiastic power, on the other hand, appears to be trying to "perfect" the mimetic doctrine that all true power implies, by means of the mediating operation of the image as it gathers about itself a consensus of voices. What the church is looking for is not power, strictly speaking; what it aims for, on the contrary, is the power of something that will provide *authority*. For power is nothing other than the appropriation of iconic authority and its symbolic fertility.

The icon in its graphic drone, in the brilliant authority of its repetitions, embodies the endlessly demanding nature of the sovereign labor of the gaze. It bears witness to the belief that can be found across perhaps the whole history of the great sites of vision, that what makes a painting is that epiphany in absence that only occurs during an eclipse. What is an eclipse? An object comes between the viewer and the sun and darkens the world of empirical forms, while its outline is illuminated by the fire that it hides, but whose brilliance we are momentarily able to contemplate.

Icon doctrine is not in the least naive in relation to the faith that it attempts to engender. The economy does indeed imply a condescension toward the most popular forms of belief, and it negotiates with the most disturbed and disturbing thoughts that drive our pleasure of seeing. But this is an educational and functional condescension that does not obtain its power from a strategic, cynical manipulation of our desires and drives. On the contrary, the economy tries to locate all the levels of our perceptions in the unity of a divine plan. It is as concerned with the salvation of our body as our soul. They are all one.

Iconoclasm, on the other hand, appears to have tried to separate what the economy had unified. This is why the accusations leveled against it, and which made it an enemy of the economy, do not mean that it should be seen as an enemy of religion in general; rather, the rejection of the image is equivalent to a rejection of life itself. Constantine is not suited to life, and his conception of the world is no more so. At least, this is what we are meant to believe. He has only one concept, uncircumscribability, to defend himself with, and even that is not linked to the architectonic organism of the economy; consequently, he does not, so to speak, measure up. He would either have to accede to a lay conception of the basis for his authority, or else produce an economically legitimate theory of signs, as the Reformation did.

For the iconophile, the incarnation is *imaginary*; it is the entry of the natural image into the flesh of the visible image (iconicity), which allows the redeemed image to return toward the redemptive image. The meaning of this redemption is therefore really to bring humans to that inherent similitude that was their destiny within the plan of creation. The icon participates in the salvation of the image. The emptiness of the iconic Parousia does not in any way eliminate the obligation to portray it or its legitimacy; on the contrary, it situates it in another register, because it interprets imitation and the relation of similitude as being removed from any effect of duplication. The icon is neither metaphoric nor redundant. It is an economy of the image, a working, functional organization of its salvational power.

If the icon is double within the unity of a name, that is because dual unity is the very essence of the model. Christ is two in unity. This mysterious unity of two natures is at the heart of the presentative figure of absence. The duality of which we are speaking has nothing to do with the one that opposes body and soul, or matter and spirit. It concerns the union of the Word with humanity. In this respect, the Apollinarist error, which confused this with the union between body and soul, must be avoided. In iconic doctrine, the body is no longer considered to be a prison or tomb for the soul, and it therefore does not concern itself with that metaphor and its dialectical outcome. The carnal body and the iconic body cannot become a prison or tomb for the Word. On the contrary, they are its economic instruments, the material figures of the Redemption.

This union of the Word with humanity is not a reduction of divinity to the limits of humanity. That was the error of the Nestorians. It is no longer the ghostly union of divinity with a single human appearance. That was the heresy of Eutyches and the Docetism of the Monophysites. The natural image of the Father and the human image of the Son are one and the same image, in the sense that the relation "son of" is equivalent to the relation "image of." The icon satisfies the demands of both *homoiôsis* (image of the Father) and *homoiôma* (image of the Mother), that is, the demands of formal resemblance and material resemblance.

The dual unity of Christ, of the Word and the flesh, is composed of all the real characteristics of humanity (body and soul) and all the essential attributes of divinity, yet in a way that does not mix them all together. This hypostatic union can only reveal its mystery in full daylight by means of a single, mediating term, a relative, that puts the Word and the flesh in relation to each other: Christ during his earthly life, the church by means of its institutions, and the icon in the totality of the created, living universe.

What, then, is an enigma? The perceptible manifestation of the mystery; a crypt for the gaze, the cradle of the imaginary.

4

Sacred Precinct and Profane Space

What is the economy of the site that icons occupy? Between the holy of holies and the profane world, how does the economy negotiate the definition of iconic sacredness? Exempt from consecration and worthy of prostration, the icon inhabits an abstract space and becomes the connecting tissue that causes nature, grace, and reason to communicate with each other.

If the iconoclast is a true enemy of the sacred, that is because two opposing conceptions of sacredness are current at the same time. In order to understand this better, let us turn briefly to the work of Benveniste on the Latin and Greek terms referring to the sacred, and the Sanskrit terms that correspond to them.[1]

In respect of the Greek material, Benveniste concentrates specifically on *hiéron* and *hagion,* the sacred and the holy. The sacred—*hiéron*—occurs in relation to the terminology of sacrifice and venerated places or people. "*Hiéros* everywhere belongs to the domain of the sacred, whether this quality is attached to it by a natural bond or associated with it by circumstance."[2] On the other hand, *hagion* indicates rather "that the object is not allowed to be violated in any way." Benveniste therefore introduces it as the "negative" concept of the sacred, that is, prohibitive, in opposition to the *hiéron,* which would be its positive correlate. The interdiction that applies to the definition of the *hagion* protects it from any human contact. This is the sacred as purity. Things that are *hiéron,* on the contrary, are sometimes associated with the *hosion,* that is, a sacredness legitimated by law and an institution. In the same way, the *hiéron* comes into contact easily with the profane by means of sacrifice and human legitimation. Even though they had previously been profane, things that are *hiéron* can become sacred by the effect of ritual. The *hagion*, on the other hand, is both holy and sacred in "essence" because it is occupied by a transcendent principle that guarantees its purity. The counterpart of this, however, is that its pneumatic transcendence keeps it at a distance from human intervention. If the threat that confronts the *hiéron* is one of excessive proximity to the profane world, the one that hangs over the *hagion* concerns devilry or magic, which itself is a result of the ambivalence that is so strong a feature of the field of prohibition and impurity.

We thus have two individual principles of sacredness that are used differently by the opposing parties. Let us now examine these differences in an attempt to understand the role that the icon played for the iconophiles in their efforts to ward off the double threat facing it: is it a profane object stripped of all holiness, or rather an idolatrous object haunted by a diabolical presence? Is it holy or sacred, and by what means?

In the relevant texts, each of the adversaries makes highly distinctive uses of the *hiéron* and the *hagion*. The iconophile party uses the two terms in a system arranged according to their function and movement. This circulation of the sacred, which is a characteristic of iconophile thought, has a natural foundation in the icon, which serves as a major pathway for the circulation of sacredness in general. The term *hiéron*, however, is almost entirely absent from iconoclast texts. Only the *hagion* functions as a fixed reference point, and it serves as the basis for the ban on the image. It is a negative concept, or better, it is tied to prohibition, faithful to its Indo-European root *yaozdata*, which involves "the idea of a rigid conformity to the norm . . . [and which] is the result of an operation that confers ritual purity."[3] It is noteworthy as well that Indo-European also links the term with the vocabulary of law.

The use made of these two words in the *Antirrhetics* and the *Horos* of the council of Hieria demonstrates how broad Nikephoros's accusation against Mammon is:

Do I have to say that these synods have been overturned by these criminals? In their violence against the whole mystery of the Economy of our Savior, they have trampled on our customs, our institutions, and everything that is sacred [*hiéra*].

Without the least shame with regard to the Church of Christ and our divine dogmas, and having disdainfully dismissed every sacred tradition [*hiéran paradosin*], they utter vain words against the glory of the only Son, words that only confirm their stupidity, words inspired by a lack of belief towards the Father, or better to say, by their apostasy.[4]

If the enemies of the icon have no place in the field of the sacred, they will consequently be unworthy of sovereignty. In the following analysis we will consider three aspects of Nikephoros's proof that the iconoclasts are sacrilegious. The first concerns the written tradition, and within that, the close relations between the iconophile conceptions of the holy and the sacred. Here we will approach the iconoclasts' suspicion that the holy (*hagion*) is idolatrous, and examine their restrictive interpretation of the eucharistic sacrament. In the second place, we will look at the nonwritten tradition in both its oral and graphic forms, in order to see how the iconophile conception of the sacred opens on to the "iconic economy." This specifically concerns sacredness as it relates to images, and therefore the Christological meaning of the economy, because the iconoclast "does nothing but desecrate the totality of the Economy of Christ our Savior as well as the sacred symbols [*hiéra sumbola*] of our faith."

Starting from these premises, the third aspect of iconoclast sacrilege will be self-evident: the very image of iconoclastic life is impious and blasphemous. Mammon is the Antichrist; he is the opposite of the holy man. Sacredness is thus envisaged here as holiness. The holy man (*hagios*) shares the concept of *mimésis* with the image. What is a sacred imitation? Constantine is caught in flagrante delicto in daily profanation. Nikephoros implicitly ends up with a mimetic definition of the *hagion*, mimetic in that the image functions as the imitation of the workings of its prototype. The image imitates the prototype in its action of sacralizing the profane world. By linking holiness directly to the sacredness of the iconic relation and no longer only to pneumatic inspiration, iconophilia thus develops a direct grasp of holiness itself.

Hiéron, Hagion, and Tradition

Constantine's attack on the sacred functions in essentially two ways: institutional transgression and spiritual profanation. Institutional transgression concerns the church as bearer and guardian of both the written and nonwritten tradition. This tradition (*paradosis*) is converted into law according to several criteria: the selection of saints who transmitted it, and the ratification of scriptural, patristic, and conciliar texts that elevated mores and customs into an obligatory article of faith and universal confession over the long term. In effect, the scriptural tradition has no more importance than the oral tradition and the repeated customs of generations of

Christians. These criteria constitute the unshakable and insuperable character of tradition itself as sacred. From this perspective, the sacred is based in the institution and could very well be identified with whatever is consecrated, that is to say, with everything that ritual and the institution ratify. To demonstrate that Constantine-Mammon has transgressed the institutional universe is to attack him on the same ground on which he stands: the law. Was he, after all, not careful to convoke a synod and to grant all possible forms of legality to both his system of thought and his decrees? The iconoclasts unquestionably paid great attention to issues of legality and accused the icon of not forming part of the ritual universe of the sacrament. Thus at the iconoclast council of Hieria (754),[5] the bishops clearly state that it cannot bear the title of sacred, because "no sacred [*hiéra*] prayer has blessed it, which would have made it pass from a coarse thing to being holy [*pros to hagion*]; it remains coarse and without honor."[6] It is difficult to know from this, however, whether the institution (and therefore the law) is on the side of the *hiéron* or the *hagion*, that is to say, on the side of the human practice of sacralization or the divine working of direct selection. The iconophiles must therefore prove two things: that the iconoclasts are unaware of the sacred, and that they pervert the holy.

The Anti-idolatrous Tradition

For Nikephoros, the Old Testament is above all else a warning to the Jewish people against idolatry. However, the texts also abound in examples that, in his eyes, prove that God loves images that contribute toward his own glorification. He considers the struggle against idolatry to have substituted precisely the impurely sacred with the purely sacred. Purification occurs. This is to say that in relation to the sacred, idolatry constitutes a particular category that coincides not with the profane but the damned (*tà enhagè*). In other words, the holy very quickly risks being contaminated with the damned if there is no intervention by the workings of the image, which, thanks to the Son, placed the divine in contact with human law. Without this saving access to the *hiéron*, whose positivity functions as a mediator, the partisans of the *hagion* are kept in the confusion of a sacredness without a "symbol," which lacks the economy of the "relative" (*katà skhésin*).

The field of the forbidden is therefore left behind for what is henceforth permitted, the authorized, which in turn becomes a dogmatic obligation that if not obeyed will constitute a betrayal of the New Covenant. This is why, says Nikephoros, the iconoclasts, just like the idolaters, "mix everything together, confuse everything, the pure and the impure, the profane and the holy [*bébelon kai hagion*]."[7] It may be surprising to us to see the iconoclasts being placed together in the same category as idolaters, but matters become clearer when we examine the vocabulary of sacredness and malediction that underpins the accusation. In ancient times everything was *hagion*. Then, "Wood replaced wood, the temple replaced the temple, sacrifices replaced sacrifices; in the place of everything that is impure and profane there is a substitution of things that are holy for us [*tà kath' hémâs . . . hagia*]."[8] Thus it is the very introduction of the sacred into the interpretation of tradition that allows a full understanding of the types of sacredness itself. This is why, being completely within the *hagion*, the iconoclast is, to the iconophiles, paradoxically in exactly the same situation as anyone else without symbolic capacity.

On the other hand, the written tradition that condemns idolatry is the same one that also opens up the sacramental field of the imaginal contract with God, because God ordered the making of images for the whole temple and chose the filial image to invest sacred space. In Nikephoros, as in the Hieria text, whatever is consigned to writing and unanimously confessed bears the name dogma (*dogmata*). But in iconophile texts, the dogma inspired by the Holy Ghost takes on the value of law by constituting the foundation of the field of the *hiéron* itself. In this framework, the image will occupy a twofold place, because as we will see, it is marked in every place and every circumstance by the category that is inherent to it: the double. This double nature is a result of its participation in the holy even as it remains the womb of the sacred. This circumstance arises from its relational status, as it circulates continuously between institutional authority and the objects that incarnate it. Neither signifier nor signified, it is the major pathway that sets their similitude in relation to each other. Thus in Nikephoros, the sacred is given the responsibility of making the power of the *hagion* to symbolize that similitude both visible and institutional.

Thanks to this development of the sacred, the holy stops being a purely negative authority and becomes a disciplinary, dogmatic, and ritual corpus. This is more than just a minor benefit, because the *hiéron* also deprives the *hagion* of its power of potential malediction and impurity. As we have seen, the holy could be shared with idolatrous paganism, which was well acquainted with the animist magic of the diabolical cults. In other words, the devil himself is not without *hagion*, and whoever lacks the "economic" category of the *hiéron* will find himself mixed up in a sabbath of infernal forces. The iconophile institution and law are therefore fundamentally associated with the development of the hieratic signs to which the *hagion* will henceforth owe its univocal, verified purity. In reading Nikephoros we come close to believing that the sacred's point of departure is the profane itself, just as Christ's humanity remains the center of the incarnation. The clergy who, more than anything else, constitute the hieratic field therefore come to be preferentially invested with the function of sacralization itself, including that of the law. It even appears as though the *hiéron*'s claim to be the specific "cause" of the *hagion* granted the very power of legislation to the church.

It is therefore not simply by chance that all through the Hieria text the accent is continuously placed on the ensemble formed by the terms *hagia, dogmata, nomoi*, and *prostagmata*, that is, the holy, dogma, the law, and the decree. Thus one reads about the impious iconophile, whether cleric or lay, "that he falls under the blow of imperial laws since he is the enemy of divine decrees and adversary of the church fathers' dogma."[9]

The Sacramental Tradition

Iconoclasm thus explicitly tries to link its own legislative power to pneumatic holiness alone, without any ecclesial mediation. Any intervention of the clergy in the iconoclast *hagion* must therefore necessarily pass through consecration. In a long refutation contained in the second *Antirrhetic* that responds to the Hieria argument concerning icons that have not received any priestly consecration,[10] Nikephoros explicitly accuses Constantine of having confused the icon with the eucharist.[11] The debate seems to revolve entirely around the notion of circumscribability.

On the one hand, Mammon does indeed describe the eucharistic species as a "true image" (*ten alèthèn eikona*),[12] and he speaks of the "bread of the eucharist as a non-deceiving image" (*apseudè eikona*).[13] This truthful icon is the one of the carnal economy of Christ-God (*tês énsarkou oikonomias Khristoû toû theoû*). In reading Nikephoros and the *Horos*, however, it emerges that Constantine considers the only memorial (*mnémê*) to the economy to be the eucharist insofar as it is a sacrament (*hagiasmos*). The question, however, as Nikephoros himself always recognizes, is not whether the mouth in communion is in the process of devouring the infinity of the

Word itself. It concerns rather the interpretation of economy, which is the sacralization of the profane world by the power of the incarnation. For iconoclasm, the eucharistic consecration linking the pneumatic holiness of the mystery directly to the liturgical activities of the priest remained as a "*princeps* scenario," so to speak. (Let us add, to anticipate ourselves momentarily,[14] that this consecration also presupposes a specific place: the sacred precinct of the consecrated temple.)

The term *oikonomia* appears five times in the Hieria text.[15] The first refers to the salvational economy (*sostiken oikonomia*) in a global way. A little further on, Constantine uses it as a synonym for *dogma* to refer to the incarnation. Then *oikonomia* becomes the equivalent of the sacramental mystery of the transubstantiation. In the passage concerning the eucharist for Maundy Thursday, the following appears: "*to pragmateuthen mystérion en te kat'auton oikonomia.*" Then again, "the truthful icon of the carnal economy." The last usage concerns the nonconfusion (*to asynkhyton*) of the christic economy. In other words, the linkage is crystal clear for Constantine, who ties the holy to the eucharistic sacrament in the name of the economy. It is the *hiéron* that is in his eyes confusionist, and the term *hiereus*, or officiating priest, then appears in its ritual, authorized function. Nowhere is *hiéron* used in the neutral or plural, as it is in Nikephoros, who elevates it precisely to a categorial dignity concerning the animate as well as the inanimate world (*tà hiéra*).

Nikephoros, however, argues strongly against a "symbolic" interpretation of the eucharist. The positioning of the icon as a ligament between the pneumatic and the profane allows him to raise an outcry when it comes to the issue of real and consubstantial presence. The iconoclasts, he thinks, truly profane the host. It is clear for him that the universe of consecration is one of consubstantiality and sanctification, and that it should never be confused with the universe of the *hiéra*, which is one of sacralization. The icon can never have a mediating function in the procedure of sacramental sanctification.

Nonetheless, iconophile thought remains fundamentally nonseparative. It concerns mediation, the symbol, and sharing, and consequently Nikephoros has to elaborate an argument about the eucharist itself that links it to the *hiéron*: "The rest of us [Orthodox] do not say that this [the bread and the wine] is the image or portrayal of his body, even if this comes about symbolically."[16] He therefore introduces a primary relational concept on the subject of the eucharist itself. He also carefully avoids the term *hagion* other than to describe the Holy Spirit who presides over the mystery of the transubstantiation. Finally he says: "How and by what would one recognize that great, immaculate, and venerable victim, the purifying sacrifice that saves the world?"[17] Thus the *hiéron* infiltrates the sacrificial and pneumatic field of the eucharist all at once. To refer to the sacrament itself, Nikephoros prefers *teletès* to *hagiasmos*, that is, fulfillment rather than sanctification. He thus holds to his objective: even if the eucharist has nothing to do with icon, it cannot constitute an autonomous practice of sacredness by itself only. It needs the ecclesiastic institution to achieve its symbolic fulfillment.

For Nikephoros, the bread and the wine are the profane species par excellence. In fact, even Mammon says so: "It is not all bread that is his body or all wine that is his blood, but only that which, by the effect of priestly consecration, passes from its state of a product made by human hand to its state of a product not made by human hand."[18] "Behold this that has no need of demonstration," exclaims Nikephoros, so evident is the matter. We should understand by this that it is evident to him that in the eucharist itself, where there is no image, a passage from the profane to the sacred world is still necessary, and this passage requires not only the intervention of the *Hagion Pneuma*, the Holy Spirit, but the officiating priest as well, who relates the profane and the sacred to each other. The bread and the wine are therefore not icons, and they can never become Christ's body and blood without the mediation of a Christ imitator-mediator, Christ himself being similitude and mediation.

In this case, the imaginal (homoiotic) function is filled by the priest (*hiereus*), and ecclesiastic power therefore remains the master of the mediating, sacralizing activities. For the iconophile, then, the field of the *hiéron* is considerably expanded, because when all is said and done, it becomes the master of mediating, sacralizing activities and the producer of sanctification (*hagion*) as well. At stake here in doctrinal terms, therefore, is the very power to establish or institute, in and of itself. Only the church has the power of "limits," that is, to determine the field of the profane, the holy, and the sacred, and to perform the actions that make people and things pass from one field to the other. The church calls this power neither political nor religious. It bases it on a third term—the economy—whose placement gives it all its operational and symbolic force. Our initial analysis of the sacred, then, reveals this to be the ultimate goal of the defense of the *hiéron* in its links with the icon and the image. "In reality it is against the economy that he has declared war, and on that basis the typhoon of impiety has arisen and has not stopped growing, setting its vile doctrine against our sacred dogmas [*hiérôn dogmatôn*]."[19]

The Written and Nonwritten Traditions

The Written Tradition

The iconoclasts' profanation of the sacred consists first of all in a violation of the written tradition. Nikephoros therefore denounces impiety and unbelief, *asebeia* and *apistia*; the enemy is *anhosios, bebèlos, dussebès, assebès*: impious, profane, irreligious, sacrilegious. . . . Additionally, the accusation that the iconoclasts transgress the sacredness of the written institutions is borne by a legislative vocabulary: "Once he has become the enemy of Christ and all Christians, the denigrator of the divine laws and sacred [*hiéron*] canons established by the apostles and the holy fathers . . . " Seamlessly, Nikephoros here associates *hiéron* with *nomos*, the sacred and the law.[20] Those things that are law cannot be transgressed, and the word of tradition marks the very limit of the Christian word with its seal. "If you respect the inviolable limits [*horoi*] of our divine religion, if you keep intact and in your heart the tradition of the Catholic church, this would only be but a spark of faith:"[21] the *Horos* of the synods has set the limits (*horoi*) of every last word concerning dogma.

The words of the council thus form the very precinct of Christian thought, and to step outside of that precinct is blasphemous. In reference to the synod of Chalcedon, Nikephoros writes: "He did everything to undermine the great synod, that sacred [*hiéron*] meeting where so many men, under the guidance of the Holy Spirit, clearly set out the principle that forms the basis for the hypostasis of Christ and his double nature."[22] The councils are here evoked not to be analyzed for their respective, specific content, but so that they form a coherent, disciplinary chain that marks off the new territory of Christian thought in an absolute way. Anyone who dares pose even the smallest question that allows some doubt to arise about conciliar truths will be impious and blasphemous. These are definitive texts in the field of the sacred-*hiéron*, and they derive their validity from two criteria. The first is dogmatic and described as *hagion*: it is the inspiration of the Holy Spirit, because the grace of the *Hagion Pneuma* presided over all conciliar decisions. The second is a quantitative criterion based on forces of time and number.

Nonetheless, it is still remarkable that Constantine makes such an effort to qualify as *hagion* everything that touches on tradition, the very point at which Nikephoros so tirelessly repeats the term *hiéron*. He therefore clearly privileges institutional roots rather than the pneumatic criterion. Not that he eliminates it; on the contrary, as we will see, his goal is to interlink pneumatic holiness with the symbolic effectiveness of ecclesiastic sacredness. This concern will appear even in relation to the Virgin and the saints, the description of whom as holy remains absolutely constant. The mimetic path, however, also allows them to be made inseparable from the ecclesiastic institution.

In order to make his pragmatic argument based on time and number, Nikephoros lists "numerous" council assemblies and provides a large number of reports and citations. This is nothing other than a numerical argument, and it certainly replies fairly well to the iconoclast demand that the iconophiles produce their sources and compare them in length and number with iconoclast sources. Thus both camps produced anthologies of citations and arguments based on authority. It is striking to note in this respect that on both sides, synods were regularly called sacred (*hiéroi*) meetings. Constantine, who was, as we will see, loath to an extreme degree to utilize the term *hiéron*, uses it only twice: to describe the synod, and to describe a ritual consecration gesture where it is associated with a verb of the same root: "*aphiéroménon eis hieran hupourgian*."[23] Elsewhere, he describes everything touching on piety as *hagion*, holy, including even the synods themselves. He thus clearly privileges the pneumatic holiness of inspiration in conciliar thought, although it then falls to the emperor and the patriarchs to give the Holy Spirit's orders the form and status of earthly decrees. For iconoclasm, therefore, the *hagion* is connected directly to the *nomos*, the holy to the law. In Nikephoros, the same assemblies are described as *hiéroi*. These meetings are sacred precisely because they gather together holy men and texts.

An additional characteristic that arises from the similarity of sources and authorities invoked concerns the lists that both sides produce of councils that had taken place earlier, and that still had authority. Of course, as we have already mentioned, nobody, either then or earlier, wanted to be considered an innovator. The idea of continuity itself thus forms a part of sacredness, and the inspiration of the Holy Spirit is not regarded as being in the least innovative. Rather, it specifies, defines, and develops dogma whose apparent novelty is caused only by the sudden appearance of innovation in one's adversary. The procedure to be followed, therefore, is that in the face of any new danger, what has been true forever must be recalled and restated in a new way. This is why both Nikephoros and Constantine list the councils of Nicaea I, Constantinople, Ephesos, Chalcedon . . . that defeated and cast out of the church the Arians, the Nestorians, the Eutychians or Monophysistes, the Acephalics, the Apollinarians, the disciples of Macedonios, Marcian, Adamantios, Evagrios, Theodore of Mopsuestia, Severos, Honorius, Makarios. . . . Jews, Greeks, and Saracens too were globally anathematized, and Origen was condemned by both camps. To iconoclasm's blacklist we should of course add as well the Patriarch Germanos, John Mansour, and John of Damascus. As for the citations, they begin on both sides with the Old Testament texts of Exodus, Deuteronomy, the Psalms, and the Prophets, and are followed by the Pauline Epistles, and then an avalanche of references to Gregory of Nyssa, Gregory of Nazianzos, Basil, John Chrysostom, and Amphilochios. . . .

Thus, even though they were interpreted differently, the fact that both camps used the same texts is not in the least surprising, because all parties were in fundamental agreement on the status of the natural image, and the authorities invoked had not yet been touched by the iconic debate. The possibility of any new interpretation would therefore have to wait for the sudden turn of the economy within iconic thought.

The Nonwritten Tradition

Within iconophile thought, the category of the *hiéron* is developed most intensively and effectively not in the written or sacramental domains, but within the oral and iconic traditions. An examination of these will allow us a better understanding of the way in which the profane field, the one of human practices, comes to be sacralized. As we noted above, the criteria by which church councils become sacred are not only based on pneumatic inspiration. There is also a criterion of legitimacy based on number and repetition. In other words, both iconoclasts and iconophiles are deeply concerned with guaranteeing the "ecumenical" character of their decisions and doctrines, even if, in the final accounting, the territory of the one group is the whole universe, and that of other (the iconoclasts) is powerfully determined by the limits of Empire. This is why the numerical argument—concerning both the number of citations and antecedents as well as numbers of those who attended—is strongly connected to relations of force, the setting for which is always a crisis.

This "political" character is found again in the very nature of the argumentation: the assault of citations, the argument of large numbers, the strength drawn from duration and repetition. Thus Nikephoros is pleased to recall the frequency and number of synods attended by crowds of Christian authorities from all corners of the empire. The iconoclasts, too, are equally concerned with the legitimacy of their own numbers:[24] the council of Hieria was refused the qualification of "ecumenical" by the iconophiles, who considered it to be a "headless synod" because of the absence of representatives of the pope and the oriental patriarchs. The strength of the numerical argument was reinforced by the even more powerful one of duration. Nikephoros engages in a plea that is dispersed throughout the *Antirrhetics*, although it is in the end methodical, for the authority of repetition. This is an important matter, because as one senses, the sacred force accruing to the law is often conferred on it by custom, habit, or even more by its mythically immemorial character. It is the tradition as it "has been transmitted since the beginning by the holy apostles and our venerable church fathers and that has the force of law in the church."[25] The sacredness of everything that exists *ex archès*—from the beginning—allows tradition (*paradosis*) to become synonymous with custom (*sunétheia*). On the iconoclast side, there is an anxiousness to legitimate the new decrees on the basis of previous texts and decisions. Once based on these premises, however, it is really the pneumatic *hagion* that is directly made manifest, through the imperial will. Thus there is no place for any new intervention in between holy scripture and the legislative text. The tradition, inasmuch as it is *hagia*—holy—is defined in the same way as the law, that is, as the *continuation of a prohibition.*

Nikephoros, on the other hand, also engages, little by little, in a gentle exercise of verbal slippage on the *paradosis graphomenè*, the written tradition. This tradition consists of everything "that has been transmitted from the beginning by the holy apostles and our venerable church fathers." Everything that is originary has become a custom, a habit, a repeated practice (*sunétheia, ethos*). What becomes law by habit is part of the tradition. Thus custom, repetition (since the beginning) will first become part of the definition of the sacred, and then become even more than that, because Nikephoros, starting from a plea for the nonwritten law, will truly be able to conceptualize the *hiéron* as a sacredness that does not need the sacrament to institute and develop its effective activities. Idolatry has been kept at bay as a "false sacred"; now it is necessary to reconquer the profane in order to open it up to the iconic gesture.

Ethos, Nomos, Thesmos

Divine law and profane law communicate within the field of ethos. The term *ethos* thus appears regularly to highlight the inscription of the sacred in daily life. This is because Nikephoros wants to create a further linkage: after moving from the scriptural to the nonwritten tradition, he wants to take the final step from the nonwritten to the icon. But these slippages are smoothly made, at a good distance from each other, and done so well that the reader gains the impression of a series of cascading, accumulating arguments, rather than ones that are explicitly articulated. In fact, if the scattered texts of the three *Antirrhetics* concerning relations between the sacred and tradition are gathered together, it becomes evident that the whole forms a coherent chain of irrefutable conclusions that resemble successive breaking but overlapping waves, without it being possible to really push any one argument to its limit and thus make the argument that follows it less certain. Nikephoros structures his discourse very carefully at just the moment that he reproaches his adversary for being contradictory and disjointed—although when he does take liberties in his arguments, he loves to begin by adopting an outraged attitude. Note the chaining together of arguments and the tone in the following quotation:

> These villains and criminals accuse us with their brazen doctrine, us, who remain within the pure faith and the nonwritten tradition of the catholic church. But they must be told that the nonwritten tradition [*agraphos paradosis*] is above all the most solid of all. It is the base and the foundation of all of life's practices [*krépis tis kai hedra tôn en té khrései tou biou*] that constitute custom [*ethos*] in the long run. This custom reinforced over a long period, becomes natural.[26]

Here, the written tradition is nominally on the side of the law—*nomos* (*en graphais hemîn nomothetoumena*). The slippage is therefore effected between the written Old Testament law (*nomos*) and the tradition (*paradosis*) that imperceptibly becomes equivalent to ethos and *sunétheia*, the mores in practice and custom. From this arises an expansion that truly desacralizes the written law in order to sacralize habit:

> But we see that even the laws consigned to writing are not respected when tradition and a different practice prevail over them. In effect, in everything, custom has full power, and deeds prevail over words. To tell the truth, what is a law if not a custom consigned to writing. Conversely, custom is a nonwritten law. It is even easier to note this in the world outside of religion. In effect, even amongst the grammarians, if by chance they happen to note in a text a discrepancy between a

word and the prevailing rule, and seeing that custom is of a different opinion to that which is written down, they cite the tradition, arguing that it is the rule of the rule [*kanona kanonos*].[27]

This passage is clearly of great importance in overturning the argument concerning the supreme sacredness of the written text as it applied to the conciliar *horoi* and patristic citations. Religion, its practices, and its laws behave exactly like a living language in which the rules are both fixed by the "nomothete" and endlessly transformed by the users of the language. A language having only laws would be like a dead language, which for Nikephoros is the case with the Jewish religion. Rather, the ethos, the *sunétheia*, will be raised to the dignity of "new law" in the Pauline sense, that is to say, as the fulfillment of the law.

The work of Jérôme Kotsonis concerning the ecclesiastic economy is in complete agreement with these ideas.[28] Developing the notion of the economy in its juridical sense, he takes up Photios's definition: "The economy is the suppression or suspension for a certain time of the strictest laws or quota of the plaintiffs, the legislator making a decision in relation to the weakness of those who will benefit."[29] The economy is therefore, as we have seen, primarily linked to the occasional and the exceptional, to the *kairos* in relation to what becomes law. Kotsonis takes up the series of questions posed by Theodore of Stoudios in a letter to Athanasios, and ends with the crucial question: "Finally, we pose the question of the types of transgressions for which the economy can be of value."[30] Thus Theodore writes to Athanasios: "Is there an economy for every man and for every transgression of a commandment? Or for which ones, and in which cases? . . . And does it concern kings only, for a single fornication, or for each violation of the law?"[31]

The issue, therefore, is one of how, and in what case, that which is not sacred by written tradition can become so by custom. The objection may therefore be raised that this question is not an "economic" one, because custom is based on repetition, whereas economic practice would concern only a unique instance. Yet Theodore of Stoudios also says the following in a letter to Naukratios: "In the church fathers, some economies are temporary and others, on the contrary, are valid forever."[32] Thus this perenniality of the particular reaches canonical status under the heading of a permanent economy. None of this, however, is surprising, in that it is the incarnational model that underpins it all. Thus, custom becomes law to the degree that it forms the living, practical rule. Nikephoros, then, having wanted to prove that Constantine was a profaner of the Holy Writ, now intends to prove that he transgresses custom in its capacity as law as well.

For Nikephoros, ethos and *sunétheia* function as exempla of divine condescendence. The sacralization of custom is assimilated to the sacralization of the daily, profane world by he who accepted its bondage. Laws cannot be inflexibly applied, so great is human diversity, so fragile is the obedience of humans. In order for the law to be visible, it must be subjugated to its own conditions of application; it must, like Christ, humanize itself.

The humanization of the law is not its laicization or its weakening. On the contrary, it marks the entry of the sacred into human life. "The current word economy comes from the economy that caused the incarnation to be seen."[33] The nonwritten law, which first of all is simply assimilated to custom according to the classical topos, is finally identified with the new Law, that of Christ himself, who never cared to write anywhere other than "in hearts." "The economy is the imitation of divine benevolence,"[34] because "for us, salvation is not in words but rather in fulfillment." This is because "the substance of dogma" is not in the written letter.[35] In other words, the incarnational hierophany is superior to the legislative *akribeia* of the Old Testament *hagion.* The writings of the church fathers thus paradoxically serve to eulogize what is not written. "This was already announced by the holy prophets: having given the laws to their minds, I will also engrave them in their hearts. We know that all this was carried out by Christ, . . . and that it is only later that facts were engraved in letters."[36] The nonwritten tradition is therefore prior to the written tradition: "What written tradition would have transmitted the unanimous and daily confession of the sacred symbol of the faith [*to hiéron tès pistéos sumbolon*] if it had not first been introduced in a non-written manner?"[37]

Nikephoros then follows this with an enumeration of the practices and customs that "the harmonious organization of the sacred order puts before our eyes [*ho tès hiéras eutaxias ekdeiknuei diakosmos*]." Custom therefore prevails over law.

At this point, however, we suddenly see the following slippage: Nikephoros identifies the institutionalized ethos, sacralized by practice, with *thesmos.* The term *thesmos,* which refers to institutions, gives ethos its legislative status and implies a new notion of sacredness: that of the maternal image. Implicitly, the law (*nomos*) of the Old Testament was the holy (*hagia*) law of a father without a son who ruled by prohibition. In the economy of the new Law, however, we are dealing with a contractual sacredness (*hieroi thesmoi*). The contract that is sacred is the one that ties the heavens to the earth, first by the mediation of the mother's body, then by the mediation of the church's body. The "divine Epiphany" says: "It is necessary for the church to accomplish this, because it received the tradition of the church fathers from it." And Nikephoros continues, still quoting the Epiphany: "As it is said in Solomon: Listen, my son, to the words of your Father and do not reject the institutions [*thesmos*] of your Mother."[38] He then concludes peacefully: "Our Mother Church carries within herself the institutions that cannot be dissolved [*méter hémon hé Ekklesia eikhé thesmous én heauté keimenous mé dunamenous kataluthénai*]."

Thus the final goal appears clearly: to defend the nonwritten law is to defend the church itself as an institution of custom that dispenses a contractual sacredness arising from natural law. For him, the iconoclasts wanted to fight not only the icon, but the church as well: "But those who live in pride and unbelief falsify the definitions of what is just [*tous toi dikaiou horous*], and completely distort the church's institutions [*tous thesmous tés Ekklésias*]."

The appearance of the term *dikaion* is striking here, because it clearly indicates that the debate about the law of custom concerns legitimacy. Mammon remains stupidly legalist: "Where does it come from, he says, and what is this law [*poios nomos*] that enjoins us to prostrate ourselves in order to worship Christ's image?" For Nikephoros, the matter is clear: the law that enjoins this worship is not *nomos* but the insitution of the mother (*thesmos*).

The mother, however, is *hagia* or *Panhagia.* Consequently, the pneumatic inspiration that presided over the annunciation and the incarnation guarantees the sacredness of the maternal, and therefore ecclesiastic, institution. We thus have here a primary example of the *contamination* of the holy by the sacred. This way of thinking about contagious contiguity that causes, as we have seen, the holy and the sacred to communicate with each other, is characteristic of the "economic" system of thought, one that, above all, concerns universal propagation. The image is the essential organ of that enlightened "prudence" and that imitative, conquering economy.

In this way, the iconoclasts are expelled into an area of confusionist logomachy. They are nothing but onomatomachs. "One must not allow oneself to be dragged into fussy and highly uneducated questionings that engender logomachy and prattling. . . . That is the invention of the Greeks and infidels. In effect, similarly to the Jews who demand a sign, the Greeks chase after wisdom."[39] Mammon is thus sacrilegious in his very fidelity to the letter and to writing, that is, to the sign. The sacred is displaced at the moment of the incarnation. At this point in his argument, however, the participation of the sacred in the human world is so total that if Nikephoros were not extremely careful, he would have to admit that the hieromyst of this new sacredness, Christ, was also its supreme profaner in that he invested himself so completely in humanity. This is why the powerful spring that causes the sacred to rebound from its fall in the new hierophany is the icon itself. "Henceforth accept the icon or erase the Gospels."[40]

If the iconoclast is a slave to the sign, this is because for him, it is as though Christ's body was perpetuated solely by sacramental sanctification (the eucharist). Christ and the eucharist, indissolubly tied together, thus form the *hagion* that is both foundational and diachronic, and ecclesial sacredness is therefore excluded from the field of pneumatic signs. A doctrine of topos—a place consecrated by the presence of relics and the fact of episcopal consecration—would thus be necessary in order for the Church to form a part of the holy. For the iconoclast, the Church therefore cannot be separated from its spatial definition, from its visible body. It has limits, and its limits in turn determine what will be interior or exterior to it.

The situation is entirely different as far as the iconophile *hiéron* goes, however. It links the body of Christ in the incarnation with its perpetuation in the Marian institution of the church. The eucharist thus continues to celebrate the mystery of consubstantiality in the nonsymbolic, that is, nonrelative, sacramental universe. The *hiéron* is by definition nonconsubstantial sacredness—symbolic sacredness that overflows all the places it invests, so that neither the Word nor any womb can imprison it. It defines the space of sacredness as a space of communicative unfolding, where the church is a quasi-transcendental system with respect to the workings of divinity in the visible world.

The sacred will therefore also be immanent to the definition of authority. Temporal power will no longer draw its legitimacy from charisma or the prophetic mystery of signs, but from the subjugation of every sovereign authority to the authority that confers iconic power on it, that is, the church.

Thus the nonwritten law does not only refer simply to the oral tradition whose model is christic teaching; it is that *paradosis siopôsa*, that mute tradition that is inscribed silently in the social body itself in order to impose what would henceforth become law and would therefore be sacred. In effect, that which is just (*dikaion*) and that which is law is no longer obedience to the text that expresses prohibition, but submission to a silent system that lifts all prohibitions, on the express condition that every practice, every gesture, every thought be linked to the iconic doctrine of symbolic mediation. Practice and repetition only have the force of law because they inscribe this linkage of the visible and invisible, the inside and the outside, in the silence of the body. All these things form the essence of the economy.

The Icon: A Nonwritten Tradition

The Graph and the Evangelical Message

The nonwritten law, the *agraphos* tradition, is nothing other than this inscription of the ecclesiastic institution in a body that is simultaneously the nonwritten body of Christ and the body of every believer that becomes its abode by means of the eucharistic sacrament. As we will see, the *hiéron* is destined to become the receptacle, the container, of the *hagion.*

The inscription (*graphè*) of Christ's body in the icon is situated at an absolute remove from written law, just as it is at as clear a remove from eucharistic consubstantiality. This inscription of the nonwritten is the iconic inscription for which Nikephoros reserves the exceptional status of a symbol that mediates between sacred things and the internal threats that they conjure up; that is to say, between the *hagion* and the damned (the diabolical), between the *hiéron* and the profane (the lay). In order to do this, the icon sets the holy and the sacred in relation to each other. The icon is contemporaneous with the evangelical message. The apostles "bequeathed the speech of divine religion to us, just as, by means of painting, they also made visible and evident for us . . . the world in which the Saviour came to live on earth."

But the contemporaneity of the icon and the Gospels is not enough. Nikephoros wants to prove, in well-tried patristic tradition, that the icon is superior to the letter and even to speech: "*Opsis protéra akoué.*" This primacy of vision over hearing is a classic theme in the literature of the church fathers; here, however, the topos is overdetermined in its aim, because vision is being invested with a function that is sacred.

Elsewhere, the same topos will rather serve the pedagogical intentions of the iconophile orator: "This is why that genre of more unrefined writing, which is nevertheless clearer for the benefit of simple and crude people, was necessary."[41] However, he wants to show first that whoever is an enemy of vision, and therefore of the icon, is also an enemy of the sacred. Here we encounter the last of his slippages, which causes a sacredness that is not one of the written or oral, but visual, tradition to resurface, so to speak, from the field of the ethos. Whatever appears, is sacred: "To whatever degree reality is above speech, the imitation and formal resemblance of reality will prevail over the sound of speech to let us know things clearly, . . . since vision is more efficient than hearing in causing conviction, and is not at all secondary to it."[42]

Yet what is entirely new here in relation to the classical topos is that the preeminence of vision has as its foundation the preeminence of the icon, and not the opposite. In effect, it is not from its visual effectiveness that the icon derives its strongest argument; rather, it is by means of iconic sacredness that vision obtains its primacy. The choice of the image is in the first instance divine. It is God himself who, in making his filial Person visible, marked out the royal road of vision. The icon is evangelical because he who occupies its center is image. The sacredness of the icon is based on its divine origin. Vision is the mediating organ of similitude. Whoever aims a blow at the icon is sacrilegious, because he strikes the very essence of the Second Person of the Trinity.

The progressive abandonment evident of the *hiéron*'s criteria did not present any danger for the iconophiles, because all of its power would reappear and come to be firmly established in a defense of the *hagion.* This sacredness, which is the very one formed by the trinity of the economy, the Virgin (*Panaghia*), and the saints (*hagioi*), would in turn promote a contamination of the sacred, which would give the *hiéra* and all the sacred symbols (*hiéra sumbola*) their character of inviolability and institutional legitimacy.

For Nikephoros, the *hagion* could already be seen functioning in the inspiration that dominated the decisions of the synods. That sacredness defined a supernatural power whose presence could be seen by the effects of illumination, inspiration . . . but at no moment is that *hagion* human, even though the nature of its operations reaches the human field. It remains supernatural. The sacred, on the contrary, is economic and therefore natural. However, yet another character is added to the *hagion*'s already supernatural character: its mediated hierophany. This character is essential to the workings of the Son, his mother, and the saints, because image and icon continually sweep across the double field of the sacred and the holy. In the light of this, Constantine is described as a blasphemer who prevents the establishment of a natural communication between the holy and the sacred. Constantine considers anything that is the object of consecration (*hagiasmos*) or priestly celebration (*hieratikès teletès*) to be sacred. He is incapable, says Nikephoros, of conceiving of the sacred without consubstantiality. This is why the paradigm of the holy, consecrated image could only be the eucharist. Consequently, even the pure *hagion* transmitted to humans by divine power is submitted to sacramental actions.

The icon, on the contrary, derives its sacredness from the pneumatic breath that transfigures similitude without having any need of the sacramental institution. Its sanctity (*hagion*) comes to it from the workings of its model who, absent in his very sanctity, remains intangible and invisible. Its sacred (*hiéron*) presence among the sacred symbols (*hiéra symbola*) is the result of an intrinsic activity. With its contagious presence it generates the sacredness of the social space at whose heart it irradiates the sanctity of its model. As an icon, it is only *hiéra*, which is to say that it is owed only honor and respect (*timè*), but as something that originates in an imaginal model that is holy, it has the right to *proskynesis*, venerating genuflection, that is radically different from *latria*, worship that is addressed to its only model.

What nonsense, then, to use the term *iconolatry* to speak of iconophilia![43] *Latria* is at the heart of the iconic battle to ward off the idol. *Iconophilia*, rather, is a highly specific term, which authorizes interpretive side-slipping and enlightens us about the real side slips to which the icon was itself subjected.

The icon is therefore imbued with different levels of sacredness without ever being identical with any of them, because its function is to make them communicate with each other, as its model, Christ himself, did. This icon cannot be restricted solely to the site of consecration in the strictly institutional sense. In effect, if the icon needed the sacrament in the sacred precinct in order to be sacred, it would then derive its sacredness from two conditions: pneumatic inspiration and the ecclesiastical hierarchy put in place by the emperor. This status of the icon would then respond to the iconoclast's wishes to separate the sacred from the profane. On the other hand, the iconophile (who, let us repeat, will never be an iconolater) wants to develop a nonlocal, nonsacramental system of thought concerning the sacred, a system of thought that will render it open to the profane world that will promise a contaminating unfolding beyond precincts, borders, and the statal hierarchy. Once perfected, however, this new "profane" definition of the sacred is not, for all that, an "anarchizing" doctrine of iconic propagation. The institution will produce a mastering framework for it, will control its power by other means, thanks to an economic conception of the new symbol; for what is desired is not a frenetic doctrine of icons in free circulation, but a coherent theoretical body that will allow the icon to be thought in a univocal way, from a point of view that is as much spiritual as strategic, that is, as a major mode of investing the imaginary and sovereignty in a controlled space, and all that in an endless mobility between places that are either under threat or remain to be conquered.

The Icon and Its Sacred Site

The icon concerns a particular category in which immediacy and mediation are alternately linked to each other. The icon is immediate, as is the gaze, and it mediates, as does the gaze of whatever it renders present. It is the site in which the sacred circulates in its polymorphism, to the point where it is integrated as a profane object, but imbued as well with sacredness. The definitive text that makes this dynamism, this iconic mobility, come alive is found in the third *Antirrhetic*, where Nikephoros engages in a display of virtuosity on the topology of the sacred.[44] In it, he comes to the foregone conclusion that whoever knows only the pneumatic sanctity of consubstantiality and the sacrament totally misinterprets the notion of the sacred itself. This will lead the misinterpreter finally only to know and practice within the category of the profane, and consequently to blaspheme. But the text is also extremely important because it leads the reader to conceive of the ubiquity of the sacred, the modal nature of the question of the interior, the exterior, and the relations between sacredness and beauty, through the successive designations of what is sacred and what is not.

When a pious man has a conversation with the iconoclasts, he can say: "it is worth honoring the divine symbols [*theia sumbola*], because the things which are placed in the sacred temples are sacred [*en tois hierois oikos anakeimena hiera eisin*], just as the things in these places [*en tois*] that are spread before the divine altar or somewhere else [*heterothi pou*] in the sacred precinct [*hiérou*], and that are portrayed on the curtain [*kata*] as on every other material [*en heterâ hulê*] are venerated as holy [*hagia*] together with those places [*sunproskoumena*]. All these things were made together by Christians in the beginning." They say [the Iconoclasts]: "we can see in

[*en*] these places icons of wild animals, of domestic animals, of birds and of other living beings. And we venerate the sacred things insofar as they are sacred [*hiera hôs heira*] and not because of these motifs [*tauta di'ekeina*]. So, even if we see the icon of Christ, we do not venerate the icon but what is sacred [*hieron*], and that is why the icon must not be venerated outside these sacred places" [*ektos touton*].[45]

Even before analyzing the text any further, it is striking to note the language that Nikephoros puts in the mouth of Constantine, the language of the *hiéron*; Nikephoros will of course later catch him in flagrante delicto when he makes the error of committing himself from the outset to the simultaneous veneration of the holy and the sacred. Constantine was loath to use the term *hiéron*, both in the *Horos* of Hieria and the *Peusis*. When he does use it, it is, despite everything, to refer to something in the sacred space that, although contiguous with the *hagion*, is not confused with it, without, for all that, creating any confusion in relation to the decor of the sacred places. His listing of the ornamental elements besides Christ's icon, however, clearly demonstrates that he has no conception of the sacred as an economic and enveloping visibility of the holy. Everything that he says gives the impression that he does confuse the *hiéron* and the *hagion*. This, in fact, is the iconophiles' major reproach of Constantine, and it is the reason that they are so partial to those passages where he shows his weakness on the symbolic level.

Second, there is a clear insistence on a vocabulary of space: inside, outside, on, elsewhere, with. . . . The issue at stake concerns the *place* of the sacred, and Nikephoros wants to be able to reply that it is not the sacredness of the places that confers sacredness on things, but the sacredness of things that is propagated in a place. What, really, does Mammon say here, in a text that does not appear anywhere in the *Horos* of Hieria and that Nikephoros cobbles together for the circumstances? He states that icons cannot be venerated outdoors. In other words, he says that there is an intrinsic sacredness whose only origin is sanctification by consecration, which makes whatever is consecrated worthy of veneration. For Nikephoros, however, sacredness does not concern "decor," to use André Grabar's translation of the term,[46] the Greek word for which does not appear in the text.

However, let us look at the continuation of the text, where Nikephoros replies to the iconoclast:

Someone could reply that the same thing [*ho autos logos*] does not apply to every case. Indeed, the forms of other living beings were not primarily produced for devotion and for veneration in the sanctuary, but for the sake of the beauty and harmony [*kosmon kai euprépeîan*] of the textiles in which they were woven together. This is what happened when, thanks to the piety and zeal of the faithful for the divine dwelling places [*peri tous theious oikous*], they were presented as a sacred offering [*anathéma hiéron*]. For, if someone adores the sacred [*hiéron*] object, he does not do this by paying attention either to the animal or to the wild beast. He knows that there is no advantage to come from them [*ouden ap'authôn onénasthai*]. But he pays attention to what is sacred [*hiéron*], giving nothing more than a look to [the ornaments]. The aim of the holy figures [*septôn*] is different. How? Because they are holy *per se* [*di'auto to hagia einai*] and they establish the memory [*mnèmèn*] of the holy [*hagiôn*] archetypes, they are venerated as sacred together with what is sacred [*hos heira tois hierois sumproskunoûntai*], but not only together with what they are part of [*sun autois*]; they will also be honored outside the holy temples [*ektos tôn hagiôn oikôn*]. But you, how is it that you are not unhappy to venerate in the sacred precinct [*en tô hierô*] the icons of the ass, of the dog and of the pig, and rejoice in burning to ashes the icon of Christ in the very sacred precinct [*autôi hierôi*]? And do you not shudder at undertaking such things, showing that you falsely bear the name "Christian?" What then could those whose intellectual capacity is mutilated and who are defective in mental performance say about the icons which are situated in the sacred enclosures [*en taïs hieraîs kinklisi*] and in the so-called *solea*, and about those which are seen on the columns and on the gates [*en tois kios kai pulôsin*], and about those which are installed in front of the divine sanctuary?

So, is it for the sake of beauty and harmony that Christians produced them or is it for the sake of specifically adapting the images to the places [*ta oikeia tois oikeiois epharmozontes*], knowing that those places [*topoi*] are places for veneration and that those icons were produced [for these places] for the purpose of veneration?[47]

Noticeable even at a first reading is the density of the text here and the to-and-froing between the terms that refer both to the sacred object and to the space, both interior and exterior, where its sacredness is established. It is readily understandable that this difficult text has attracted the attention of exegetes of the iconoclastic crisis, particularly Grabar. However, the translation and interpretation that he proposes pulls it toward a justification of decorative forms that is strongly favorable to iconophilia; moreover, this robs the text of its polemical and properly economic dimension. This is so to such an extent that Grabar echoes in his own text the patriarchal plea by speaking of fetishism and animism when describing iconoclast thought! A little earlier, as we have seen, the iconophiles had no hesitation in treating their adversaries as idolators, against all logic. Now it is the modern historian himself who accuses the iconoclast of superstitious iconophobia.

If Nikephoros takes the trouble to defend the "topology" of the sacred so fiercely, however, it is because his adversaries are neither naive nor fetishists. Is Christ in the icon like the lamb, or like the griffin that decorates the chalice? Or again, is he like the plants, the animals, and the different motifs embroidered on the hangings? In other words, is he dissociable or not from the sacred space to which he belongs, from the profane space in which he stirs, from the matter that serves as his support?

In the first part of the text, Nikephoros talks of *sumbola*, by which we should understand not only icons, as Grabar does, but all the objects, the whole of the sacred abode's sacred space, with its liturgical objects, decorations, and ornaments. The *sumbolon* is iconic, so it causes the *hiéron* and the *hagion* to communicate with each other. But everywhere it is involved with the universe of profane signs, sacralized by consecration or by contiguity and community with the sacred world. What characterizes the *sumbolon* above all else is nonconsubstantiality. Nikephoros therefore has to establish distinctions among the symbols, because his new objective is the methodical appropriation of space by the sacred, owing to a principle that is both active and contaminating. He begins by insistently marking off contiguities: in, in front of, above, below. Then he marks off global features, or the formation of a common system: these are the verbs that begin with *syn* (*sunproskoumena, sundiagraphomena, sunexeirgasthésan, sunproskunoutai*), thus indicating that sacred "symbols" cannot be dismantled. In a sacred place, something profane that does not deserve worship or respect cannot even be considered to subsist. This contamination of the sacred comes from its close linkage to the pneumatic holy, which is infinite, spreads everywhere, and therefore possesses, in principle, ubiquity. This is so to such a degree that by respecting the *hiéron* of the sacred places, one reaches *so to speak* the holy (*hôs hagia*), which is a phrase that inevitably evokes the passage stating that in relation to the icon, an absence *hôs paronta* is equivalent *so to speak* to a presence. This *hos* is the "as if" of the mimetic economy.

The first blunder of Constantine, therefore, consists in the desacralization of the interior of the holy places, and the profanations to which the iconoclasts give themselves over are the proof of this. But, replies Nikephoros, in the holy place itself, it is absolutely necessary to distinguish the different species of *sumbolon*. If every sacred, nonconsubstantial element is called *sumbolon,* it is still necessary to know how to differentiate between three terms—decor, support, and icon—that is, between what is on top of, below, or neither on top of nor below but "in relation through" (*skhéseôs*). There are three forms of symbolic relations: the consecration of the profane, the temple, or a liturgical object; contamination by the sacred (this is the case of profane decoration on a consecrated object); and iconic grace, which renders sacredness by the privileged relation between the icon and the prototype. What differentiates the two last cases is the concept of support. *Sun, en,* and *kata* refer to a whole topology of contact between the sacred and the profane that is only resolved in what Grabar calls an "aestheticism." He bases this on the expression "*kosmos kai euprépeia*" (beauty and appropriateness), a topos of the argument for the beauty of holy places, which recurs twice.

But matters are not so simple, for in the case of the icon, beauty poses an entirely different problem owing to kenosis. In effect, if the icon is a memorial to the incarnation, that is, to God's assumption of human misery, his splendor can only be spiritual, whereas in the case of the ornamentation of objects and liturgical places, beauty is not only the motif of decoration itself, it also becomes an anagogical factor in the contemplation of divine splendor. Luxuriousness and beauty enter into a relational conception of the symbol in anagogical mode, which spreads the pleasure of seeing by contiguity in order to carry it to spiritual fruition.

What Nikephoros tries to demonstrate above all, then, is that the iconoclast conception of the holy is separative, in the sense that it generates obstacles to communication and symbolic mediation. The sacred, which has nothing to do with this in his eyes, is essentially a symbolic category, which is to say that in conformity with the Christological economy, the sacred is profoundly acquainted with kenosis and transfiguration. Kenosis refers to that hollowing out of divinity and the sacred of which we spoke earlier and concerns the ultimate profanity: death. In a sense, it could be said that death, which escapes all symbolization, is substituted by the category not of emptiness but of a hollowing out, to which economic dynamism provides the possibility of reversal. What resists all symbols is then symbolized, and the transfiguration is that living resurrection of the world that by pneumatic grace allows humans and things to appear anew in the time and space of the sacred.

If Nikephoros is to be believed, Constantine venerates the profane and profanes the sacred. Once again, what separates is the same as what mixes together. This theme, untiringly reprised throughout the *Antirrhetics,* is haunted by a diabolical contradiction, itself *diabolê*: division, separation—that is to say, the inability to mediate, symbolic inaptitude, and therefore the impossibility of setting things in relation to each other without them becoming confused. It is therefore not surprising to see that the "diabolists" are champions of consubstantiality. Thus Grabar, taking up Nikephoros's argument again, considers in turn that Constantine "tends to confuse the representation and the thing represented, and to make the religious icon slip towards the magical image," from which a type of "fetishism" arises. He continues, saying that Nikephoros, "as an ardent polemicist, may perfectly well have distorted the thought of his adversaries," but that, all things considered, he was probably correct, because "in this, the iconoclasts come close to traditional beliefs that in the Near East are perhaps more deeply entrenched than elsewhere!" After this, he concludes that the Orthodox, "educated in the school of Greek thought," as was Nikephoros, did not wish to run the same risks and preserved the icon without confusing it with the idol or "the magician's effigy." We believe, however, that it is rather because he ran the same risks that he worked so energetically to produce a doctrine that could protect it.

On reading Kitzinger's study of the cult of icons before the iconoclastic period, the most striking feature is precisely a growing tendency to superstition on the side of the burgeoning iconophilia.[48] There is a clear absence noticeable in the expansion of object worship of a confirmed symbolic dimension. In other words, it is not so much the iconoclasts who obliged the church fathers to produce a coherent doctrine of the symbol as the crowd of the faithful living in confusion. Kitzinger begins by noting the considerable growth of the icon between the sixth and eighth centuries, and goes on to remark that the result of the attribution of "magic properties to an image is that the distinction between the image and the person represented is to some extent eliminated," because "the image acts or behaves as the subject itself is expected to act or behave."[49] He points out as well the icon's prophylactic and apotropaic character, and the fact that there is a marked increase in the numbers of acheiropoietic icons during the time under consideration. Finally, he concludes that as time passes and the cult of icons expands, its material bond with the sacred disappears.

Now, this is an extremely important point. The icon participates in the *hagion* with everything that that entails concerning potential demonism and virtual diabolism. The iconoclast, on the other hand, expels what is holy in order to avoid talismanism and animism. Nikephoros, however, rehabilitates it in the symbolic field of the sacred, where it will moreover constitute the element that runs transversely to all sacrednesses. Kitzinger acutely notes that as the contact between image and spectator becomes more and more intimate, so it is not that particular relationship that the apologists try to explore and justify. On the contrary, they raise the icon above human needs and anchor it in a transcendental relation with divinity. Thus the artist will make abodes for the Holy Spirit; as Leontios of Neapolis says, "I render honor to the abode of the Holy Spirit."

This assimilation of the icon to a dwelling place (*oikos*) is a constitutive element of its relation to the holy. Just as the holy temples were the institutional abodes of the *Hagion Pneuma*, so icons become the mobile dwellings of a power that their matter does not limit. The contiguity of the holy and the sacred is of the same nature as the content to the container, whose iconic graph inscribes the threshold that separates and unites them. This is why Nikephoros is extremely careful to distinguish the relation of the decor on the vase that is decorated from the relation of the icon to the figure that it shows. In the first case, on top of and below have a specific contiguity: the support is a container sacralized by its place and function. Its decor is distinct from the container and does not participate in the least in the content. It arises instead from a surplus over the content, and by contagion enjoys the respect (*timê*) that is owed to the support. In truth, the decor maintains an "aesthetic" relation with the support, by which we should understand that beauty and harmony do honor to the sacred function. Appropriateness and beauty—*euprépeia* and *kosmos*—are only circumstantially sacred and have anagogical value.

What fed this anagogical interpretation was a Plotinian conception of the image: "Whoever sees the perceptible universe also admires the intelligible world that he sees reflected in it, as someone who contemplates a painting."[50] The gradual passage from the contemplation of beauty to the contemplation of being finds its precise topical formulation here. The gaze of the faithful is taken under control, from the spontaneity of its immediate pleasures to the end of the voyage, which will place it in the hands of the angelic powers. In this sense, then, the beauty of the decor has a protreptic and pedagogical intention.

On the other hand, the fundamental conception of the icon is clearly distinct from any thought concerning decoration. This means that the wooden panel and Christ do not have the relation that a support has to its decoration, of container to content. In the temple, the consecrated abode communicates to everything that it contains the sacredness that it itself obtains from everything that made it a *hiéron* in the first place—that is, the relics enclosed in the altar, without which it is not sacred, and the liturgical sacrament that dedicated it to an eponymous saint. In other words, the temple is sacred because it contains relics (*hagia*), but it communicates its sacredness to everything that it contains that was originally profane: it simultaneously becomes a receptacle and a dispenser. However, the ensemble of the sanctuary, which is unsurprisingly described as *hiéron hagion*, maintains its symbolic economy, its capacity for causing the sacred to circulate interior to its consecrated precinct only. Thus the whole mechanism that communicates between the different levels of sacredness remains unified and therefore dependent on the institutional framework. The result of this is that the sacred remains totally isolated from the profane, because from the moment that one enters the sacred precinct, one way or another, the holy and the sacred share places, objects, signs, gestures. . . .

In order to part from this precinct, however, Nikephoros finds a subtle means: the term *sumbolon*, he says, is a homonym. The polysemy of the word *symbol* allows the container and the content not to be mixed with each other. If the symbol is taken as a container, then the sacred spreads out from it and cohabits with the profane in a manner that is economic. Among the "symbols," the icon occupies a highly distinctive place. It forms part of the *hiéra* that are venerated as such (*hôs hiéra*), but by means of the procession of imitation and memory, it also forms part of the *hagia*. The icon is therefore neither only in the field of the holy nor the field of the sacred; it is between the two and makes them communicate with each other along two paths: the homonymic relation and the archetypal mnemic relation (*eis mnèmèn tôn archétupôn proïenai hagiôn*). There are therefore two means of communication: one is based on its mimetic form, the other in the interior attitude of the contemplator. In common with all other symbols, the iconic *sumbolon* is therefore nonconsubstantial, but it also has the peculiarity of communicating directly with its own cause (*aitia*), the prototype. In other words, there is no linguistic remove here of the sort that separates the signifier from the signified; rather, the icon as a symbol becomes the manifestation per se of the cause that gives it its meaning. This amounts to saying that the signifier is present in the icon, even if it is necessary to add to this "relatively."

This relative immanence of the holy in the sacred is specific to the iconic symbol. In contemplating a decorated object, therefore, the ascent of worship to the supreme and holy source can only take place by a series of successive abstractions, each based on the other, in order to detach the contemplator from the perceptible world; conversely, on the same model of the incarnation, to which the icon is the memorial, the movement of contemplating the icon leads the contemplator toward the world. Starting from the cause (*hagion*) evoked by the imitation of the prototype (a formal imitation, *homoiôsis*), the contemplator is anagogically led to the sanctification of the perceptible world.

The icon brings humans to the world, in that this world is the one of salvation. Therefore, the homoiotic movement, which confers holiness on the icon owing to a mimetic sacredness, is complemented by a second mimetic movement, one that travels from the iconic sacred to the profane, in order to redeem.

The icon moves toward the world; this means that it leaves the temple and spreads beyond it: "*ou sin autois monon alla kai ektos tôn hagiôn oikôn.*" Not only is worship performed in and with the holy place, but also outside of the consecrated holy abodes. This irruption of the icon outside of the sacramental field is a central aspect of the iconophile economy, one that strives to invade the profane field in order to appropriate it for itself.

Thus the icon is endowed with a power that is both centripetal and centrifugal. It is centripetal because it captures the holiness of its model with its forms and centrifugal because it dispenses and spreads the sacredness that it incarnates by contact and contamination. This, in fact, is one of the major functions of the economy.

How, then, does the capture of the model's holiness function in the icon? Here, Nikephoros tries to link together the things that he had initially needed to separate, that is, the formal concern regarding the immanence of the sacred. In the icon, Christ is not a mere decoration, but his form must respond to a certain number of requirements appropriate to symbolic ends: *ta oikeia tois oikeiois epharmozontes.* Christians are always careful to avoid rupture, disharmony, maladjustment. The icon painter is not any old decorator, but an artist who maintains a privileged relation, governed over by the Holy Ghost, with the prototypical cause. This is so to such an extent that the formal choices for portraying the holiness of the prototype cannot be separated from the existential *mimésis* that governs holy life.

In the production of pictures, pneumatic inspiration works as much by prayer and contemplation as by the direct intervention of the *hagion.* Hagiographies provide us with some examples in which as the artist sleeps, so the prototype appears in a "homonymic" dream, bearing the traits by which he will be portrayed in the icon. This first guarantee of resemblance presided over by the direct intervention of the prototype is then reinforced by a gesture that offers a second guarantee of authenticity: the inscription of the sacred prototype's name on the icon (the homonymic *épigraphè*). "Hagiastic" contamination therefore occurs simultaneously by resemblance and homonymy. To accord the icon this "transitional" status, the texts call it *septa,* pure.[51] The pure and holy icon thus meets the internal conditions that its mimetic participation in the incarnation demands.

In what sense is beauty sacred? The making of the icon, as we have seen, remained closely linked to a system of measurements. There is a sacredness in repetition and number. "The transfer of measurements ensures the transfer of powers," notes Kitzinger. Thus number and name are the foundations of the authentification of the sacred. These two foundations give the icon its symbolic definition, whereas pneumatic inspiration alone, having guided the hand that "copied" the model, may leave the contemplator of the dream or apparition in a position of nonproductive worship. This is not, however, the intention of economic thought, which is different in this respect from the acheiropoietic icons. The iconophile, *having a relational conception of the icon and a transitional conception of the sacred,* venerates the holiness of the Holy Face, *even as he prefers to develop an hierophany that is made by human hand.* This iconic hierophany is more eager to sacralize and invest what surrounds it than it is concerned with maintaining the charismatic purity of the acheiropoietic images, which will become in turn an iconic model.

In relation to the place of the sacred, neither the time nor presence in the temple of icons or objects touched by pneumatic grace form the object of iconophile discourse; rather, it is the always mobile link of a progressive and uninterrupted sacralization of profane space by iconic symbols. It is this link that is problematic for iconoclast thought, which sees in it, correctly, a sacredness that escapes hierarchic control and the control of the institutional universe of the sacraments.

Independent of liturgical control, the icon incarnates that "unvested power" of the monks that Peter Brown discusses, which is a parallel power that escapes both imperial and episcopal power.[52] In his analysis of the crisis, Brown also manifests a tendency to identify the icon progressively with the holy man. This identification is extremely enlightening in relation to the interpretation of the mimetic sacred of the holy and to an understanding of the violent antimonasticism of the iconoclasts. But this unlinked, unvested power, such as he describes it, no longer fits the icon. The sociopsychological analysis that constitutes the rest of his study of the holy man leads him to follow Grabar and Kitzinger in privileging the icon's magical and thaumaturgical character. On the one hand, the force of his argument arises from the fact that he does not separate the iconic function of the sacred from the social and political fabric that it reinforces; in his opinion, danger arises from the fact that the sacred causes an expansion of a power parallel to all hierarchies. On the other hand, however, there would nevertheless appear to be a great difference between iconic sacredness and the holy man, although they cannot be separated at all in the genesis of the iconic function. It is in this that the comparison between Nikephoros's text and the life of St. Steven the Younger is highly instructive, for the very use of the terms that refer to the icon and the holy man make it seem as though the system of thought regarding the sacred is working hard to separate the icon from its living model, the holy man. "Holy men and icons were implicated on an even deeper level. For both were, technically, unconsecrated objects."[53] Brown is in a position to argue for this identity because he had asserted a little earlier that "the icon merely filled a gap left by the physical absence of the holy man."[54] He illustrates this concept with evidence from Gregory Nazianzos and Basil, who had described the saint as being a statue. The saint, immobile as an icon: the stylite tradition had long provided a model for this conception. I disagree with none of this. What is important from our point of view, however, is the genesis of the iconic system of thought. It is not the saint who stands at the origins of the icon, but the image that is the cause of what is holy. This is true even if it is indeed through the hagiographic accounts that iconic reality can be seen emerging historically, little by little and with growing precision. The holy man, still named *hagios*, does manifest his relation with the *hiéron* in many ways, but in an unstable, confused, and (to take up Brown's word) inarticulate fashion.

In this paradoxical performance, the icon, on the other hand, manages to escape institutional space and establish the space of symbolic linkage itself. A thinker such as Nikephoros cannot be considered the defender of a subversive and turbulent conception of the icon. Rather, he will, so to speak, gather the powers reaped by the holy man and redistribute them economically among the different authorities, as that economy decrees.

Conclusion

Nikephoros's conclusion is clear: "We Christians, . . . we know what we prostrate ourselves before: we venerate what is 'sacred' as 'holy things' [*ta hiera sebomen hôs hagia*]." The *hôs* here represents *diabainei*, which refers to the movement by which the cult that one offers to the sacred ascends to the prototype ("*epi to prôtotypon*"); this is the anagogical relation that travels from the sacred and the consecrated to the sacrosanct per se. Such is the economic working of relations (*skhésis*). It should be identified not with a relativism lacking in spiritual nobility and serving immediate interests, but with a relativism that economic thought has made tip over completely into the mimetic sublimation of divine condescension.

In short, the unremitting effort that Nikephoros puts into proving that the iconoclast Mammon is the enemy of the sacred corresponds with his intention to formulate a specific sacredness against the sacredness of his opponents, in which the image has a structural function. Iconoclast sacredness, as all sacredness, has a double character. This duality is interpreted by its adversaries as diabolical duplicity, division without mediation. Constantine V and his disciples recognize on the one hand a pneumatic, direct power, and on the other an institutional body of signs aimed both at guaranteeing the authenticity of the sacred and mapping out its disturbing ambivalence. The system of iconoclast signs passes through two systems of gesture, each subordinated to the other: the first is the mimetic, imperial system, which is nominated directly, and the second is the system of sacraments, dispensed by the clergy who do not share in sovereignty, but depend on it. This is a sacredness that is hierarchized in a linear way, and its duality (pneumatic and semiotic) has no mediator other than the emperor himself.

Nikephoros renders this imperial production of the sacred derisory and contradictory in order to oppose it to another duality. Whereas iconoclasm only recognizes the *hagion*, iconophilia formulates a subtle theory of the circulation of sacrednesses on different levels. But this theory, which makes the *hiéron* the centerpiece of the new *iconocracy*, is not set up in a purely theoretical way. It is the journey of the reader through the texts that allows the coherence of the "weave" to be progressively seen. What is the *hiéron*? It is the principle of mastering the *hagion*'s turbulence and the sacralization of the profane world, which is haunted by other turbulences. This amounts to saying that the sacred is an agent that brings order to the holy and puts it into a well-tempered relation with the real world. This is why the icon would become the appropriate symbol of the *hiéron*'s epiphany. It epitomizes and actualizes in itself all the major workings of the sacred: to contain the *hagion* without enclosing it, rendering it visible without releasing it so that it is beyond control, tying it indissolubly to a fertile and contaminating definition of space to be ruled over and space to be invaded. To say that the icon is a symbol means, strictly speaking, that it is the very agent of the symbolization of what is holy. The attribution of sovereignty to the keeper of iconic sacredness therefore corresponds well to the ecclesiastical institution's objectives, which make the sacred, good order, and the economy inseparable within a mechanism that substitutes one for the other, or, if one prefers, by a concatenation of equivalences proper to the economy.

In order to deprive the emperor of iconic fertility in the order of appearance as well as representation, the iconophile institution makes use of the weapon that it is still in the process of inventing and that it never stops trying to perfect.

5

Iconic Space and Territorial Rule

To attempt to rule over the whole world by organizing an empire that derived its power and authority by linking together the visual and the imaginal was Christianity's true genius. The church, founded by Paul, was apparently the first to provide a response to the problems of iconocracy that we are considering here. These concern the entire operation which, in giving its flesh and form to something, the very essence of which is a withdrawal, invisibly takes possession of all earthly, visible things. Having already examined the question of the theoretical energy involved in this enterprise, we now turn our attention to its pedagogical and political effectiveness. By virtue of the economic unity of the system, an uninterrupted pathway between the spiritual and temporal worlds was made possible; they are one and the same when considered from the point of view of the economy.

The incarnation of a God appearing in an image in the form of a son founds both a new theology and a new politics. The Pauline conception of the *eikôn tou theou,* the Son who is an image of God (and who constitutes a body that founds a new kingdom), inspired the church to a doctrine in which images were given the responsibility of making institutional space visible. This space develops a worldly or planetary calling under the more abstract title of the universal. Catholic thought, which in Greek is nothing more than the category of universality itself, envisages no more and no less than the conquest of the world beyond the barrier of time, borders, and languages. We are today the heirs and propagators of this iconic empire, yet effort is nevertheless still required on our part to understand how the practice of the icon has infiltrated its smooth and efficient operation.

In promoting the visibility of God in his christic incarnation, and in identifying it simultaneously with the ecclesiastic institution, St. Paul truly opened the iconocratic field up to the designs of empires. Here is the Epistle to the Colossians (1:15–18):

> He is the image of the invisible God, the firstborn of all creation; for in him all things in heaven and on earth were created, things visible and invisible, whether thrones or dominions or rulers or powers—all things have been created through him and for him. He himself is before all things, and in him all things hang together. He is the head of the body, the church [*hé képhalé tou sômatos tès ecclèsias*].

Yet how did the icon succeed not only in making an institution apparent, but, by its very spatiality, rendering visible and real a fertile, matrixlike formula for the invasion and domination of territory?

The icon itself, by virtue of its physical, tangible reality, constitutes an extraordinary treatment of space. Every graphic decision carries meanings that are both doctrinal and institutional. We have already seen examples of its educational use and its capacity to convince people immediately of its own truth. However, it also puts in place an extraordinary yet real, tangible system that is thoroughly imbued with a design for the appropriation of Christianized territory. The question it poses is distinctively modern, because it is none other than the question of the empire of the gaze and vision, which is what I call "iconocracy."

By iconocracy, I mean that organization of the visible that provokes an adherence that could be called a submission to the gaze. I choose the term deliberately. Customarily, those who destroyed sacred images are called iconoclasts and those who defended them iconophiles. In respect of the latter, however, I prefer to talk of iconophiles only when considering the spiritual and philosophical arguments that determined the battle in favor of icons, and of *iconodules*, that is to say slaves to the icon, whenever the stakes are considered from the educational and political points of view. *There is no iconodule but for the iconocrat*; there is no slave but for the master. In the struggle for mastery and control over iconic production, the two camps constantly accuse each other of being slaves to the idol, because each would like to seize power. One thing, therefore, is certain: to talk of iconolatry is to commit a serious error that shows a radical lack of understanding of the spiritual and political problems of iconicity. As for the iconoclast, it is clear that his hatred of the icon has its source in the unshakable attachment to what he considers to be the pure, true image.

The image, with its capacity to strike as a lightning bolt in the service of power, is not content simply to suspend the word and overwhelm by silence. Here and now, in the corporeal world where it addresses the issue of the incarnation, it proposes a definition of the entirety of space where power is deployed. For the church, following Paul, had interpreted the image of God as the advent of a glittering reign, as *basileia, a plan for the occupation of space.*

Michel Foucault's philosophical exercise on a painting by Velázquez is well known. The chapter entitled *Las Meninas* in *The Order of Things*, which opens his whole meditation on representation, is in fact the subtle description of a painting approached as a staging, a production. This is a classic scenography in which looks are exchanged, reveal themselves, and hide themselves in a pictorial space that has become a metaphor for royal space. But the monarchy in question is not so much that of King Phillip IV of Spain as one founded by the sovereignty of the gaze of the painter Velázquez, who commands the visible to become invisible in a double elision of the places of the king and the subject. Foucault discovers in this image the visible structure of an imaginary space and the institutional logic of an invisibility that is submitted to iconic organization. Yet strictly speaking, in this analysis there is nothing that is relevant to the nature of the iconic itself. In Foucault's view, Velázquez's *Las Meninas* exhibits something new, yet the secret of which a methodical and reasonable *ekphrasis* would, to some extent, reveal and describe. In this sense, it is possible that the brilliant analytic description could make one believe that it has left nothing unexplained, and that it releases the philosopher from a confrontation with the object itself. Although this statement may seem excessive and paradoxical, the fact remains, however, that the surplus yielded by the contemplation of the painting is nonetheless almost of a different nature to the satisfaction that one derives from its understanding. The pleasure of the drawing, of the forms, of the color—in a word, of all the pictorial devices—is added to the deciphered enigma of its meaning, "as though adding to youth its flower."

We may well, however, disagree deeply and essentially with the idea that both the problems posed by painting and the solutions that each work offers are quite so independent of everything that makes the painting visible and readable. The plastic value of the painting, the ensemble of material procedures, would in that case be nothing but the surplus value of its meaning.

Yet what brings us to reflect on the technique of the icon is precisely something that takes us beyond the technical operation of a scenography. The technique of its material production, "the making of the meadow," as Francis Ponge said, is a productive unwinding of meaning. The manipulation of materials and styles, the placing of color and lines, bear with them stakes that are as much spiritual as political. Foucault skirts the greatest difficulty that discourse about images encounters in addressing himself to images that generously offer their representativity to the philosopher. The icon, on the other hand, not representing what it renders visible, issues a summons to philosophy with an enigmatic specificity. Will it also allow us to grasp something that, later in the history of painting, emerges as an enigma specific to painting?

A different explanation might well be offered, however, to the effect that a painting ought to be understood as something that links the invisibility of the image with the question of the incarnation. Just what is it that takes bodily form in the visibility of the painting? In the preceding pages we outlined the mimetic and kenotic consequences of the relations that tie the flesh of the icon to the body of the resurrection. Our path then led us to an examination of icon doctrine in holy and sacred space. Now we turn to the icon in public space and its economic existence with regard to established power. Here, we will compare conceptions of the icon and its material technique to the idea of a territory that has been invaded or submitted to rule.

In relation to the manufacture and use of the icon, its devotees maintained that what was at stake in it in imaginary terms could not be separated from its material form. On the question of repetition, for example, the Byzantine image presents a fundamental generic difference to *Las Meninas.* In that unique masterpiece, a repetition arises from a temporality internal to the mirroring operation of the image. The problem of duplication is included in a rhetoric of signs that would bring joy, not to mention semiological delight, to an orator. Yet for all that, *Las Meninas* resists and remains a picture, which is to say an enigma whose power is never exhausted by the intelligibility of its signs.

The repetition to be found in the Byzantine icon, on the other hand, is both institutional and real. The icon must recopy a model that is, for the most part, another icon, to which it is totally and unchangingly subservient. As a result of this, moving back along the chain of icons, the necessity arises of decreeing certain images as being both foundational and miraculous. In other words, to the question of whether, in every image, the notion of imitation requires the existence of a real, or even imaginary, model, and whether the problematic of the true and the illusory demands consideration by an ontological tribunal, Foucault responds adroitly, thanks to Velázquez, by the drafting of a specular scenario in which the comings and goings are organized from the starting point of the portrayal of a mirror in a scene where the looks cleverly intersect as they exchange the sovereignty of their respective fictions. The native exteriority of the scene is abolished in the rhetorical interiority of painting itself.

The Byzantine economy, however, is entirely different. Byzantine iconography creates a repetitive and fertile plastic world where the mirror is the invisible quiddity of being, *not represented* because not representable. What is shown, rather, puts in place the visible formula of something that will ensure the stability of an empire. In opposition to Kantorowicz's conception of the sovereignty of the artist in the Renaissance,[1] I propose a kenotic practice of virgin space, within which is incarnated the sovereignty of an institution that will make of the flesh a body, *corpus Ecclesiae.*

Both the iconophile church and imperial power produced irrefutable signs and emblems of their own power. Let us now turn to a few examples demonstrating how it was possible to make the transition from a plastic space to a territory, the generating principle and concept for which is harbored by the icon. In effect, the problem concerns the invasion of profane space by an authority that ought to have restricted itself to churches and monasteries, and ought also to have limited its right to concern itself with moral life, religion, and salvation. Such, however, was not its intention. Besides its spiritual message, Pauline thought carries within it a universal, conquering message that no wealth or power of this world should be allowed to escape. The role that the icon plays in this conquest still appears to be both foundational and definitive.

Icons of Christ and the Virgin were frequently associated with imperial power, although this phenomenon dates from well before either the Quinisext council or the relapses of the iconoclast crisis. The meaning of this association, however, was radically modified during and after the crisis, as will be evident from the examples to which we now turn. First, we will examine a few instances of imperial coinage; then we will study two specific portrayals of the Virgin and child, the Virgin of Tenderness and the Virgin of Blachernai.

Coins and Seals

The invasion of the space, of the territory, of trade by the image of power is a theme that preoccupies evangelical thought itself. The well-known episode of *reddere Caesari* is found three times in the Evangelists: it appears in Matthew (22:21), Mark (12:17), and Luke (20:25). Here is Matthew's text: "They handed him a silver piece. Jesus asked, 'Whose head is this, and whose inscription?' 'Caesar's,' they replied. He said to them, 'Then pay to Caesar what belongs to Caesar, and to God what belongs to God.'" It is absolutely clear in this passage that the image engraved on the coin marks out the space of both an exchange and an obligation. The text thus clearly distinguishes between spiritual and temporal power, and we have every reason to believe that this distinction was fairly faithful to Jesus' thought and to the spiritual nature of his teaching.

What becomes of this tradition, however, with St. Paul? His text says: "For the same reason you also pay taxes, for the authorities are God's servants, busy with this very thing. Pay to all what is due them—taxes to whom taxes are due, revenue to whom revenue is due, respect to whom respect is due, and honor to whom honor is due."[2] Here, the issue is no longer one of separating God from Caesar: profane exchanges and spiritual obligations are mingled together in a list that designates all collectors or receivers of taxes as having been given their responsibility by God (*leitourgoi theou*). It is no longer a question of giving Caesar his due, but of taking his place. The icon played a determining role in this takeover and we will now examine the question of how it did so.

André Grabar, in his study of the imperial cult in Byzantium, maintains that the Christian cult imported wholesale the whole system of the cult of the emperor in order to render it to Christ and the *Theotokos*, the mother of God.[3] Thus emperors and empresses had themselves represented in the company of Christ, the Virgin, and saints, both in the profane world and in holy places.

In this connection, the first object to show the emperor and Christ side by side is a consular diptych dated to 540. The field of numismatics, however, allows us to determine that Christ's face first appears on a coin in the period immediately after the meeting of the Quinisext council. This appearance relates to a "revolution" that took place during the reign of Justinian II: until then, the gold *solidus* had represented on its obverse the bust of the emperor, and on the reverse the iconography of a Victory carrying a cross, which subsequently became the cross potent on steps. It was in 692–95 that Justinian II famously released a *solidus* that is described in the following way in the catalog of the British Museum: "Obverse: Justinian II, facing, bearded. Wears crown with cross and long robes of lozenge pattern; in l., small *mappa*. Reverse: Bust of Christ facing with cross behind head. Hair and beard flowing; wears tunic and mantle; r. hand in act of benediction; l. holds book of Gospels."

"Revolutionary" though this appearance on a coin was, it had, however, been preceded by the portrayal of Christ and the Virgin on seals surrounded by an oval frame that have the appearance of the shield carried by Victory figures. An image inserted into circles or ovals such as these is therefore called an *imago clipeata*: a shield image.

These choices of emblems, these novelties that appear on coins and seals, clearly show the connection between the iconography and the founding signs of both economic life and political institutions on objects whose essence is circulation itself. Thus the holy image circulates throughout the empire, yet is also limited by it, because the empire, in turn, determines the frontiers of its validity and its worth. Furthermore, the circular form of the seals and coins refers not only to the consular shield of the Victory figure, but also to the enclosure of the disc shape that denotes both totality and infinity. It can be found again in the icon of the Holy Face, which shows Christ with his circular, cruciferous nimbus.

These effigies, carrying the double symbolic value of both mercantile worth and christic presence, go hand to hand and place to place, traveling throughout the entire empire and marking by their passage and use a network of exchanges, obligations, and credits. It is not, therefore, simply by chance that the iconoclast emperors immediately marked the advent of their reign with the release of a new coin bearing an iconography that propounded an idea that was thoroughly political in nature. Older models are repeated, representing on one side the image of the emperor, and on the other the cross potent on steps. But alongside these, one finds a coin that, for the first time, suppresses the cross in order to make room for the son of the emperor: Leo III on the obverse, and Constantine on the reverse. This is not a matter of purely and simply suppressing the cross, which was, in fact, the sign favored by the iconoclasts to replace the icon. Rather, it concerns the placing in circulation of a model for the transmission of power that owes nothing to arbitrary choice, usurpation, or charisma. This hereditary, dynastic handover of power constitutes an entirely new notion of monarchical continuity and is one of the elements of the iconoclast conception of power. (In reality, however, dynastic continuity remained extremely precarious in Byzantium, although dynastic desire did reappear on several occasions.) This privileging the relation of father to son at the expense of the mother's relation to the son refers back to the Old Testament legacy that makes the king the direct emanation of paternal will, directly transmitted from the divine will to the birth of the princely heir. The maternal, ecclesiastic institution, however, clearly saw in this the threat weighing over its foundational role in the sacralization of temporal power and was determined not to lose that power. The religious ceremony at which emperors were crowned would therefore come to be used to reestablish the signs of the institutional transmission of civil power by the maternal authority of the church.

Let us note, meanwhile, that shortly after the triumph of orthodoxy (which is to say, the triumph of the image), although it took some time for the icon to regain a broad dispersion and resume its dominance, there was an immediate release by Michael III of coins carrying the effigy of Christ. In other words, the triumph of the icon was interpreted, without the least doubt or delay, in terms of a very close association between the church and temporal sovereignty. No power without an image. Additionally, the figure chosen and put in circulation, Christ and his mother, was one that had acquired particular power during the crisis. Even outside of the strict domain of icons themselves, then, christic iconography constituted a graphic formula for the inscription of the visibility of that which becomes law.

Thus in a few centuries, the *reddere Caesari* became a *reddere Christo*, which must be understood as a "give to the church." The image is therefore in the same situation as coinage itself, a substitute for value, cash circulating, waiting for nothing other than to be placed in international circulation. It is not a metallic yardstick, because what it causes to circulate is not the abstract equivalent of merchandise whose value can be estimated in material production. It is, rather, a material object that harbors an abstract value, one that is completely imaginary. In this sense it resembles fiduciary signs that incarnate, without the least fanfare, the effects of faith and of credit, rather more than coin of the realm, always restricted by the limits of territory, habit, or time.

Icons of the Mother and Son

In order to investigate this economic and globalizing process in greater depth, let us examine two traditional iconic models portraying the *Theotokos.* The first is the Virgin of Contact, the *Glukophilousa,* still known today as the Virgin of Tenderness. The second concerns a scene in which the Virgin points to her son at her breast, yet does not touch him; it is known as the Virgin of Blachernai, and it is the heir to the earlier Virgin orants. These two icons are laden with meaning both in the fields of spirituality and Christology, and in the setting in play of the space where temporal power is decided.

What, then, of the drawn lines that inscribe the face or the body in each of these cases? Each step of the iconographic technique, each plastic element of the icon, is invested with a double spiritual and temporal meaning. The icon is a map of the occupation of space, an interpretation of the incarnation in which each element has a purpose. The duplication of the iconic vocabulary corresponds to the express vocation of the icon, whose repetitive essence consists in the implementation of a dual conception of the invisible world by virtue of its very visibility.[4] The visible is one, but the invisible is two. The image, in its unary evidence, offers a noncontradictory demonstration of something that, without it, could not be simultaneously thought without contradiction. The invisible is double because it addresses itself to the question of being from its position as nonbeing, at the very moment that it allows a glimpse of its nonbeing in the luminous flesh of an object. The icon is a symbol, which amounts to saying that in the economy of its *map of the occupation of space* it also aims at being a *map for the occupation of the spirit.* From now on, the desire of all rulers will be to have in hand the key to all signs and all symbols. Realism and theatrical specularity have no place at all here. The icon is a system for the inscription of the *hic et nunc* of institutional presence. This presence is itself designated as the authority that makes the body appear as the incarnation of duality. Henceforth, duality is the very being of meaning. In fact, shortly after the end of the iconoclastic crisis, it would eventually become possible for the church to establish itself on the principle of dyarchy (the sharing of temporal power with the emperor) and to appropriate symbolic hegemony for itself by assuming God's power here on earth.

Périgraphè, or circumscription, is a line that imprisons and reduces what it contains at the limits of time and space. Let us now, rather, consider the graphic line, which is nonperigraphic in nature, examining it from the point of view not of the phenomenological void that constitutes the gaze, but of the indeterminate retreat of borders that limit all space of whatever sort. Thus, Gregory of Nazianzos writes:

Whoever does not believe that St. Mary is the mother of God, is divided from divinity. Whoever claims that Christ passed through the Virgin as through a canal, without having been formed in her in a way that is both human and divine, divine because it was without the activity of a man, human because it was according to the normal process of pregnancy, he too is a complete stranger to God.[5]

In the preceding paragraph, Gregory had also enumerated the contrary attributes that characterize the hypostasis as being first "at once terrestrial and celestial, visible and spiritual," and then "*khôrèton kai akhôrèton,*" which the "Sources chrétiennes" translates as "perceptible and imperceptible." More precisely, however, it means "that which occupies space, and does not occupy space," "space" here being *khôra*, the place that one occupies in the visible world. Thus Origen says that to be born of a woman is what permits every man to say that he occupies space (*khôra*).[6]

Thought about the Son is thought about the image, thought about the image is thought about place and space (the icon), thought about space is thought about the bodies of women under the double sign, already broached, of virginity and maternity. The question that we will investigate here is how that iconic womb would become swollen with space over which to rule and give expression to the full power of an institution in which real women would have hardly any place because their strength manifests itself as the pure, empty substrate of a power that they do not share.

The Virgin of Contact

The space designated by the term *khôra* refers to the body in its capacity as both content and container. This is because the verb *khôrein* (*khôran ékhein*) means both to occupy space and to contain something. In other words, to say that the iconic line shows the *khôrèton* is to say that form is something in which the content allows itself to be seen thanks to the visible edge of its container. This form that is an edge is the zone (*zonè*), which is, in Greek, the peripheral belt of contact between the womb of the mother and the body of the child. It therefore becomes important to assert that Christ did not pass through his mother as one traverses a canal; that would suppose two forms: the form of the canal and the form of Christ. No: the virginal womb and the child are one and the same form. The actual womb of the Virgin, strictly speaking, formed a precinct around that which is infinite, limitless. Inscription is therefore the perfect characteristic for determining the space of something that has none, the *akhôreton.* It makes manifest an unfathomable enigma: the virginal womb gives its form and its borders, its limits and its characteristics, to a son that it neither touches nor encloses.

Such is the ecclesial space that is made ready in the icons of the Virgin and child. In these icons, the mother and child adopt different postures. One of the best known is the Virgin *Glukophilousa,* or the Virgin of Tenderness, which shows the areas of contact between the two at their maximum. Their bodies are fused, intertwined, the two faces together, cheek to cheek, to the point where the child's neck is extremely distorted. Here, we see an iconography of interior space, where Christ's humanity appears completely in the contiguity of the child's face to its mother's. This almost inclusive contiguity is accompanied by an extreme care in making all other anatomical references disappear in the geometry of the folds of the clothing. In the *Vladimirskaya,* for example, no corporeal envelope is visible. The fall of the drapery is formed by a strict organization of geometric planes, so that a linear, repetitive architecture results, where successive inscribed waves, fitting closely into each other, spread the circular and centrifugal effects of occupied space. This inscription of the folds shows us not only an unusual interpretation of human anatomy, but also an invisible extension of the tucks and folds of the world in the graphic architecture of a shadowless body.

The Virgin's clothing is as beautiful as heaven and earth, as vast as the universe. The space (*khôra*) of the virginal body where Christ finds the form of his carnal periphery, the membrane that defines his terrestrial place, and the space of the consecration of the ecclesial body are all simultaneously identified with each other. The *Glukophilousa,* the Virgin of Contact, is the scene in which the body manifests the sacralization of this contact, this contagion. In fact, contact is a general characteristic of this iconic formula. Everything that it "touches" is struck by the very fact of its presence in a contiguity that is made into a continuity. The icon does not simply show this contact, it also creates it in the very thaumaturgy of its presence. There is a constant relay between looking and touching, as well as a mutual limiting of each by the other. Most mosaics cannot be touched, but icons are often close to the eyes, carried about, carried on one's person.

The development of portable icons actually served to increase this space of contact and contagion. Wherever there is an icon, the gaze of God is present. It does not need a sacred architectural institution. Outside the church, it transports this holiness symbolically to all places; it brings it into existence invisibly and with supreme power, wherever it is.

The institution of the icon, which it is not possible to frame or pin down, is the small-scale model of an ecclesiastic institution; it permits the production of rules for an open and profane space, which the church can traverse in all senses and appropriate for itself. Against this invasion, the iconoclast emperor, careful to preserve his temporal prerogatives, clearly asserted that only those things that relate to sacramental space and are consecrated are holy. He wanted to restrict the power of the clerics to the limits of the church, and the church within the borders of his own empire. For the iconophile, on the contrary, everything that the icon invades becomes sacred and therefore the property of ecclesiastic power. The icon is centrifugal and invasive: by propagation, it spreads the infinite principle that it includes all the way to infinity, without limiting it. Thus the church, a sanctuary built in the image of the Marian body, cannot become *horos, peras*, an enclosed and circumscribed precinct. Furthermore, the limits, the borders (*horoi, perata*) of the empire could not ever become the boundary markers of a temporal power reduced to a national territory. In other words, within a framework whose stakes are political, the vocabulary of the icon's graphic inscription, which categorically opposes *graphè* to *périgraphè*, becomes a finely targeted instrument for the institutional inscription of a lifting of the limits on the propagation of ecclesiastic power.

As a result of these principles of iconic production, it happens that from its place within that territory, the church develops an independence with respect to all interior boundaries, and thus an access to territory beyond the profane space of this world, which it can conquer without limits.

The icon has no frame; no limiting structure surrounds it. Only the plastic principles of the inscription of the Word govern it, giving it its ecumenic and catholic (that is, international and universal) power. The process of globalizing the image across the whole world has begun. It is the mode of the universal communication of truth, and it becomes the legitimate property of all places and all nations where it establishes its "optocracy."

The Virgin of Blachernai: The Virgin of Noncontact (Platutera)

The iconic model of the Virgin of Blachernai goes back to an older type of Virgin, called the Virgin orant. This image shows the Virgin facing the viewer, her hands open toward the heavens. At the beginning of the ninth century, after the triumph of orthodoxy over iconoclasm, the *Theotokos* appears in the position of an orant, but wearing on her breast a miraculously suspended bust of a nimbed Christ, which she does not touch. As André Grabar justly remarks, this nimbus, so unrealistically suspended, is no longer the triumphant shield of the *clipeata* icons. Created after the triumph of orthodoxy in 843, this late image, he comments, "could not possibly represent any real scene. For even those images, some very old, which show the Virgin actually holding a type of shield with the young Christ portrayed on it do no more than imitate Roman images of highly-placed people who themselves also carry the triumphal *clipeus* with a portrait. The image of Blachernes, however, does not itself reflect any possible reality, as the medallion with the bust of Christ is not held up by any physical means."[7] Grabar then goes on to conclude that the scene is in fact a portrayal of the conception.

Yet how can this icon, which shows absolutely nothing real, be referred to as a representation of the conception, and therefore as the founding moment of the incarnation? In these scenes, where the body of the Word detaches itself from the Virgin's clothing, his nimbus functioning to render her womb transparent, it becomes necessary to link economic thought to iconic choices. Iconic models do not refer to realities; all are imaginary, and all are involved with a unifying conception of celestial truths and temporal realities. Here, I would rather return to the descriptions that refer to this iconic model as "*platutera tôn ouranôn, khôra tôn akhôrôn,*" or "wider than the heavens" and "space of that which is not in space." These epithets refer to the Virgin's body carrying God's body in the position of the orant. The Russians call this Virgin "the Virgin of the Sign"; it could also be named the Virgin of Inscription, of the Graph. This iconic type simultaneously shows the presence and absence of contact. In order to contain the body of God, a body larger than the heavens is required, a space for something that does not have any, a place for something that is everywhere, a visibility for something that no one can see. The pairs of oxymorons follow one another as the dual nature of the Word is formulated, and this, in turn, is essential for establishing the dual power of the ecclesiastic institution. The invisible church is therefore invisible in two senses, the one spiritual and the other temporal. The borders of the visible simultaneously impose the invisibility of the spirit and the incommensurability of restricted territory. The ubiquity of the Virgin's gaze, as the icon's title indicates—*peribleptos*, she who sees all around her—generates the ubiquity of the ecclesial gaze, which seeks to reign over heaven and earth in their entirety, and which overflows whatever might impose limits on human kingdoms. It must see everything. The iconic gaze is thus synoptic. Not only is it the epiphany of what no eye can see, but it also keeps watch over what no eye could ever take in. Circulating, circular, encircling the infinite—the icon is intended for all, in all times, in all places, and in all idioms. Breaking the spell that punished Babylonian pride, it meets up again with the foundational polyglotism of the spirit that had been redistributed to everyone by grace at the pentecost.

The Virgin of Noncontact is the figure in which the equivalence of inside and outside, the near and the far, is played out. She is the Virgin of the Oxymoron. Her womb is transparent, allowing one to see her entire economy, which is to say, her son. What her bosom presents, without containing, transforms the maternal body into a cosmic womb in the form of a boundless encompassing. This mysterious suspension of the Word is the very image of the incarnational economy that relates the doctrine of the incarnation (*caro*) to the body (*corpus*) of temporal power. The Virgin of the sign is the Virgin of the conception of a concept.

The iconoclasts did not reject all images, but they did reject, very specifically, images of the Virgin, Christ, and the saints, as well as their cults. Concerned with tightening the national borders and decentralizing administrative power, they set about controlling the empire by means of military and administrative reform. This was the reform of the themes, which entailed the distribution of land to the peasant-soldiers who defended the empire as they protected their lands. This, in turn, forms yet another map for the occupation of ground surface, where the emperor delegates military, administrative, and fiscal responsibilities to strategists who are more his executors than representatives.

An important concept at the iconoclast council of Saint-Sophia (815), as P. J. Alexander stresses, concerned the emperor as *mimètes tou théou*, imitator of God,[8] an idea that has a whole Pythagorean tradition behind it. If the iconoclast emperors put such zeal into their rejection of the icon, then, it is because they wanted to contravene the principle of dyarchy, or the sharing of power with the church, by radically separating temporal from spiritual power. The iconic economy, by contrast, permitted an ongoing practice of sharing and delegation. The principle of the king as the sole, true imitator of Christ, however, remained in force, as can be seen clearly in the *Ecloga* of Leo III, for example, which implies a singular reading of Psalm 82 (81), making it favorable to this mimetic interpretation of royalty. St. Jerome, however, resists such an interpretation, commenting that "God does not say 'you are gods' when referring only to kings and princes, but to all of us who have a body,"[9] although Eusebios, on the subject of the same psalm, is of the opinion that *théoi* relates to *hègouménoi* and *archontés*.[10]

A large number of church fathers also interpreted the image and imitation of God from a legislative and juridical point of view, as Kantorowicz notes.[11] He cites, among others, Pope Damasus (366–84), who says, "*Omnis res dei habet imaginem*." He also quotes Basil on the subject of the interpretation of the homonymic argument: "The emperor and the icon of the emperor are not two emperors . . . ; in the case of the identity of the emperor with his icon, this identity is accomplished by mimesis [*mimètikos*]."[12] In the first and second centuries, it is the Pythagoreans who develop this idea. Thus, Sthenidas of Lokri: "God is the first king and natural legislator. The king only becomes him by imitation." Ladner remarks that the caesaropapist tendency never prevailed in Byzantium, except at the exact moment of the iconoclastic crisis, and even then, only in a highly complex way.[13] But even there, the caesaropapist concept should be questioned for its historic relevance. It would be better to say that what interests the iconoclast emperors is to become, in the name of a fight against the idols, the absolute masters of political, juridical, administrative, and military representation, and the sole practitioners of earthly mimesis. For the people as a whole, the sign of the cross would have to suffice; for the clergy, the celebration of the eucharistic sacrament; for the king, administration and justice. The people must make do with dissimilarity; the clergy must be content with consubstantiality. Only the emperor has access to similitude, and the iconoclast *tekhnè* could be nothing other than the art of governing.

It might be said, then, that for the iconoclast Constantine V, the icon, far from being as empty as it claims to be, takes possession of space in its entirety by means of the *périgraphè*, to the degree that it also sacralizes it. For him, all plenary illusion will be brought to a halt by a deserted sign, a truly open form, tearing space without circumscribing it. Emptiness cannot ever be shown as being contained, and form has a horror of emptiness. Thus iconoclasm develops a cruciform semiotic, which places the emperor and Christ at the exact point where the spiritual and temporal worlds intersect, as well as at the crossroads of all the routes that engender a given territory. It is at these crossroads that the emperor places his statues. The cross is not the sole memorial to divine torture, but it is the *sign* of a strategic space that refers not to mediation, but to the localized and efficient presence of generals and watchmen who conquer and control the territory that they have under their watch. This semiotic is nothing but the other face of domination.

It was imperative, therefore, for the church as an institutional body that the icon triumph. And triumph it did. Henceforth, for the Christian world, the *theocracy of the visible* becomes the key to all authority, which is to say that it becomes a doctrine, both theoretical and strategic, of exchanged looks and imposed visions. The church, apparently, was well able to support and defend an unimpeded alliance between sovereign and sacred roles, on the one hand, and its economic role, on the other, thus submitting to its control more warlike roles, which it designates as unsuited, by themselves, to mediation or symbolization.

Such "ecclesiastic" phenomena, then, shaped all subsequent theoretical constructions and practices aiming to produce conviction in submission and blind adherence in servitude.

Conclusion

As is well known, Christ stated that his kingdom was not of this world.[14] Such spiritual words, however, did not serve to establish any church.[15] Rather, Nikephoros, the champion of iconophilia devotes himself to an active, effective reinterpretation of the subject of taxation, one that is worthy of Pauline rhetoric. In effect, the church's enemies could only "stupidly" satisfy themselves with Christ's phrase in an attempt to thwart temporal power. Once more, we are reminded that the enemies of the economy understood nothing of the evangelic message, and most of all, of the necessity of understanding it economically.

Here, then, are the words of Nikephoros, giving us a magnificent prosopopoeia of Christ the king, which reverberates like the drums of a triumphant despotism; the king of the universe announces that he is abandoning all the usual signs of terrestrial royalty in order to reveal an empire of his own symbols: a brilliant light, glory without limit and without borders, cosmic monarchy, ubiquity and perpetuity.[16] The text resonates like the voice of an icon traversing the borders of space and time:

Contrary to those earthly and mortal sovereigns who acquire a temporary and less important glory, my kingdom will not be interrupted like those kingdoms that are founded in this poor world, and whose glory fades like the flowers of the fields,[17] and which finally corruption and death will replace. Moreover, the thoughts and unstable opinions of the mob have deprived them of their dignity, and they have been subjected to ill repute and to innumerable misfortunes and difficulties. In fact, none of those who rule the world and life here would be found in my kingdom, and nothing that could be observed in the history of these [earthly] kings. No votes of the *demes*, no elections by the people where human opinions often prevail. . . . None of the symbols which mark such dignity can be found in me, symbols which are corruptible and perishable: no purple robe, no crown set with precious stones, no sceptres, no raised thrones, no radiant spectacle. No chariot embossed with gold, nor the public honors of an escort. [I have] no troops bearing shields, no spearmen, no sounds of acclamations coming from those who either precede or follow me. [I have] none of these transitory and human things which usually occur in earthly power. Consequently, my kingdom is not of this world. Poor in appearance, humble to those who see it, I lead few disciples, an inglorious group composed of poor men and fishermen, but it is a sublime group, which excels in everything perceived by the mind. I am the son of God, the all-powerful king of the universe. I am his most legitimate child and his radiance.[18] I bear the same glory and honor as my Father, because I am the inheritor of the paternal glory. Sharing the same throne with my Father, I am situated together with and equal to his glory, and I possess the prerogative of kingship. That is why I am the king and the master of the universe. Neither is my kingdom then of this world, nor does my power resemble in anything the powers of this world. My authority is not circumscribed. I am the master and the Lord not of this or that people, land, or city, but of angels and of humans and of the earthly, the celestial and the subterranean realms at the same time. Every knee bends to me.[19] Everything is under my feet and there is nothing that escapes my hand, because my kingdom is without limit and without end.

This is the truth and there is no other. This is believed and proclaimed by all faithful people. Where would the plans of providence regarding earthly things be, and how would the affairs of our lives be governed, "if there is not in God's hand the depths of the earth?"[20] Everything is held under his authority and is administered by him not only as God but also as man; as has been said: "I will make the nations your heritage, and the ends of the earth your possession."[21] It is also said, "For he is king of the whole world,"[22] and again, "Look, your king is coming to you, humble;"[23] at Jerusalem it is said, "righteous and saved is he."[24] It is written again, "the righteous Lord is in the midst of your people,"[25] and again, "the Lord will reign forever, your God, O Zion, for all generations."[26]

This astonishing demonstration of power that Nikephoros puts into the mouth of the image of the Father reveals his true project to us: to make of the economy a program of universal conquest. It would take little for these words to be put into the mouth of some ruler from the domain of science fiction today, or some fantastic doctor to whom one could assign the most devilish paranoia. But what is this about? A charismatic voice arises in a tone of untroubled legitimacy to announce to us that if his kingdom is not of this world, it is because the entire world is his kingdom. This ecumenical power is the one of the selfsame symbolic deployment that establishes the idea of economy. The relation that all the "images" of the world maintain with those things made of flesh and soul that make up humanity overflows national borders for ever in order to carry out an ecclesial *incorporation.* Does the failure of those diabolical doctors of science fiction not arise from the fact that they always lack access to the image? Always invisible, disfigured, masked, monstrous, and occult, as soon as one sees them and they make themselves heard, their ruin is certain. Teratological figures of invisibility, they constitute an off-camera population that terrorizes the living. They are positively diabolical. It took a long time before images of the devil were produced, because hell is first and foremost completely invisible. The powers of evil assume many faces, yet have none that they can call their own. They are *aprosopon,* exiles from the face and the status of personhood, and in this connection we will shortly witness a surprising historical example concerning the Jewish face.[27] The enigma of the icon, however, has nothing to do with the occult. It is this that also resolutely sets the icon in opposition to the talismanic image, which summons invisible forces forth in order to diminish them and ward them off by rendering them visible and audible, and which in turn causes them to "switch sides."

Besides demoniac invisibility, however, a complementary tradition also exists within the Christian imaginary. The devil too knows the power of images and makes use of them himself. He disguises himself in visible form to seduce and to tempt. He apes God, shows himself, and makes himself heard. For lying, diabolical images do, in fact, exist: they are the ones that the holy man will confront during his fasting hallucinations in the desert. Whoever has been tempted only by the world does not yet know true temptation, that of the false image, the diabolical image that comes to besiege the spirit and the flesh far from any earthly reality. The great variety of pictures that are inspired, paradoxically, by the diabolic seductions of the image is well known. Implicitly, iconic thought recognizes that between the clarity of doctrinal distinctions and the earthly vitality of the imagination and desire, there is space enough for all manner of confusions and temptations. Is an image that bleeds and that heals you all that different from one that persecutes and kills you? As in the investigation of the economy, the investigation of iconic power meets its own spiritual limits and must appeal to a principle of distinction that has no place in the image. The later tradition of spiritual exercises, aimed at repressing the excesses of a "pseudonymous," enticing imagination, also bears witness to the church's long-standing concern regarding iconic temptation.

Who would be able to negotiate with life and history while being assured of escaping everything that leaves a mark on our finitude, our weakness, our mortality? Who could escape desire? The image of God itself is capable of falling into sin, and the iconoclasts no doubt had good reason to mistrust and denounce it. Yet iconic doctrine is not only the first real system of thought concerning the freedom of the gaze in its encounter with painting, it is also the first meditation on idolatry, conceived no longer as a divergence from this or that religion, but as an anthropological fact from which no one can escape.

In the prosopopoeia that we have just examined, the passage concerning the renunciation of all that makes up the visible glory of this world for the universal and sovereign appropriation of the whole universe is resoundingly clear. The paradox here is only an apparent one, because invisible omnipotence is based on the interpretation of the visibility of the incarnate image. It is the image of God demeaned in man that was saved by this image of the man who recovered his place in God. Henceforth, the image will form part of all plans for redemption in the universe as a whole. It will prevail over all other modes of communication. It is the discourse of silence and submission, the discourse of emotion and conviction, the discourse of proof and noncontradiction. And if the image is all of this, one understands that there can be no question of it being left in the hands of the public at large. It demands a monopoly on its production, its programs, its messages. Only the master of the image, whom I call the iconocrat, will know what is right, good, and equitable to render visible in it, which is to say, to make known and to cause to be believed in relation to it. As Serge Gruzinski says in connection with this point: "If the image comes up against so many stumbling blocks, it is because it is the manifestation of a structure that exceeds it everywhere. It is the expression of a visual order, and, even more, of an imaginary in which conscious and unconscious assimilation is synonymous with occidentalization."[28]

Because the invisible has a universal value, all that is necessary for each and every iconic hegemony to be legitimized is the production of a dogmatically sanctioned means of making it visible. Anthropology has confronted us with the relativity of our reason. To the vertigo inflicted by the discovery of the limits of a triumphant logocentrism, the image has brought the consolation of a federative, universal, and pacifying *tekhnê*. There are arguments that claim that the church has lost everything in our world because it no longer rests on the same doctrinal and spiritual certitudes that it once did. This, however, is to misunderstand the very bases on which despotisms of every kind now repose. It is to forget that the church bequeathed a dual concept concerning duplication itself. The economy explains the most elevated works of art just as well as the most oppressive uses of visibility. It is ecclesiastic thought that makes heard the voice that says that the image is "the best and worst of things." Will we be able to respect its enigma in order to maintain our own liberty?

PART III

IDOLS AND VERONICAS

The two preceding sections of this book, on the general concept of the economy and the iconic economy, inevitably raise new questions about the modernity of patristic thought. This is a field that is still wide open, and it is to be hoped that the material presented here, which is more than a thousand years old, will provide a basis for understanding the origins of all of today's sites of vision, in all their grandeur and misery.

It is not my intention here to attempt a global interpretation of dominant visibilities or to paint a picture of all our iconicities. Nonetheless, with all sectors of contemporary production being so completely dependent on the practices and doctrines of imagery, it is incumbent on us to attempt understand both its promises and its disappointments. One thing, however, is certain: today, there is no alternative system of thought concerning the image capable of competing with the theoretical and political power of the one that the church developed during its first ten centuries.

Most attempts at theorizing the icon and the image have until now simply consisted in manipulating vocabulary in order to hide the total absence of anything new to be said. On the one hand, it is true that there is no novelty in thinking that does not evidence a reworking of language, and the Byzantine example demonstrates clearly how necessary it is to fight and debate within a language in order to make it say what is innovative within a system of thought itself. On the other hand, when the frenzy of neologisms overtakes an entire group and becomes, rather than the sign of an innovative restlessness, the standard of an overcautious collective, one may legitimately wonder whether the interest in forming a single group has not prevailed over the true desire for fresh thinking. For a long time, semiology has taken us strolling amid the latest conceptual blossomings in new parks of meditation, but we have very quickly found ourselves in an old French garden where only the gardeners change, delighted to be promoted to the new rank of landscape artists. But of a truly new landscape, nothing.

We have always been, and are still today, heirs to a Christian iconocracy that was spurred on, at its very core, by profaners who were attracted to it. If we want to do more, or if we simply want to do something else, the entire task still remains before us. Who, indeed, can claim to have accounted for the philosophical and spiritual aspirations of our century by simultaneously unifying several disparate theories and producing a *critical* tool that is both valid and well suited to the latest iconic productions? We tinker about between marvel and anxiety, between technical revolutions and an unassuaged thirst for revolution itself.

All the same, there is an urgency about all of this, failing which, systems of thought will continue to suffer balkanization. Some people dream of the icon, of a redeemed body or a new ethics, whereas others get drunk on numerical virtualities and take themselves to be the new Mabuse. The former sound the soul's knell at the sight of the works of the latter, who in turn, lamenting the retrograde and timorous incompetence of the former, continue creating a world that they no longer have the means to think through. The work still remains, and I, for one, do not claim to have done it.

What, then, can I add to all this? First, I will pause at the one point on which the two Byzantine sides agree—their mutual condemnation of idols and idolatry—in order to investigate what that condemnation signifies. Following this, I have included a brief report on my efforts to articulate what patristic thought can bring to the study of a few examples of modern works in the fields of painting, cinema, and photography. What exactly are our icons today, our iconoclast signs, our idols?

The following, therefore, are a few elements of a work still in progress that I have added here, in order to avoid ending the book on a note that may give the illusion of closure, and to open it up to the consideration of all those who, like me, feel that talking about the image is the most difficult task of all, particularly at a moment when visual productions have invaded the world of spirits and bodies to the point of depriving them of all hope in relation to the image itself. The church fathers taught us, at least, that seeing and showing are not enough to exhaust the definition of the image and visibility. Just what can we be similar to today? How can the order of similitude be redefined?

For this reason, I have gathered together these several texts, written over a period of time. Most of them, however, have been altered slightly because my approach has been transformed as my research has progressed. Nonetheless, all have their place here because they all bear the mark of my exploration of the Christian world, and each in its own way shows the continuity of both my philosophical concerns and my unresolved questions. All partially illustrate the long dependence of our vision on Christian thinking about the image and icon, whether this be to develop its conceptual potential or to elude its traps. Striking to me is the revealing recurrence of certain themes: the quest for the acheiropoietic image (the veronica); the violent return of the problematic of idolatry in the contradictory modes of fascinated adulation or destruction; and again, the complex interweaving of theoretical aspirations, lucrative management, and the political administration of iconicity within economic relations. And last but not least, the problem of the incarnation, which was at the heart of my entire meditation on the visible and is still before me, although it should be borne in mind that patristic teaching puts us perpetually on guard against any confusion of the incarnation with the materiality of the visible. What is the flesh of an image, and what is it that is formed in the gaze that we cast upon it?

To the degree that this work was primarily intended to expand on the foundations of Christian thought regarding iconicity, the texts and reflections that follow are only brief variations on themes. They were inspired by irregular encounters with objects or with readings that provoked afresh either my hypotheses or simply my questions.

6

The Idol's *Delenda Est*

The "theology of the icon," the backbone of oriental Christianity, was obsessed by one problem: how to harbor the icon from the slightest suspicion of idolatry? This is why it was possible for the cult of icons to be based on a radically abstract theory of iconic appearance. Iconoclasm and iconophilia are not opposed to each other in the same way that a generalized, unconditional adoption of portrayal would be opposed to a radical aniconicity.[1] All had only one goal: to defend the one true icon by establishing the truth of the image. The icon without reference to the image is by itself neither true nor false, and it bears no relation to ontological questions of any sort. It is *imaginarily true.* The iconophile imagination differs from the iconoclast imagination in the definition of the visible, because for the latter, there cannot be a true icon of a true image, but only a sign. This sign is of the order of a mark or a gesture. Nonetheless, the fact remains that all, iconophiles and iconoclasts together, universally condemn *idolatrous fictions.* For both, it is claimed that the imaginary is linked only to the symbol and sign, and knows nothing of illusionist mimesis and immanentist fictions.

We have seen that the notion of similitude in the icon is completely imbued with a phenomenological conception of the gaze as the constitutive aiming of a circularity of exchanges between the essential emptiness of the icon and the breach that contemplation brings about in the spectator who gazes at it. It could be said that what the icon imitates is not the vision that humans cast at things but God's imagined gaze that is cast upon humans.

Similitude is not resemblance. The icon is referred to as an "economic," or relational, symbol and not as an imitative entity; as for the sign, it claims dissimilarity by abandoning to the foundational image the privileges of consubstantiality. The icon is not a part of the object, any more than it is a representative convention.

Iconophilia condemns idolatry and attempts to maintain no relationship of any sort with it. Its entire theoretical effort is driven by this concern because it is the chief accusation made by the opposing camp. Equally, what strikes Christians from the Orient first when they consider western painting is its profane character, which they immediately denounce as idolatry. They believe that the icon's symbolic articulation, thoroughly imbued with the relational economy, has been completely betrayed by optical substitutes. Alternately phrased, for them, western knowledge about vision has replaced the doctrine of the gaze. This is so to such an extent that in the place of the symbolic remove that governs iconic mediation, a persepectivist distance has been substituted that assigns places in space to subjects and objects alike for an eye that mimics the supposed distance of the subject from the object of his or her thought. A theoretical mimetic has become a specular mimetic, and the certainties of salvation have given way to rhetorical virtuosities and the unstable pleasures of illusion. Or this, at least, is how an orthodox adherent might situate western art.

The corporeal reality of the sacred *is* corporeal reality in that it is sacred, in that it is the object of a scopic exchange where the body only allows itself to be seen gloriously and miraculously. There is no more contact between the divine prototype and its icon than between the icon and its human model. In any case, what is called the incarnation is neither an immersion in the flesh nor an idealization of matter, but rather something like the gaze's imitation of itself when it is haunted by the desire to be seen. *To become flesh is here nothing other than the obtaining of a certain gaze in the empty space where he who accedes to existence when he enters the field of what constitutes him for the gaze of another is incarnated.* Being in possession of the existence of his flesh only by virtue of the sole fact of another gaze requires that that gaze be endowed with an infinite thirst for imagining. Such is the thirst of God, a pure image given to the thirst of the humans whom he consigns to his imitation. The imaginal relation gives birth to the flesh of being. The symbol is, strictly speaking, imaginary.

In forging this doctrine of the incarnation as God's "imagination," Nikephoros is not surrendering himself to some metaphysical reverie or poetic meanderings. Rather, within the terms at his disposal, he discovers the relations that bond both formations of the imaginary and symbolic productions tightly to the constitution of the body itself. However, once economic thought had succeeded in linking a meditation about the flesh to the constitution of each and every body, including the constitutional body, the result was that this appropriation of imaginal powers by the authorities became a reality, as they sought to order and control the collective belief by seizing hold of the body's genesis in the gaze. A sudden upsurge of iconocratic power consequently followed, along with its inevitable correlate and dreaded consequence, idolatry. Considering that the Byzantine debate was centered on the incarnation, it must be acknowledged that for both camps, the icon was situated on the side of the body. But because the ecclesiastic institution was not willing to renounce the linkage of imaginal flesh to the ambiguous benefits of the management of desiring bodies, individual as well as social, it had greater difficulty than its opponents in escaping from what I earlier called strategic and political "slippage." Thus the church struggled on that narrow and vertiginous border that places the icon on the outer banks of idolatry while keeping it at the heart of the worldly visibilities whose generator and vital organ it had become. Negotiating between the symbolic and diabolical would always be a subtle endeavor.

It consequently became urgent for the Christian people, whom the church was trying to subjugate in this way, to be assured that the icon imposed on them was safe from the slightest suspicion of idolatry. Idolatrous were the Jews, the Greeks, and the barbarians; idolatrous was everyone not Christian, even the iconoclast Constantine himself, which makes clear how much the enemy of the incarnation was himself no more than a body without an image. He is therefore turned into an idol lover, with the energetic army of iconophiles resolutely maintaining that they have nothing in common with him.

For everyone without exception, then, the watchword is irrevocable: the idols must be smashed. It is only with their material disappearance that the threat of their powerful fiction disappears too. This implies two things: first, that they are feared because they have power, and second, that it suffices to smash them in order for that fear and power to disappear. In other words, they are not simply smashed: in fact, *they are killed.* The history of idols is never without murder, and the idol is by definition neither an abstract dynamic of the sign nor a living economy of symbols, but the turbulent and expired existence of destructible, sacrificed bodies.

Who, in that case, is an idolator? It is always the other, or more particularly, the people. It is never the leaders, whose ambitions induce them to take themselves for gods, rather than to worship them, or even to derive from that divine worship exemplary benefits for the representation of their own power. Idolaters are neither emperors nor patriarchs. But the faithful, the believers, the credulous, the superstitious, these are the idolaters, a feverish mass, inspired and subjugated at the same time, who do not have ears for the too-subtle doctrines of the incarnation and consubstantiality. The idolaters are all those who bend the knee, who prostrate themselves, who worship, who touch and sway to the point of ecstasy. They have seen the icons cry, have seen them bleed, have seen them kill. They have seen their own hemorrhages and leprosy disappear at the single touch of a divine object. Their blind eyes have once again become piercing, their tongues loosened. They have even been revived from dead. They carry with them effigies, amulets, phylacteries, and talismans. They are called fetishists, and they do indeed often resemble them. They travel the world searching out and preserving relics. They spend time with icons and contemplate them, eyes brimming with tears; they notice the incorruptibility of holy cadavers. They are all there in their thousands, those who believe in the pleasure and suffering with which the bodies that incarnate them are imbued; they take action, invoke, make, and sacrifice. They deploy a new force in which, for them, no activity is improbable. Everything is possible for those who believe. The popular imagination rediscovers the archaic divinities that have always caused it to maintain with the visible matter of the world operative relations of a violent effectiveness. Demons and wonders! Nature appears to defy itself—or rather, to defy everything that is predicated on it.

Idolaters, fetishists? It is not by chance that these terms carry with them a heavy history of colonial conquests and the justifications of genocides and repressions of all sorts. Figures worshiped by the other always inspire hate and a destructive rage.

The iconoclastic dispute is perhaps nothing other than a convulsion concerning the meaning and fate of idolatry itself, and this is not a restrictive definition, because it makes clear that what is at stake in the debate both has perpetual validity and is thoroughly modern. Whoever wishes to rule must, above all else, be a good manager of idolatry. What does this mean, if not that he must administer worship to his advantage by eluding the fate of all idols, which must, in turn, be sacrificeable, and indeed, always end up by being sacrificed. Christian thought managed to arrive at an interpretation of the christic sacrifice (that is to say, the putting to death of the image itself) that allowed it to bring into the world an indestructible image that no one else could destroy. Jesus rises from the dead, and his icon is indestructible. Whoever destroys it behaves like an idolater. It is for this reason that Constantine is referred to as an idolater without a hint of paradox, he who rejected all cult rendered to the true image and who, by destroying it, treated it as an idol. The idol's emptiness is not kenotic; it concerns the question of bewitchment, possession, and exorcism.

The idol is defined by the theological dictionaries as being both an image of falsehood and a false image of the truth. In the first case, it is an image of the truth that is being defended; in the second, there is a rupture between truth and the image. In the iconoclast conflict, the bond between the truth and the image was maintained by both camps. This was inevitable, because both remained faithful to the Pauline message of the Son's imaginal economy. It is therefore visibility that is the problem, and not the image itself. In truth, no cult of visibility can escape the question of idolatry, and the iconoclasts therefore treat their opponents as idolaters. But how can the iconophiles reproach the iconoclasts with the same thing? Simply by invoking the fact that they only have eyes for matter, that they are only capable of that gaze particular to idolatry; unable to look at things in the correct way, they pretend to condemn them, the better to hide their paganism and their passion for the world. Thus Grabar, the great iconophile expert, ends up finding them to be animists! I think it is now clear that the entire debate is at the other extreme from this problem, because it is really the iconophiles who have the most work to do to escape the suspicion of idolatry. They succeeded philosophically, but when it came to the management and administration of the goods of this world, they found themselves battling with what I would call the idolatrous economy of the visible. Symbolism must manage the diabolical; it is in this sense that I said earlier that the world belongs to God, but the devil has usufruct of it, the pleasure of its uses and the mastery of its pleasures. We can thus say in this sense that *one of the functions of icon doctrine was exorcism.*

The church had no intention of separating itself from the power of belief in, and effectiveness of, the idol. That idolatrous people whom we are told that God hates, that he punishes, that he condemns, the church decides (in the name of the economy) to accept into its camp. Economy: a diabolical negotiation in which total turmoil will come to be inextricably linked to the imperatives of both salvation and strategies that alienate. The double language of the icon: abstract thought endowed with unequaled spiritual virtue, and simultaneously, an unsettling manipulation of matter. Byzantine hagiography abounds with examples and prodigious accounts that tell of the thaumaturgical, irresistible power of imitators and imitations. These accounts, whose purpose is intended to be edifying, are full of that ambivalence, that double language proper to the icon, of the spiritual purity of the image and the mad worship of things.

Those who are mad for God are never far from the devil, who endlessly visits them anyway in order to tempt them. Suffice it to look at the anchorites, alone, emaciated, in the middle of the desert: it is no longer the world that assails them, it is the demon of images who comes to besiege them. It is temptation. But what is temptation? Nothing other than an image, an apparition, a diabolical hallucination. The true proof that the saint of the desert submits himself to is vision and the capacity to discriminate between the images that assail him. The ability to be portrayed, and portrayal itself, are the devil's preferred instruments. A rendezvous is made with desire.

The moving fragility of that flesh that is discovered in the experience of passion; all the passions.

~

In the film *Andreï Rublev*, Tarkovsky movingly demonstrates the way in which temptation is linked to the vocation of iconographer. No icon is possible within passion, but it is also true that no icon results without that infernal crossing of the universe of temptation, despair, and death. From the very first images, as in all of Tarkovsky's films, a trinity of men set off walking, and they travel the road that separates us from hell in order to rediscover the anagogical path that separates us from salvation. A trinity of men leaves in the darkness, searching for another trinity that alone can take them back to their state of foundational image and restore them to their iconic vocation. Tarkovsky must himself have thought of his own cinematographic vocation at the heart of this infernal, redemptive pilgrimage. In his own way, he both posed and resolved the question of the incarnation, which he never separated from the transfiguration and the resurrection. It could also be said that the issue he deals with concerns the passage from passion to compassion, that is, to that imaginal affection that takes us back to similitude with those whom we do not resemble.

~

For the idolater, the icon is neither true nor false in relation to something that is foreign to it. As an icon, however, it is always true and itself produces its own authentification by the brilliance of its effectiveness. Yet it also resembles something that is neither true nor false, something that is not yet sure, and doubtless never will be. The product of uncertainty and anguish, of the desire for fusion with the spirit of mystery, it is something in which that uncertainty and desire find their forms and are resolved by a reticulation of the visible that governs the signs of its ritual actions. In this way, those who are called idolaters expect a real service from their idol and will destroy it if the contract is not fulfilled, if their expectation is disappointed, or if it is replaced by a new, stronger divinity to whom they will then turn. This is why idolaters inspire such great terror. But in whom? In the living idols of power who dread the death of their annihilation. But the one and only God also fears idols; he shows his anger for them and he demands their destruction. Jean Pouillon describes the fetish as a "trap for gods," that is, as a means of tying the immanence of the sign to meaning.[2] I would add, however, that in the case of the idol, this trap for gods is only a trap because it condemns the gods to death. The all-powerful God of monotheism knows this well, he who hates idols and idolaters. He knows that idols are the death of God, the limit of his power, his very powerlessness. Thus the idols maintain a double relation with death. Destroyed by the iconocrats, who feel severely threatened by them, they expose themselves to fracture, to being smashed, and to the death whose signifier they intrinsically are. And what they inform us of when they have finally been smashed is the futility of the divinity they were charged with enclosing. The God of the Bible, however, could not tolerate such a fate. Let there be no image if it is impossible to produce one that is definitively indestructible. Paul actively concerned himself with this issue, and thanks to him, it proved possible for the church to establish itself within the power of its own virginal, decay-proof iconocracy.

Idolatry is the quintessential cause of horror. The same abomination is found in all monotheisms, whether in Hebraic texts, the message of the Koran, or in Christian thought. Idolatry, which is denounced as the creation of false gods, the sacrilegious worship of matter, and the satanic adherence to magical and talismanic thought, functions to give shape both to figures of terror and legitimations of hatred. The power of the idol values the fact that its destruction can only confirm its infernal recurrence. It is as insurmountable as our mortality.

When talking of idols, Nikephoros is always careful to say that *they do not in the least resemble anything true.* Always pseudonyms, their power is mysterious, far from all the imaginal and iconic similitude of the enigma. The icon is a memorial to life, through the transfiguration of its flesh, whereas the idol, from the start, is a memorial that makes a dead person's body present and consequently belongs to the shadows. I refer here to Jean-Paul Vernant's analysis of the *eidôlon* and the *colossos,* in which he describes the *eidôlon* as the "category of the double."[3] "The double," he writes, "is something entirely different from an image. It is not a 'natural' object, but neither is it a mental product: neither imitation of a real object nor delusion of the spirit, nor creation of thought. The double is a reality exterior to the subject, but which in its very appearance is opposed by its unusual character to familiar objects, the ordinary decor of life."[4] As shadow, smoke, or a shaped effigy, the *eidôlon* forms part of the invocations of death and the gestures that establish our commerce with the dead. The idol retains all these characteristics in Christian doctrine, which constructs iconic thought in a term-by-term opposition to the signs of a Greek paganism that cannot be separated from sacrificial rites. The icon, however, refuses to be a double by administering dual thought in an entirely different way, that is, by the economic path. But on several occasions, we have seen how the refusal to duplicate did not necessarily escape the traps of duplicity. Would the church itself not one day succumb to the temptations of photographic duplication, so strongly dreaded by those familiar with ways of thinking about shadows?[5]

The idol's often three-dimensional nature puts it on the side of things, manipulable objects, a part of which escapes direct or frontal vision. It belongs to a world without life, light, and voice, without everything by which, *a contrario,* iconic nature is defined. It is also often on the side of dolls, that strange population of duplicating objects and replicas produced in the threatening heat of feminine manipulations. The sorcerers are never far away. It is not by chance that the ecclesiastic iconocracy put an icon of a mother without depth and shading at its center, full of a being who does not fill her up. This suppression of the idolatrous empire doubtless forms an intrinsic part of the diversion of all feminine power for the profit of a power that had the cunning to put the icon of a woman at its foundational center. Are women not full of the mysterious vitalizing power of the body's matter, women who are worshiped but whom it is also necessary to destroy? A deceitful and reptilian woman who will be forbidden from deceiving. . . .

Idolatry is a space of incessant mobility, traversed by burning eruptions and an exterminating roar. It is the very place where the fascination with the feminine is linked to the mystery of life and the sideration of death. It is what doubtless maintains the murderous spectacle of the corrida in the Christian countries most frightened by the pleasures of the body, and which take as much pleasure in temptation as in mortification and sacrifice. One kills for the benefit of a lure, in the proof of what is said to be a truth. One rejoices with the idolaters, and their festivals are strangely traversed by a macabre joy, a desperate elation. Carnival is the carnivorous jubilation of bodies at the funerals of transfigured flesh. The idol's essence is antieucharistic: for hopes of resurrection, it substitutes the strict repetition of calendar rhythms—for idols have their seasons. The arena is a key site of Christian idolatry, a place where the death of what one had previously worshiped is applauded. Do women always know their place in this sacrificial rite? There are "ways of the cross" in existence that come close to mimicking that same operation in sacrificial celebration: the exquisite murder of the worshiped image.

~

Picabia.[6] Man Ray's photograph shows him to us, the victim of the corrida, the animal powerful and naked, the one who really wants to die under the banderillas and sword of the priests of art. . . . That disrespecter demands respect because he is going to die.

Everything was possible for him because reality had for him neither philosophical status nor theological dignity. It is nothing other than that stupefying despair of the body that encounters its mortality at the moment it climaxes. The work of a powerful and serious sensualist who has nothing childish about him. . . . He was never fooled, all the while dreading that he doubtless would be. The work that passed through his hands that were not in the least capable of holding on to anything, the hands that lose things, that squander . . . even his talent; he loves to see it slip between his indifferent fingers.

In Spain there is a desperate love of idols. . . . There, the theater of suffering becomes the site of a true distress strangely mixed with the dawning of pleasure. Spain has the secret of that painful idolatry. A violent paganism inflates the veins of the beautiful Spanish women. Picabia is of those women. The animal sacrificed in the arena is God's victim, his favorite, powerful and seductive. Picabia comes from there. . . . The women, the bulls, the machines, everything is only a self-portrait. Picabia was born without sin of that idolatrous soil that is never scared of blood, and that maintains with death relations of brazen seduction and sublime coquetry.

A Spanish laugh . . . just before the cry that was supposed to suspend everything rings forth, before great art collapsed in turn beneath the artist's dreadfully wounded body.

~

Idolatry cannot be separated from feminine power, as though iconic power, the power of its maternal virginity, had repressed what makes it formidable and could only doom it to destruction. This repression endlessly returns and spreads in broad daylight with the daily swarming of idols that can only be mastered to a greater or lesser degree: the misleading fantasies surrounding a star, the gleaming paganism of a Spanish procession, or even the expiatory sacrifice of Marilyn Monroe or the methodical organization of the virginal transfiguration of Michael Jackson, who appears to want to rise from the dead before he has had a chance to be killed. All are ephemeral, for all worship leads to murder.[7]

Everybody agrees on that *delenda* worthy of Cato: the idol must be destroyed. I would say that the definition of the idol is nothing other than an image that must be killed. History abounds with accounts of the breaking of idols, to the point of the most recent current events, where accompanied by singing, idols and flags are destroyed, yet not without the reestablishment of iconic cults. All the troubling ambiguity of the return to orthodoxy is there in the countries that have just destroyed their idols. It is the act of an idolater ready to substitute one idol for another.

When an icon stops being an image, it becomes an idol and demands a sacrifice. The iconoclasts destroyed icons to prove their idolatrous nature, which is to say, to demonstrate their mortality. For the iconophile God, however, the icon is indestructible.

Whereas the destruction of the martyred Christian body allowed us to see its whole economy, and by the same token, its redemptive function, the idol, once destroyed, admits its emptiness and shows its nothingness, its truly cadaverous nature. Empty of grace, it refutes the kenotic vacuity of charismatic entrails. Broken idols never become relics. Thus each piece shows the nothingness that haunts it. Deserted by the spirit like a broken toy, a dismantled machine, it is now devoid of mystery, the very object that never raised itself to the height of a decay-proof, unbreakable enigma. No one believes in it anymore, the object that endured only through the single motivation of passionate belief. The idol is nothing other than the fate of an image caught in the flux of passion. The passion of Christ's sacrifice is its reversal, its redemptive inversion.

But can we be so sure that in the secret intimacy of our incarnations, objects respect the order, given to them by the church, not to give in to the evil spell of confusion?

Melancholia, Nostalgia, or Fate: The Sign, the Symbol, and the Idol

From the preceding discussion, it emerges that there are several areas around which both the production of images and our considerations of iconicity can be centered: the anti- or defigurative iconoclast *sign*, the icononphile *symbol*, which can be both figurative and abstract, and the *double*, which is the idolatrous object. In all three cases, we are dealing with distinct figures of sacredness. However, *this has nothing to do with the classification of objects; rather, it is about a distinction in an imaginary relation to invisibility.* The same object can pass from one status to another; the question is purely one of interpretation and custom, and in this respect, it is worth noting that the church fathers had already specified what amounts to purity of intentions in the production and interpretation of the visible. In relation to images, everything depends on the role that we decide to make them play; by themselves, they have no power of decision. It is for this reason that I do not see any reason to fear any one sort of visible image more than another. The image offers itself; it is up to thought to avail itself of it. What is to be feared, however, is the power that we cede to those who have the monopoly and mastery over its manipulation and interpretation. The true masters are the masters of signs and symbols; idols can always be destroyed and replaced. It is in the interests of power, however, to disguise those idols as signs and symbols of meaning and truth in order to ensure their permanence. Those who rule fear idols, inevitably doomed to sacrifice and quick to revolution.

What, then, do partisans of the sign do? They sacralize mourning, and here I stress that it is mourning and not death that I speak of. They produce both works and discourse about melancholia, privileging the emblems of lack and the yawning gap in the name of an irreparable absence. These are often works of tearing, opening, and incompleteness. They are also often works of insolence, laughter, and derision. Denouncing all idolatrous ceremonials, they do not harbor iconic dreams and iconophile ambitions. I would number among their ranks the dadaists, the "abstract" expressionists, the supporters of art brut, and the champions of Pop art, surprising though such a combination may appear. The champions of the sign are in fact always far from abstraction, even when they work in a nonfigurative mode, because they are ignorant of the withdrawal that haunts iconic life. The emptiness left by the figure of mourning and the emptiness that the workings of grace demand can never be confused with each other. In other words, the emptiness of the sign has nothing kenotic about it; it is only that definitive remove that separates us from the immanence of a meaning.

All practitioners of the sign have in common with each other the melancholy of mourning and the annihilation of all the indulgences of memory. Their object is no longer the manifestation of a presence, but the sign of a definitive incompleteness and an unbroachable remove. The doubt that haunts it does not concern expression or expressiveness but the very possibility of communicating meaning or the existence of truth. Madness, misinterpretation, nonsense, contradiction, skepticism, and tension all give these works their own violence that often makes them revolutionary or antiestablishment figures both in the field of art and in the social field itself. Endlessly suspicious of the unfaithfulness of memory, laughing at the certitudes of science and all forms of apodicticity, iconoclast signs underpin works that at first sight do not present any stylistic kinship with each other. These signs make fun of styles, can adopt them all, put all of them to the test, and then easily separate from them without nostalgia. Lovers of codes, virtuosi in their use, they can invent them in order to enjoy their combination and their multiplicity all the more, with no last resort or ultimate return, no project, no regret. The melancholic is not nostalgic, unlike the iconophile partisan of the symbol.

I spoke earlier of the shape of sacredness. What would it be here? It is a negative sacredness marked by the seal of profanation, driven by the dynamism of sacrilege and the breath of blasphemy. What is this other than the sacredness of desire itself seizing control of all the routes offered to it, without regard for idealizations or institutional conventions, whatever their nature? The kingdom of signs does not know censure and punishment. It is always sovereign in its own domain and does not claim ongoing continuity. It is the art of princes without a church, an art of fighters hostile to all feudalism. The melancholy of Don Quixote who peregrinates against idolatrous winds and iconic seas. Marcel Duchamp.

Something else entirely is the lineage of lovers of the image who do not renounce the illuminations of the iconic symbol, "symbol" here being taken in the sense that I will call *nikephorian.* Convinced of the image's invisible naturalness and its carnal economy, they put themselves at the service of its complete manifestation. Figurative or not, the iconic symbol treats absence in an entirely different way, because it makes it a deliberate object, produces its trace, illuminates its imprint, and prepares its resurrection. Their concern is not melancholic but nostalgic. Something is lost: it must be refound. Something is forgotten: it must be remembered. We are in exile: we must return to our country of origin.

Technicians of the transfiguration, the producers of icons hold forth either openly or secretly about truth and salvation. Partisans of a redemptive art, they begin to be the redeemers of art by themselves. Balancing between the hopes of anamnesis and the despair of nostalgia, they are people of memory and gravity. Their violence is not that of insolence but that of the call to order and a return to sources. All through the ages, these artists have had the ability to put to the image the question of its own origin and destination. They work, they make pictures. They plead for the spirit and promise liberty. And then they take this liberty, not fearing martyrdom. Their joy, as much as their dereliction, bears them witness; their cause is universal enough to justify their solitude. Figurative or abstract is unimportant to them, because the operative figures of life, truth, and meaning must be found here and now. This is a form of that economic reasoning that historically has managed the visibilities of our incarnation. Abstraction, in the stylistic sense of the term, is only the explicit figure of the historical retreat from threatening idolatry. It is a spiritual and virile art, always faithful to its iconic mission.

Ranged within this lineage are all the meccas of visibility that persist in the iconic economy, from Michelangelo to Malevich. All fought for an authentic visibility safe from idolatry. This is a fight that still continues and will last for as long as the hope for freedom of spirit and the conviction of truth endure. Error dies hard, and this made the nonfigurative painters of the beginning of the century iconoclasm's last champions. Anyone loyal to visibility is an iconophile, especially when it speaks of invisibility! The iconophile is always driven by faith, although that faith need not be religious or assume the insignia of theology. The issue is simply one of faith in the image and enthusiasm for the imaginary, and that enthusiasm can also be for God's face, science, or technique . . . it is always a symbolizing elation and an economically productive dynamism.

Sacredness here is the sacredness of life itself, assumed in the flesh of its passions and its expectations of grace. The icon maintains its relations with the enigma without faltering. It requires hermeneuts of transubstantiation of all sorts, because life arises from matter. Iconophile art is always a eucharistic procedure that transforms matter into a living image and a redemptive gaze. In his study of Jawlensky, I. Goldberg notes that still life goes hand in glove with trompe l'oeil as far as inanimate things are concerned.[8] "Has anyone ever seen a trompe-l'oeil crucifixion?" he asks. To this pertinent question, I would reply that the still life is undoubtedly the iconic genre in which the modern scenario of the imaginal incarnation is played out to the greatest degree. These inanimate, consumable things echo in their silence the solitary voice of the crucified flesh. Warding off idolatrous fictions, the still life reactivates the iconic question by casting off, little by little, the yoke of specular representation. It constitutes a major step in the reconquest of iconicity within European art, in a spiritual form that is all the more new, no longer being religious. Goldberg demonstrates this point brilliantly in the faces painted by Jawlensky, and this leads me to suggest the *Gioconda* as the first still life. This did not, however, prevent its transformation into an idol, arousing destructive rage with its changeable moods. In this sense, it is exemplary of the narrow limit that separates all iconicity from the fate of the idol, a threat that is entirely absent from the world of anti-iconic signs. From the perspective of the sign, the question of the flesh of the image is eliminated; from the perspective of the symbol, slippages between incarnation and incorporation are inevitable. If the flesh does not take on bodily form, the passage from the speculative to the institutional is impossible; if on the contrary, it does, the figures of idolatry invade it forthwith, and the whole fascination with consumption and sacrifice begins.

In the face of these two attitudes, melancholic or nostalgic, disjunctive or mediating, the idol looms, offered for worship and sacrifice, an inexplicable object, its mystery resisting all hermeneutics. It holds forth unintelligibly about the body, belief, and pleasure. It renounces the immortality of redeemed flesh in order to promote the mysterious vitality of the corruptible body and intangible shadows. The idol is neither melancholic nor nostalgic because it has no soul and is unaware of its states of being. Active, functioning matter, it mimics the immanence of death even to its final remains. Inanimate, powerful, it materializes mystery yet does not incarnate it. It incorporates it and disappears with it, carrying it along in its silence and returning stubbornly to show the physical obstinacy of its powers and threats. Any visibility can become an idol and all iconocrats tremble to see it return. And return it does, because it is nothing other than the *figure of fate* itself. Will we ever stop wanting to destroy it? In order for that to happen, we would have to stop loving it. Having nothing to do with the field of similitude, it stands in the field of the double, of resemblance. In a word, the idol resembles us. Like us, it wants to be loved, and like us, it knows that it must die.

To say that the idol is fated is simply to say again that it was as impossible for partisans of the sign to do without it as it was for partisans of the symbol. Imaging matter, inescapable power, the invisibility that it harbors no longer has anything economic about it. Its function does not lie within the legitimacy of management or the justice of organization. It spills out, it wanders around. In the profusion of its effects, in the seduction of its promises, it shows itself off under the threat of its own disappearance. It is nothing but living energy that is spread in the intimate knowledge of its own annihilation. It only lives by repetition. It loves the incandescent rituals that accompany both its glory and its sacrifice. It loves the blood that sacralizes its indignity and in which its contract with human desire is inscribed. Does this energy not bring to mind that *hagion* that the iconoclast wanted to keep in the protective secret of the temples and tabernacles, and that the iconophile dared to manage and transform, the better to administer wisely its profitable turbulences? The living relation between art and women hinges on it.

If access to symbolic linkages is what marks the advent of the Law, then the impossible confrontation of the idol and the Law becomes more understandable. When Moses descends from Sinai for the first time, the Law is smashed when it comes face to face with the idol. When Moses returns with the Law for the second time, it is the idol that is smashed. This incompatibility of the Law and the idol is reinforced by the Law itself, which expresses the prohibition on the idol, for the idol threatens the Law.

The idol can only erect its monuments on the signs of its own abolition. It establishes its scenarios in broad daylight, the very ones in which, endlessly broken, it erects its own fragments into cenotaphs of belief itself.

The image is thus nothing more than the shroud found in a deserted tomb, on which our desires for resurrection continue to be inscribed.

Doctrine has eliminated idols but not idolaters, under pain of eliminating humanity in its entirety. It has simply classified the objects of sacredness into good and bad objects, trying to give itself the means to use that energy and to prevent it from turning back in an attack upon itself and the legitimacies that it institutes. Nevertheless, there will one day be objects that we will no longer have the right to destroy without damning and condemning ourselves. True iconoclasm is in fact an *idoloclasm* intended to prevent us from embarking on paths of destruction.

We thus find ourselves once more located within a strange topology of authorities to be both destroyed and respected. Even as theoretical thought establishes the institutional power that terrorizes that hard-won freedom that it wants to be able to control or even annihilate, it also makes possible the entire field of productions of the imaginary and, indeed, of our hopes of freedom as well. This is why the question of the image, the icon, and the idol is so harrowing for us: it addresses us simultaneously about both life and death.

Such is the image in all its economic power, deceitful and truthful at the same time. It institutes a series of wide-ranging questions regarding the relations between our desire and our identity. Is "know thyself" essentially a "know thy image"? In order not to appear to be succumbing to some rhetorical vagueness with this question, I would rather say that it is probably the case that the type of visibility chosen by each and every person clearly shows the relation that he or she maintains with his or her essential similitude. It would be possible for such a point of view to underpin a history of narcissism within which both the anagogic or deadly figures of our freedoms and servitudes, our despairs, and our utopias would unfold. A sort of political economy of narcissism that would not, in any shape or form, be the account of an accidental drowning. Philosophical thought about the image is after all perhaps only a way for Narcissus to learn to swim.

Artists today seem to be traveling the lush and contradictory territory of images, icons, and idols in all directions. Passing from one to the other without even always knowing it, they once more explore the domain that Pauline thought had already defined two thousand years ago. Is it possible for us to imagine rearranging the forms and functions of the visible in an entirely different way? For that to happen, it would be necessary for us to overturn the economic architecture on which all these combinations rest, and which was able to give a place and a function to what threatens it: the idol. Were we to take the liberty to think the image otherwise, would that not be only by leaving behind the terrain of monotheism?

7

Ghost Story

"The story began in 1898. The first photographs revealed a positive image of an enigmatic face belonging to a mysterious man who had been crucified. The shroud had silently waited for more than eighteen centuries to be revealed, both spiritually and photographically. It was sixty years as well since Daguerre. . . . Finally, at the appointed hour, the discovery took place—providentially—at a time when the excesses of the adolescent human sciences sometimes even cast doubt on Jesus' very existence."[1]

This passage, of course, refers to the Shroud of Turin. The text, which is one of hundreds like it, is by René Laurentin and comes from the preface to a work by Antoine Legrand published in 1980. A few years later, the famous shroud was definitively dated. It was made between 1260 and 1390 and is not in any way a "natural" image, or acheiropoieton, not made by human hands. To a great many Christians, however, this fact makes no difference at all: the shroud is and will always be Christ's authentic burial sheet.

In this chapter I would not simply like to give an account of the history of a false relic, but to show how photography was then experienced as a magical operation (as it is still perhaps considered to be), capable of capturing the invisible in a direct way, without human intervention. Although this may be astonishing to us, we should not in the end be surprised that a technical object with an attendant group of optical and chemical procedures should have become the providential instrument for the revelation and proof, both objective and material, of the presence of the divine and the sacred, of death and resurrection.

The case of the Holy Sudarium is exemplary in this connection in that it simultaneously renders visible the principle of eternal life and the figure of death. Here, photography was put to the service of the unrepresentable in order to reveal the invisible. In relation to this—or, rather, when faced with this object—the fantasmatic workings of a segment of Christian society, of the faithful and their leaders, produced a body of assertions and beliefs that leaves precious little to choose in comparison with the most remote forest or desert tribes who demonstrate a sacred terror before, and violent rejection of, photographs. Photography, or etymologically "writing in light," produces a strange eclipse of consciousness as the luminous impression becomes an inscription of shadows. In that photography works with the double, it is not in the least surprising that it should arouse the impalpable figures of the land of the dead and demons. But the fact that Christianity, officially so concerned to eliminate all talismanic beliefs, was able to produce and preserve so doubtful an object allows us to glimpse something that the economy felt should be exploited. Long embarrassed by a suspect relic that it had no means of rendering fruitful, it left it sheltered in reliquaries, awaiting its moment. And that moment came one night in 1898. Then, the predatory apparatus of the shadows became the means through which the illumination of the soul was spread. Leaving the abject dread of the double to the pagans, the church was finally in a position to hail the collaboration of technical know-how with its own redemptive mission.

In order to understand this fully, it is necessary to bear in mind the major stages of thought concerning the true, natural image that gave rise to the belief that the photographic apparatus had come—"providentially" as Legrand said—to perfect and fulfill the imaginal meaning of the universe. Here, let us attempt to uncover just what it is that has fed the fantasy of an acheiropoietic photography from the end of the nineteenth century to the present, making it do more, even, than take over from the tradition of the veronicas. For, on examination, we receive the impression that it is tradition itself that has at last found its legitimating medium.

The oldest tradition concerning the image not made by human hand dates from the middle of the sixth century. There is a document entitled "The Teaching of Adaï" that mentions a Holy Face, and we find an account confirming it in Evagrios's *Church History*,[2] which talks of an icon that is *theoteuktos*, made by God. However, before taking up Evagrios's relatively late story, it is worth inquiring about the genesis of this tradition, which, before it became one concerning an acheiropoietic Holy Face, was itself preceded by an earlier story related by Eusebios in his *Church History*. It is, of course, impossible to discover the facts underlying these stories, but the chronological sequence of the accounts and the ways in which they come to be modified in accordance with the economic necessities of the times can be discerned.

The text of Eusebios's *Church History*, dating to around 325, recounts that the king of Edessa, Abgar, ill perhaps with leprosy, wrote to Jesus asking him to come and cure him. Jesus replied that he would send his disciple Thaddeus to visit him, which he did after the resurrection. Thaddeus did indeed cure Abgar, but there is no allusion to an image or a portrait.[3]

In 1848, W. Cureton discovered a Syriac document among the manuscripts of the British Museum, which he published under the name of "The Teaching of Adaï."[4] It was republished in a fuller version in 1876 by G. Philips, after the discovery of a second Syriac manuscript in St. Petersburg. The d'Addai text, which appears to be later than Eusebios's version, repeats the account of the king's illness and petition, but now his messenger, Hannan, makes a portrait of Christ that he brings back to Edessa, where it becomes the object of great veneration. The image is not acheiropoietic, but the text does make a specific connection between the incarnation and Christ's "iconic tolerance." Ewa Kuryluk remarks in this connection that "The Christian culture of Edessa and, more generally, of Syria and Cappadocia was shaped by the clash of two major traditions: the non-iconic attitude of the Semitic population, which was prone to succumb to the Monophysite heresy . . . and that of the Greeks devoted to depiction and hence supporting the orthodox line. . . . The controversy was reflected in the legends of Jesus' letter and portrait."[5]

It is not until the sixth century (536–600), however, with Evagrios, that first mention is made of a miraculous image, that is to say, one not made by human hand. In that account, Hannan embarks on his trip and attempts to accomplish his mission. Christ, however, occupied with his preaching, cannot make the journey. Instead, he dips a piece of linen (mandylion, mindil) in water, passes it over his face, which is then miraculously inscribed with its imprint, and gives it to Hannan in order to cure Abgar. Thus was born the Holy Face. Shortly thereafter, it was used to replace an idol on Edessa's ramparts, then immured in order to escape destruction by the pagans. Then, in 545, after it had saved the city from siege by Chosroes, Bishop Eulalios had a dream in which its location was revealed to him.[6] It was extracted from the wall, and a double miracle was noted: the lamp that had been enclosed with it was still burning, and the tile on which it had been placed also bore the imprint of the divine face. Henceforth there would be two Holy Faces: one on a piece of linen, the other on a tile.

After this account, the image reappears regularly in theological texts and sacred tales. At the council of Nicaea II (787), for example, which sanctioned the first reestablishment of images during the iconoclast crisis, it is mentioned as a justification for the painting of icons.

In the tenth century, Constantine Porphyrogenitos had the mandylion brought from Edessa to Constantinople, and from then on, each year on August 16, a liturgical service was celebrated in its honor; thus the following words occur in a sticheron of the Vespers: "Having portrayed your most pure face, you sent it to the faithful Abgar who wanted to see you, you who according to your divinity are invisible to the cherubim." Henceforth humans would be able to see what the angels themselves cannot contemplate, and this because, by the effect of his light and grace, an image of God was painted.

From this point on, what came to be known as icons of the Holy Face were spread throughout the Christian world. According to the texts, the icons were made by human hands but were modeled directly on the mandylion. In Rome, one of these icons, said to have been sent by Stefan Nemanja II, Grand Zupan of Serbia, to Pope Celestine II in the twelfth century, was called the True Icon, or in the vernacular, *vera icona*, or veronica. Worshiped in Rome until 1527, when it was destroyed by the soldiers of Charles V, it was then replaced by the story of the Veronica cloth, the best-known image of which is still the Franciscan one of the fourth station of the way of the cross.[7] From this moment on, the story becomes a western one, and no further allusion is found to it in the East, where the two Holy Faces, on fabric and tile, are considered to have been lost after the Crusader's sack of Constantinople. In Eastern Christianity, icons made by human hand take over from them.

The change from the Holy Face to the Shroud took several more centuries to be justified, and it occurred within the western tradition (although even in the East there was no lack of stories attesting that Christ's shroud had not been destroyed or lost after the resurrection, and mention was still made of it as a relic: in 1957, Mgr. Pietro Savio published more than seventy-five sources attesting to its existence between the second century and 1204).[8] In order to justify the transformation of the acheiropoietic Face into a full image of the body, however, it was said that the shroud had been kept in Edessa since apostolic times, but folded up, in order "not to show that it was a burial cloth." Only the part showing the face could be seen, and it was called "Abgar's veil."[9]

It is, as mentioned, in the West, however, that the issue comes back to life, so to speak, particularly at its beginning. We move now to the fourteenth century, at Lirey, near Troyes; the widow of Geoffroy I of Charny returns the shroud to the canons of Lirey, to whom it had originally been brought, so it is said, by the Knights Templar, and they offer it for popular worship. The bishop of Troyes, Pierre d'Arcis, however, makes clear his opposition; he warns Pope Clement VII of the imposture and requests that ostensions of the false relic be prohibited. By a bull of January 6, 1390, however, the pope authorizes ostension, although only on condition that the object be proclaimed not a shroud but a painting: *Pictura seu tabla.* The shroud is eventually returned to the Charny family, but thirty years later, Geoffroy's son again repeats the request for ostensions. Again, the bishop of Troyes denounces the shround as mystification and states that he knows the artist. The Vatican, however, demands that the bishop keep a *perpetuum silentium* on the subject, and henceforth, with this silence as security, the shroud is placed on exhibit.

In the centuries that follow, many stories evidence a belief in the existence and authenticity of the shroud. None of these stories could be challenged, however, because the object itself was locked in a reliquary, immured, and protected by iron gates at Chambéry's Sainte-Chapelle. Any direct contact with it or ostension of it was therefore impossible. Then, on December 3, 1532, a fire broke out. The shroud, however, was saved, and even though the burn traces can still be seen, the Lord's body remained intact: "Many did not want to believe the unbelievable: the reliquary was completely melted, but the divine effigy was intact." It was at this moment, or shortly thereafter, that Calvin wrote: "When a sudarium has been burnt, another can always be found the very next day. . . . It is even said that this is the same one that had been there before, and that it had been saved from the fire by a miracle; but the paint was so fresh that, had there been eyes to see it, it would hardly have been worth lying about."[10] Subsequently, during the plague of Milan, Duke Emmanuel Philibert of Savoy had the shroud removed to Italy, from whence it would never return. To this day, it is still to be found in Turin.

What, then, does the shroud look like? It is a linen cloth 4.36 meters long by 1.1 meters wide, yellowing, with several patches. With the naked eye, there is nothing, or almost nothing, to be seen: the confused traces of a body 1.75 meters tall. The decisive ostension, however, took place on May 25 or June 2 of 1898 when a lawyer named Secundo Pia was eventually granted royal authorization to photograph the shroud. A first attempt failed because some frosted filters broke. Then,

> On the evening of May 28, a pane of glass that had been positioned at the request of Princess Clotilde to protect the sacred cloth from candle and incense smoke had been causing some bothersome reflections. At 11 p.m. Pia took a fourteen minute exposure, and then a second of twenty minutes. At midnight, he left the cathedral and immediately enclosed himself in his darkroom. He dipped the glass plates in a developing bath. Suddenly, the negative in front of a red lamp caused the true face of Christ, which no-one had contemplated for more than eighteen centuries, to loom before his eyes.

Pia wrote: "Enclosed in my darkroom, I experienced such intense emotion when I saw the Holy Face appear on the plate for the first time that I was paralyzed."[11]

L'Osservatore romano of June 14, 1898, greeted the Savior's appearance in the same terms that usually accompany accounts of a miraculous apparition, and Pope Leo XIII declared that "this providential event is appropriate to the present age and will favor the awakening of religious sentiment." It is at this time as well that the science entitled sindonology was born, patronized by the great names of Christian science: Paul Vignon, professor of biology at the Institut catholique de Paris, René Colson, *répétiteur* of physics at the École polytechnique, Armand Gauthier of the Académie des sciences, and Yves Delage, also of the Académie des sciences. Laws were formulated, phenomena were described. This culminated in 1931, when Vignon created an international commission for scientific research on the shroud, consisting of 110 members.

Before returning to the recent demystification of the shroud, it is worth noting the degree to which even the most experienced researchers were swept along by a wave of fantasy. Here are some examples: "They crucified cadavers in dissection halls. They experimented with whips and crowns of thorns made of bushes from Palestine until they obtained imprints similar to the ones on the shroud. In this way they were able to identify the direction of the blows and the positions of the body that had received them. During the 1950s they hung volunteers who had a passion for the same research on a *patibulum.* Legrand even had himself hung on a cross. He contracted tetanus, and speaks discreetly of it in passing."[12]

A strange ceremony was thus instituted, a sort of scientific liturgy in which the doctors' role makes one wonder about the necrophiliac complicity of the surgical profession. For example, Dr. Barbet, who published *La Passion de Jésus-Christ selon le chirurgien* (The Passion of Jesus Christ from a Surgeon's Point of View) repeatedly experimented on amputated limbs:

> Having just amputated the arm of a healthy man one third of the way down, I hammered an eight millimeter nail (a nail as used in the passion) into the center of the palm, at the third intermetacarpal space. I gently hung forty kilos from the elbow. After ten minutes the wound had stretched, and the nail was at the level of the metacarpal heads. I then gave the whole ensemble a very slight nudge, and I saw the nail suddenly break through the point in space narrowed by the two metacarpal heads and easily tear the skin all the way up to the corner. A second gentle nudge ripped through what was left of it.[13]

The "lightness" of the officiating touch will, of course, be appreciated here! What is astonishing in this passage is the degree of medical relentlessness in the attempt to justify the miracle; for, after all, if a miracle there had been, it would certainly justify leaving the bodies of amputees respectfully in peace! There were, however, even greater obscenities to come in connection with the historical events, and it is to Legrand that we owe knowledge of them. A doctor himself, he had himself hung from a cross by the wrists until he was nearly asphyxiated. He developed congestion as a result and had trouble seeing.

> In March, 1948, after a lecture in the amphitheater of one our great national institutes in which I had described Christ's positions on the cross as he struggled against death, I was completely astonished when a student from Luxemburg, M. R. Geiser, who . . . had been deported to Dachau, asked me if I myself had not also spent some time there. . . . The description of the agonies of the crucified that I had just given coincided exactly with the tortures he had seen inflicted on other deportees in the winter of 1943–1944.

This, in fact, is the terrifying formulation of both the natural and supernatural effects of iconic *mimêsis*: the deportees serve the cause of the divine image. But this was not enough for Dr. Legrand, who published an article entitled "Du gibet du Golgotha à ceux de Dachau" (From Golgotha's Gallows to Dachau's) in the periodical *Médecin et Laboratoire* on December 19, 1952. "Notice," he proclaims, "that since the angle of Christ's arms is more open than those of the victims at Dachau, the traction force of the arms would have been insufficient to raise the chest." And he ends by noting that neither Christ nor the deportees could have had erotic fantasies in their death pangs, as some evil souls have suggested. The reader of this text oscillates between nausea and suffocation; surely some spiritual or scientific voice should have been raised to put an end this appalling delirium.

But no; a profusion of texts continues to describe the passion, to reconstitute it minutely, minute by minute, as though it were a crime on television: spittle, wounds, fractures, asphyxia, hemorrhages . . . nothing is missing. Even the Nazis cooperate in this endeavor.

Nothing, however, comes close to the miracle of photography, which remains the absolute paradigm of revelation. In 1931, Enrie, nicknamed "Christ's photographer," took the best trichrome photographs yet of the shroud, and in 1936 he published *Le Suaire de Turin révélé par la photographie* (The Shroud of Turin Revealed by Photography). From that point on, a scientistic madness erupted on claims of a power that was magical. God, the Father painter, had inspired the invention of photography in order to reveal the realm of the invisible, the soul of the world. The chemical miracle is thus transformed into a spiritual miracle, and science, which might well have carried humanity off on a tide of luciferian or atheistic pride, becomes instead the ground of revelation itself. At just this time, the Virgin herself was sighted on several occasions, and St. Theresa of Lisieux had herself renamed St. Theresa of the Infant Christ and the Holy Face. Photography additionally proved to be an inexhaustible source of proofs of the visibility of spirits, which fed a growing interest in magnetism, spiritualism, and the occult sciences. Photographs were taken of auras, of ghosts, ectoplasms, good and bad spirits, angels and the damned, and the souls of the living and the dead—the shadows of the world emerged from the shade. Photography thus became the providential unveiler of the invisible, the netherworld, and the lens lent a scientific, unwavering character to what would henceforth appear as the very object of photography itself. Here is Paul Claudel, in "La Photographie du Christ" (The Photography of Christ):

It is not only an official document, as the minutes of a meeting would be, an official decree, duly signed and initialed: it is a tracing, an image carrying with it its own guarantee. More than an image, it is a presence! More than a presence, it is a photograph, something that has been imprinted and that is unalterable. . . . *For a photograph is not a portrait made by human hand.* . . . It is, physically, he who imprinted this plate, and it is this plate that subsequently comes to take possession of our spirit. . . . It is difficult to believe that this detailed, negative impression of Christ's body, caused only by some randomly spread herbs on an unprepared cloth, is a phenomenon that is purely natural.[14]

As this passage makes clear, once "it is physically he who imprinted this plate," then the authenticity of the shroud becomes a secondary problem: the miracle is produced solely by the direct intervention of God on the photographic plate, which henceforth functions as the mandylion itself. All the essential elements of this story are now in place, and the photograph has come to replace the "Holy Veronica" of the Franciscan tradition. We are at last in a position to be able to ask how photography came to function, then as it still does now, as a producer not simply of acheiropoietic images, but ones in which the effect of their "real presence" is accompanied by a rhetorical and scientific system that is wholly unique.

At root, the belief in this particular capability of photography is based on the wholesale transfer of a technical vocabulary into a spiritual one. Light, developer,[15] darkness, lens—all these terms induce a dreamlike state of being. The same is true of the photographic apparatus as was true for the optical and specular vocabulary of the Renaissance: the technical object is a doctrinal matrix. Here, however, the obscurantist incompetence and stubbornness of the proselyte no longer have anything in common with an intelligence at work as it attempts to grasp hold of a model of intelligibility. The collaboration between the mirror and a system of thought is far from the giddy complicity of fantasy and photography. But let there be no mistake: the church is not the victim of its unconscious desires, which, after all, can only resemble our own. Rather, it consciously manages the collective unconscious in order to derive redemptive profit from it: these are times of doubt, of materialism, and of atheism, and something must be done to mark God's intervention in history.

The power of rhetoric is such that the keenest efforts and most advanced technical refinements were necessary in order to prove beyond doubt that the shroud was a fake. At present, nothing is sufficiently rigorous to overcome the deception of something that plain good sense had been enough to refute for centuries. Let it be said in passing that we seem to believe that we are not in a position to dominate an object until we understand how it was made and brought to a state of perfection. *Qualis artifex periit!*

Photography, then, seems to be powerfully linked to a history of credulity in, and attachment to, the real presence or existence of what it shows. And it does this with infinitely greater force in relation to something that reveals the Truth in the *negative.* In effect, the terms in which photography is described, the procedures by which it reveals what left an impression on it—resemblance; two dimensionality; the passage from light to a darkness that is so revealing, as is the one from the revelatory darkness to the charismatic light of presence; the symmetric and specular nature of the image with respect to its model; the seizing and holding of the moment that evokes eternity so well; the image of what died yesterday and remains alive today; the image of what will live always, despite everything that annihilates us today, in a word, this opposite world so similar to ours that is shown to us, mimetic and painless—all this is everything that turns photography, as a providential invention, into a redemptive and authentifying technique. It is worth noting in passing, incidentally, that these are all the selfsame features that provoke repulsion, terror, and sacred dread in many other societies.

All this would be incomprehensible if it were not for the fact that we have been so firmly attached to the image for centuries, and that this has occurred under the all-powerful iron rule of the church's economic imagination. For if the church, in its supreme authority, saw fit to push credulity to the limit in the face of all likelihood, in the face of all the irrefutable proofs concerning the dating of the shroud, this is because once again, exactly as had taken place during the iconoclastic crisis, it could not bring itself to renounce the benefits that were thus made available to it. It is because this image has power that it is necessary to defend and protect it. It is not because it is true that it has power. It is because it has power that it becomes true, *that it must be true.*

What, then, is its power? It lies not only in the miracles that it has performed, the protection it has dispensed, the conversions that it has effected. Indeed, far from it. All these things are secondary benefits, so to speak, gathered along the course of history, and which it certainly has no monopoly on. All relics or miraculous images of any sort can be invested with equal or similar power. Rather, the Shroud of Turin has such exceptional, privileged status because it is related to photography, the imprint, the reflection, to filiation and the resurrection, because it concerns the capture of shadows and therefore the transformation and salvation of science itself by means of divine collaboration. Science and technology are put at the service of faith; once again, it is the image that must be massively believed in, without protest and without speaking. *Perpetuum silentium* is the watchword before the image that speaks the discourse of univocal, frontal, and mimetic evidence.

Is the church, then, in the process of inventing the myth of photography as mystical evidence and final proof of what is true? It would not be for the first time. The iconophile victory was a violent and authoritarian victory of symbolic power over those who, with the exception of the eucharist, rejected all the magic of real presence. The church, however, saw things differently, because it took the long view of the issue: the iconic delegation of power, a filiation that is mimetic and redemptive, forges the iron for the sword of victory from the production of images of all sorts. Thus is belief procured, and obedience too, and silence with them both. No objection, no doubt. It is he who rejects the invisible who is blind. The shroud makes the natural image visible without broaching its foundational invisibility, and the proof of this lies in the fact that, by inversion, it passes into negative form. Negative theology has at last found its photochemical double.

Let us return now to two essential points regarding photography's iconic magic. The first concerns real presence, the second, negative thought. What is the status of the acheiropoietic image? For an iconoclast, the Holy Face is a direct and sacred imprint of the body. It is a sign of, and memorial to, divine humanity that prohibits any other portrayal. If the iconoclasts had been faced with the Holy Sudarium, they would not have recognized it as an argument for figurative portrayal, because it concerns, as does the cross, a negative sign, resemblance to which would be holy, venerable, and nonreproducible. For an iconophile, conversely, the shroud is a sign of divine assent to the criteria of similitude and the redemption of that similitude. For the former, it is, as a negative sign, heterogenous to the model of which it is the imprint. It can only refer to the passion. For the latter, it is homonymous and homogenous with its humanity and with the symbolic status that transforms (*métamorphôsis*) the negative (death) into a positive (life). It is proof of the resurrection. Consequently, both the Holy Face and the shroud permit doctrinal authority to transform an index into an iconic symbol. Photography thus miraculously becomes the organon of this specifically targeted economy, by means of a sort of lexical traffic between a technological vocabulary and a spiritual vocabulary. In conformity with the economy in its most intimate modalities, and in the enigmatic brilliance of its manifestation, the cadaver becomes a sign of life, the shadow becomes a source of light, the invisible is promoted to visibility, and art is one with nature.

For the triumphant, iconophile church, photography is the scientific coronation of that divine assent to redeemed similitude. The image of the shroud makes God's humanity truly present, and therefore his incarnation and resurrection as well. Miraculously added to the sacramental magic of the eucharist that transforms the bread and wine into the body and blood of Christ, is an imprint of body and blood that deserves the same respect as the host and to which it adds the criterion of similitude. *Hoc est corpus, hoc est sanguis.* Photography is the modern tool of transubstantiation par excellence; it is also a most extraordinary instrument for the treatment of still life. I mentioned earlier that it was possible to see the still life as an antieucharistic manifesto in its portrayal of the sacred species: in its silence, our gaze gleans the signs of our "resounding futility," and the body of our appetites feeds on its figures of hunger and is enchanted by its iconic melancholy. The negatives of the shroud show us the body and blood of the sacrifice and engage in the work of animation, of reanimation. They convince us that this corpse is breathing, and that each image is fundamentally miraculous. We are essentially imaginal and acheiropoietic by nature, and photography invites us to rejoin with our own similitude, also not made by human hand.

Photography, without word or gesture, but rather by the effect of light only, performs a nonsacramental eucharistic operation because it can manage without transformative words and can actually show the body and the blood. The believer's eyes commune with it and are opened by it. Yet all this does not fully account for its magic. Added to it, amazingly, is the fact that the revelation of the truth functions in the negative. The torture victim's body, invisible to the naked eye, suddenly appears clearly in the darkness. For it is a corpse that we are dealing with, and that corpse has now been revived. The image, in its mode of manifestation, must therefore reverse its own content, and the negative is then interpreted as *negation.* This is because the corpse in question is not that of a dead person, but the body of he who is life, who revives and saves, who the shroud can only show in a process of inversion. Photographic magic comes about by the transition from a technological gesture (dip the plate into a developing bath) to its rhetorical equivalent. It is nothing other than a homonymic slippage, and the iconic economy has taken full advantage of its effects; it is the homonymy of the visible negative and the negativity of the invisible. To produce a negative—that is, a negation—is to act positively, because by respecting the prototype's invisibility, one gives oneself the means to reverse it into the positivity of the truth. Photography is a chemically apophatic art!

Magical thinking always functions by equating the image with the word, a making consubstantial with a saying. This is the magic of desire. Photography acts without words *like* a magical formula, a deliberately mute abracadabra that produces an abracadabra-ing that functions as a muzzle.

Before coming to any further conclusions, however, let us pause to examine the procedures that determined that the shroud is definitely a fake. NASA, the CNRS,[16] and other bodies of world science had to set to work in an attempt to establish the definitively historical origins of the shroud by means of a precise dating. Before even entering into the details of this issue, however, it is worth noting that these definitive conclusions did not in the least shake the convictions of those who believe photography to be acheiropoietic; the church still refuses to this day to make any official statements on the subject. We will return to the question of just what the difference is between an acheiropoietic fake and a true work of art once we have discussed some of the facts concerning the dating of the shroud. Perhaps one does not exist—except for the stubborn sindonophile.

Since 1946, the dating of certain objects by means of the carbon 14 method has been possible. Because carbon 14, a radioactive isotope, deteriorates progressively through the centuries, the percentage of its deterioration through time can be recorded. Its measurements are very sensitive and relatively accurate. In order to determine the percentage of carbon 14 in the shroud, however, it would have been necessary to cut a forty-centimeter piece out of it, so a mass spectrometer, which allows the isotope to be measured on the tiniest of samples, was used instead. On October 13, 1988, in Turin, the mass spectrometer, which separates the carbon atoms by using a process of acceleration and magnetic traps, yielded a result: the cloth was made of linen dating to a period between 1260 and 1390.

These results, however, were soon contested, and it is worth paying attention to the objections. The scientist Eberhard Lindner, faced with the conclusions of the spectrometer, took up a theory that had already been advanced earlier, according to which Jesus's resurrection took place like a flash, an atomic explosion, a thermonuclear emission, which turned the proportions of carbon 14 in the sudarium upside down. In 1902 Arthur

Loth had already spoken of "an electrical action, a photofulgural photography or some phenomenon of radiation,"[17] and in 1966 Geoffroy Ashe hypothesized that at the moment of the resurrection, Christ's body radiated such heat that the shroud was scorched. In March 1977 as well, Ray Rogers spoke of a photolysis-flash of a thousandth of a second, the same one that had forever fixed the shadows of those seized by the death flash at Pompeii and Herculaneum, and Hiroshima to the ground. We have, of course, already seen several examples of the many infernos within which people have been prepared to recognize the shadows cast by the resurrection and redemption. Photography, too, using either natural or artificial light, also proved capable of providing a sacred image not made by human hand; now the nuclear flash is close to finding its sacred model and permanently fixing the shadow cast by our immortality.

In order to confirm the results of the mass spectrometer, the thermoluminescence technique was also used. A piece of the shroud was exposed to a quartz or aluminum crystal emitting light at a certain temperature, and the light then given off by the cloth was interpreted to establish a chronology. Yet another test, the potassium-argon method, in which the respective proportions of the elements that remain at the end of a given period allow for an exact dating, was also employed. All the measurements agreed: the Holy Shroud dates from the end of the thirteenth or fourteenth centuries (1260–1390). The fantasy, however, remained resistant, with some even querying how a fourteenth-century man had mysteriously been able to endure the whole of Christ's passion so that this bloody testimony might be bequeathed to humanity.

The shroud, then, is a work of art bearing all the characteristics of a fraud designed to provoke popular piety and to obtain all the familiar benefits of pilgrimages to miracle-working relics. And if, indeed, it is a true work of art, damaged and worn though it may be, whose contrasts really are more legible in a photographic negative, then the problem is simple as far as this particular object in itself is concerned, although questions remain regarding its production.

However, this description of the whole affair has been necessary in order to allow us to formulate several more fundamental questions on the subject of photographic magic. A little earlier I asked the question of what the difference is between an acheiropoietic fake and a true image. Once it has been recognized that the Holy Shroud is a fake, have we thereby established what a veronica, a true image, is? Are those who flee before the camera lens for fear that they will be deprived of their soul or that someone will gain knowledge about their life—or rather, a power over their death—not also truly alive to the question of the iconic economy? Their shadow, their reflection, their double, beyond all rhetoric and narrative, whether hagiographic or not; they do not want to give these things to the first ones who happen to come along, the tourist, the ethnologist, the journalist, all of them citizens of the empire of images, of that world in which how to dominate, subjugate, and kill with their help is so well known. Are they always so wrong when they see in these people predators who do not have the least respect for similitude or shadows?

The problem that the Shroud of Turin poses concerns the cause of the image and its double foundation in a gesture and a model. Whether the model was, or still is, real, or whether we are dealing with a divine body with perceivable or fabricated exteriority is not the problem. We are not raising the question of faith, but of belief. Of what gesture, what authority, is the image the effect? When the worshipers of the Holy Shroud claim that it is an acheiropoietic image, they are saying two things: first, that the beauty, the perfection of the result cannot be made by human hand. Even more than this, though, they are saying that the very nature of the image, on analysis, does not allow the trace, the mark of any producing gesture to be seen. If photography corroborates this claim, it is because it itself is interpreted as not being the result of any material cause, any gesture. Not made by human hand thus means that the hand, specifically, counts for nothing there.

In the nineteenth century, however, and particularly in its second half, the identification, attribution, and recognition of fakes by art historians and experts became possible. What were their criteria? The dating of matter and materials certainly did not possess the same rigor that it does today. Instead, it was knowledge, the eye, that was exercised in order to define styles, themes, writing, graphologies, gestures, everything that concerns the relation of touch to the hand that lays it down. Impressionism, the works of Cézanne and van Gogh included, developed an oeuvre characterized by gesture and touch put at the service of an optical impression. A work is said to be by the hand of a painter, and several hands, even, can be recognized in the works of a studio or in retouched objects. In short, both signature and style are ranked in the same class of criteria for the authentification and reading of works of art. In relation to this, photography appears to be an instrument that objectifies a world seen by a body without hands, touch, or signature. Would this mean, then, that the true image, the veronica, is the product of a cause without body or matter?

Linked to this fantasy of pure, divine productivity, luminous and without a body, is the simultaneous birth of a painting that is pure, spiritual emanation, liberated of all gestural subjectivity, and which brings the question of the image back to the manifestation of inherent truth. I am speaking, of course, about abstraction such as Kandinsky, Malevich, or Mondrian thought about it. But if abstraction naturally follows the acheiropoietic fantasy of photography, it turns its back on it in freeing itself from all specular and mimetic constraints. Painting's ambitions were never more closely tied to the veronica than in the abstraction of the beginning of the century, and the canvas on which forms and colors are placed henceforth functions, in fact as well as in thought, like a veil that covers and uncovers. *On the Spiritual in Art* is the major manifesto of this purely spiritual and sacred imprint. The trace of the spirit prevails over that of the hand.

A supplementary proof that corroborates this fiction of photography as productive of an iconic effect without a gesture is the absence of any drawing. The photographic impression is nongraphic, or as might be said, agraphic, just as we say aphasic. In a certain way, it concerns the same thing. The impression leaves a stain rather than makes a line. The shroud's image bears the magic of something that has form without an outline. It shows only values of shade and light to give two-dimensional evidence of relief. In the Byzantine iconic tradition too, everything concerning the graphic line, writing, and outline is called *skiagraphè*, writing in shadows. The shroud is on the side of cloths and stains, that is to say, of those immaculate cloths on which women collect the bloody and living traces of our mortality. The *photographé* of the shroud functions without gesture or outline. Was it not iconicity's maternal, fertile roots that abstraction's great thinkers and practitioners were seeking to rediscover? And was it not the enigmatic place of the veronica that they desired to occupy? The haunting presence of the Holy Face and its negative photography endlessly preyed on the practitioners of modern iconography. Malevich and Jawlensky are in some ways its elite thinkers, but there are several others as well.

The affair that has bound photography and belief so closely to each other for a century is far from being over. What we know now is that nothing is more enigmatic than the foundations of thought concerning the image. The same is true for the claim that every image is an image of an image, that truth is measured by the yardstick of the imaginary, and that it is a long way from the image to the visible, from the gaze to vision. In photography, more than in any other process that produces images, the fundamental issues of the desire to see, and by the same token, the manifestation of what vision can only lack if the object that it chooses remains faithful to its aim, all hang in the balance.

The figure of death cannot reveal itself in the negative to become, miraculously, the figure of life. It can only lose itself in another figure, that of the death of death, in that other night of which Blanchot wrote: "It is the death that cannot be found." At best, we are immobile dancers who mark the common limit of two chasms with a suspense still mobilized by our bodies. Between the caves of reassuring fiction and the veristic abysses of trompe l'oeil there is enough space for all the anamorphoses. The Holy Shroud is an anamorphosis, and the controversy surrounding it makes us understand that all iconicity is fundamentally anamorphotic in nature. This is what the economy has become: this topological coiling of word and gaze that presents us with an ontological fantasy. The only possible reply is Stella's "You see what you see,"[18] which does not, for all that, decree a halt to the image.

Henceforth, every image that seeks to be seen can only show the spectral essence of the veronica negatively.

Is every work of art a fake acheiropoieton?

8

The Jew, Frontally and in Profile

One day a Greek painter by the name of Byzantios, on seeing me for the first time in a very long while, said, "I would always recognize you because you look exactly the same from the front as you do in profile." Is that why I am interested in Byzantium? Through those words I first grasped the ambiguity that would always mark the perception of my face by another. What did he mean, exactly?

More generally, however, concealed within this witticism lay the question of what constitutes both an outline and a look when one is gazing at another person. Speaking of which, that Greek, looking at me, Jew that I am, also confessed that he wanted to keep open all the possibilities of the undecidable, leaving me hanging between the promises and threats that a painter's eye can always bring to bear on the forms of our visibility.

At the worst moments of history, however, the scalpel of the gaze has preferred to cut out of the other an image for itself to hate. Earlier I spoke about the virtuosity of the "painter" Nikephoros when he decided to assassinate his other. He made his decision without hesitation. Nothing resembles an iconoclast more than a Jew or an Arab to suppress.

How can we understand the origins of the physical, perceptual system that forms the basis for the face of horror, impurity, and shame that through the centuries has been attributed to the facial features and bodies of those who must be hated, assassinated, at all cost? In an attempt to explain this, I will draw on several caricatures of Jews that appeared during the Nazi period. This is not, however, a study linked to racism or even

Nazism. That hideous moment in our history will for long exercise the minds of others who refuse to forget. I will rather more modestly simply reconsider a small number of texts and images, my goal being only to demonstrate that strange complicity between science, fantasy, and sublimation in the structure of organized repulsion. Additionally, and perhaps most importantly, I would like to examine the ideological roots of these few miserable, prejudiced graphics and their link to a more general history of caricature.

What are the indices that characterize the Jew's face? Where do they come from? Why do they form the intolerable portrait of a creature recognizable by its profile alone? Why can a Jew not have a face? Why are Jews unfit for a face-to-face encounter? How, according to their enemies, did their own God condemn them to this obliqueness, to this deprivation of the gaze, and is he too, perhaps, excluded from all frontality?

Let it be understood that if God prohibited the Jew from access to the image, that is because he did not recognize himself in him. The Jew has no image; yet despite everything, as was the case for Constantine, it is necessary to paint his portrait. In order to investigate this, I will also consider what were taken to be the most beautiful profiles of humanity and the marvelous face-to-face encounters so decisively established by Christianity.

This study is based essentially on the propaganda publications produced in France and distributed by the NEF[1] in 1940. The assassins there used the very principle of the game of massacre by employing silhouette and outline as weapons in the annihilation of the face.

First, I will address the question of the profile; then I will briefly comment on the triumphalism of Pauline visibilities concerning the face. In a word, I will show that the poverty, the very wretchedness, of anti-Semitic propaganda is based not on an archaic or puerile structure; on the contrary, it is based on subtleties and refinements that are the very opposite of Greco-Christian idealization, which is itself an ideology, that is to say, a strategically coherent discourse about the body and about territory.

Profiles

The most striking feature about the caricatures we are considering is, first, the fact that no matter what the position of the face, that famous nose is always seen in profile. It is linear, enormous; it plunges downward. But the importance of this caricatural emphasis, and a feature that I would like to stress here, is that it is the organ par excellence that stands out in the shadow theater of the profile. The Jew is like his nose, a figure of the shadows. A shadow in essence, he is the face of death without resurrection. His forehead recedes and is almost nonexistent. His chin disappears too; he is agnathous and has no neck. All that exists are exaggerated features: the graph of the nose and lips or jaw, to which I will return shortly. As for his eyes, they are said to have been made to look behind him.

It is clearly important that the Jew be recognizable, and recognizable he is, by evidence that is, as the expression goes, "as clear as the nose on his face." The shape on display has such a minimal area, is so asymmetric, that it is nothing more than a mortal, bestial promontory that transforms the face into a maw. He is identifiable by the shadow or the graph that outlines his profile in a space that has no depth. With a two-dimensional profile that is pinned up and outlined like a sign, that is, like the linear form that constitutes a written body, he is, as the church fathers would say, circumscribable. This scriptural condition is not at all surprising in a people of the book and the letter who have never had access to the true similitude of symbols. They are a people of the sign, always at a remove from meaning. As for corporeal delineation, it is, of course, well known through the ways in which the body is stylistically sublimated. Ugliness, like beauty, is, above all, linear. "To look elegant, or not" (*avoir la ligne*, literally, to have a line): here is an expression that speaks volumes, because it raises the question of an identity that is integrated and complete, or one that is excommunicated within a schema that can be either ideal or repulsive. This line in German is *Figur*, by which it is understood that in order to show up well (*faire bonne figure*, literally, to form a good face or figure) and to have access to the face, it is necessary to be on the right side of the line; this, in turn, concerns the silhouette where the unbreachable barrier between humans and animals hangs in the balance. This is because in French, the term *figure* refers ambivalently to the face and the silhouette, whereas in Anglo-Saxon languages, it is completely swallowed up in the linearity of an outline, in circumscription.

To have access to the face is to have access to visibility and the gaze. Being invisible, the Jew is out of the frame, beyond the visible and the gaze. Nonetheless, this intangible shadow must be located as quickly as possible. This is the indexical function of the two-dimensional shadow of the profile, whose specifics are, like a pointing finger, all those soft folds of that face of the unformed; no more than a shadow, the nose dives downward and obscures the mouth, the lip swells and obliterates the chin, the forehead flees after having blocked the gaze. It is a face, a nocturnal, crossed-out landscape, a shadowgraph that betrays itself despite itself to those who can catch it by surprise from that angle where it can no longer deceive anyone. Its profile, its finitude, its circumscribability are the paradoxical correlates of what it signifies: the imperceptibility, the undefinability, of death. The outer edges of his body are closed, it is a completed sign, enclosed, defined. It refers to death, just as Christ's uncircumscribable body, in an entirely opposite way, promises the transfiguration of a borderless face that refers to life: the borderlessness of the infinite, salvational Face that is opposed to the enclosure of the profile of mortality. The Jewish body is circumscribed, excluded from visible and redemptive inscription.

The profile is a line in a graphic and scriptural space. The Jew is recognized by his lines, writing, and form; he must be opposed, line by line, to an antithetical profile of which he is nothing more than the emaciated opposite, which is to say that he is excluded from the plan of incarnation and salvation. His body is disembodied, which is to say, reduced to its non-transfigured materiality only; he is constructed like an idol. A golden calf, he is the gold and the animal that will be reduced to nothing. It is the God of similitude who requires him for the economy of world salvation. A new *Delenda est.*

Let us now turn our attention to some racist fantasies and commonly used metaphors. Inevitably, we encounter the regressive, archaic unconscious obsessed with animality and the diabolical. But it is also interesting to move in the opposite direction, to return to the facts, both scientific and imaginary, that once produced an ideal profile. The essentially non-Jewish profile, that profile that is so un-Germanic, nonetheless haunts the corporeal image that the Aryan has of himself. I mean by this that famous profile that obsesses and fascinates the West: the Greek profile. For if there is indeed a profile that has dominated the spirit and process of the idealization, the standardization, of the body, it is that famous Greek profile, which emerges so gloriously in Greek sculpture. There, too, surprisingly, if those who are obsessed with such canons are to be believed, from no matter what angle a Greek face is looked at, it always appears, like the Jewish one, in profile. But the Greek face has the right kind of line. In Giraudoux's *Intermezzo*, the following extraordinary classroom dialogue takes place: "What is a right angle?" And the class replies, "It is the angle that the Greek nose makes with the Greek earth."

Could the ideal orthogonality of the body with the lands of empire be any better expressed? Thus the abscissa and ordinate of the world have become fixed and now await only an algebra of method for the two-dimensionality of reason to establish its well-tempered hegemony. In one stroke, the Greek nose, that famous profile, engages the scriptural order of rationality; such is the good line, the graph of the beautiful, delivered by the Greek face.

In *Gesture and Speech*, André Leroi-Gourhan describes the probable appearance of Neanderthal man: "Low wide skull, a receding forehead, enormous orbital ridges . . . the lips set very high, and the chin nonexistent."[2] The face evolves with the jaw drawing back and the facial bloc being reduced relative to the forehead and the chin. In fact, the forehead comes to dominate the entire facial structure. "The supraorbital bloc progressively loses its function as the base of the facial structure diminishes in size until it disappears altogether, for instance, as may be seen in most females today."[3] In the process of freeing the frontal and temporal lobes from the cerebral hemispheres, the key moment undoubtedly arrives with the well-known prefrontal unbarring, which causes the bony supraorbital ridge that overhangs the eyes to disappear at the same time as the brain is locked in and the ensemble of symbolic functions develop. As Leroi-Gourhan notes, "The most important palaeontological problem remains that of the freeing of the forehead in *Homo sapiens*."[4]

We can see from this description that the facial ideal of the Hellenized world corresponds to a celebration of that prefrontal unbarring as a triumph of, first, hominization, and then humanization. In the Greek Classical ideal, the nasal bridge is completely integrated into the structure of the forehead. The Greek nose does not exist; there is only the triumph of a profile absorbed into frontality, which functions as the signifier of the concept of man himself, or more precisely, as the advent of the visible body in its capacity as a sign that is identical to its own content. The conceptual, theoretical hegemony of the Greek world thus constructed an imaginary body that would continually keep at bay any paleolithic regression or animal debasement, and at the same time positioned vertebral straightening and verticality as the correlate of frontality. The Greek body is neither bent nor oblique; it is straight. It is an "orthotype," as used to be said in 1940. In this connection, it is remarkable that the Greek ideal did not develop any themes concerning face-to-face encounters, as did Christianity. In fact, in visual terms, the face-to-face encounter was constituted, on the contrary, in the very image of the unbearable face of the Gorgon, the mythological figure of deadly sideration engendered by femininity. Its antitype is the impeccably profiled face of Athena that faces up to things behind the shield of its other face. What is set up here is rather an antagonism of profile against profile, Semite against Greek, on the basis of a confrontation between two scriptural conceptions. The ideal body is really the legible, victorious sign of the logos that knows neither prefrontal barring nor bendedness, nor limpness, nor mortal shadow. It is a radiant image constructed against an erased figure.

In the Germany of Lights, that face comes to occupy an exemplary position that reliably prepares the sinister typologies of the future. Before discussing how the Jew is excluded from the Face, however, let us consider how he comes to be deprived of the right kind of profile.

The terms in which Greek sculpture is praised would be fitting for a graphology of the intelligible, for the ideal inscription of the body in a space with Leibnizian characteristics. The beautiful body is made of marble, that is, "hard and angular," in the words of Winkelman, who admired "the graceful geometrization of the face" in its ideal form in terms similar to those of Schelling:

> If we now look at this in more detail, we find that this abstract truth in the rendering of the individual forms of the human body was based essentially on expressing the predominance of the spirit corporeally as well, and thus on emphasizing those organs that have spiritual or intellectual reference over those possessing more a sensual or physical purpose. This is the basis of the so-called Greek profile, which indicates nothing other than an emphasis of the more noble parts of the head over the less noble.[5]

German philosophical texts praising the Greek corporeal ideal, too, provide us with some understanding of the rationalized fantasy of the future Aryan body. They also allow us to understand that ideological amalgam that constitutes the Jewish body as a non-Greek, indeed, even non-Christian, body; on the one hand, we can discern his inaptitude for thinking and knowledge, and on the other, his exclusion from any possibility of redemption.

The Positioning of the Jewish Profile: Reversing the Signs

We can now see how, on the basis of the triumph of the orthogonal and the linear, the profile became the corporeal paradigm of the regulators of the knowable, governable universe. As result of this, a century later, the Jewish profile would become both subject to control and abhorrent. It becomes controllable, theoretically speaking, by the very virtue of the profile accorded to it. That profile attains the status of a theoretical equivalent because it relates to the double movement of writing and philosophical definition. In order for it to become abhorrent, all that had to be done was to invert the canons that had initially been idealized. The Jewish profile is first and foremost nothing but the reversal of discourse about the Greek profile. It is the perverse reversal of bodily inscription, the writing of the body in space, logos against writing. Neither of these two profiles exist any more than the other, but the imaginary world that they relate to is inseparable from the unique discourse that constitutes them, a discourse about the body as a "pin-downable" linearity that is reversible at any moment. The Jewish profile is nothing other than the dreaded opposite of the Greek profile, so that both function mutually, as though in a mirror. Specularity functions as an agent of reversal and inversion, and the inversion of signs reveals the aberration that they hide. This reversal is remarkably illustrated in a Nazi caricature: a charming young Englishwoman, nude, reads the *Times*, and in the mirror opposite her, "Times" is quite naturally transformed into "semiT." The mirror itself is broken, and her misshapen reflection can also be seen in it.

Yet everything happens in this image as though in a new version of the Narcissus story: he discovers his image, inverted. It is the image of his own alterity, and this has the effect of shattering the mirror. And, as is often the case with tales of demons and ghosts, the mirror also serves to reveal depravity—whoever has no specular image belongs to hell and the kingdom of the dead. What is remarkable in this instance, however, is that the English girl, straight, fine, beautiful, and nude, turns out to be, surprisingly, a bent, heavy, grimacing Jew, who diabolically offers her counterpart the image of her own horrifying double, fully frontal, and with a nose about which there can be no mistake. Here, it is the mirror itself that is invested with the mission of unveiling the golden calf and of smashing the deceitful idol. How better to express this duplication of the sign whose meaning, by inverting itself, is unmasked as it delivers its truth? It is the specular reversal of a graph that liberates the image into an abyss of horror.

The Face

There is, however, also a different standard that influences the orthotype. It is to be found in the Christian tradition of the Orthodox face, and it is this face that opens the path to an impossible face-to-face encounter. Here, a new reversal of signs concerns the Jewish body again: already exiled from the logos and beauty, now it must be deprived of redemption.

Besides the fantasy sequence that constitutes the Jewish body into a non-Greek body, an oblique, bent body unsuited to orthogonal inscription with a thinker's brow, another one, no less astonishing than the first, comes into being that designates it as a non-Christian body. Just as the fate of the Jewish figure cannot be understood without referring to the world of the hellenized imaginary, so any consideration of the face must be based on the dogmatic roots that established Christianity as the doctrine of a different frontality, one of the visible image, a face-to-face encounter that succeeds because it is redemptive. For this, we must turn to Byzantium, when the question of the portrayal of a Jew's face, Christ's, was first debated. How did that Jewish face come to have access to frontality? For simply by its frontality, that Jew's face is definitively abstracted from its roots. He is no longer Jewish because he is seen face-on, as an enigma. One of the Persons of the Trinity, he is *prosopon*, God's eye and brow. He shows himself frontally. It is he who passed on his Face: his Holy Face, a direct imprint, the negative of a body that was able to win the rights to the New Testament sign, hence a salvational sign, on the two-dimensional surface of a mandylion or shroud. Enveloped in its shroud, the body is inscribed there in frontal symmetry.

Christ's body is inscribed but not circumscribed. The ordinate of the Greek nose and the abscissa of the Greek earth have become the coordinates of a new graph of the divine face, trapped in the enigma of the Face. It is Paul, the first craftsman of that face, who overcame the twin impasses of Deuteronomy and the *Gorgoneion*. Deuteronomy does not allow representation, a face-to-face encounter, or the mention of God's name, and if his name is not pronounceable, it goes without saying that the homonymy on which iconicity is founded is impossible as well. Greece also did not allow an unbearable face-to-face encounter with the figure of death. The

Greek profile is therefore also tied both to averting a face-to-face encounter and mastering it by means of the graphic linearity of an inscriptive logos of word and life. The homonymic iconicity of Christianity thus inverts the signs of the Old Testament, just as it did those of Hellenism. Henceforth, not only is the face-to-face encounter possible, it is both a doctrinal obligation and the sign of the redemption.

Christ must never be represented in profile: body flat, frontal, face without shading, each line or iconic trace producing a linear miracle. This miracle is the triumphant honeymoon of the Greek profile and God's face, a profile without edges. Byzantine iconography shows this to its greatest extent, this dazzling elaboration of the tangible operation that formalizes both the face-to-face encounter in the visible and the legitimate and legitimizing pronunciation of God's name. As Olivier Clément writes:

> The icon offers us the truth of the face. . . . The forehead is broad and luminous. . . . It unites with the eyes; the luminous ridges and long, pure lines of the eyebrows converge at the root of the nose, often marked by a sort of triangle. . . . The movement of the wing-like eyebrows is extended towards the "terrestrial face" of the mouth by the line of the nose: long, thin, composed of two lines. . . . The mouth is perfectly well-defined, without heaviness but not without density, the lower lip in general being a little shorter than the upper. . . . The cheeks are spaces of silence.[6]

The technique of the icon is entirely normative, although whereas Greek anatomy corresponds to its dialectical fate, Christ's divine anatomy deals fundamentally with economic concerns. The Greek profile has a logical and ontological goal; Christ's face has a soteriological goal. Once again, the Jew is excluded.

The Prohibited Face

The Jews were not allowed to see God's face. They were also subjected to the prohibition of all representation and all homonymy, a prohibition that deprives them forever of the gaze and makes them tip over into the unpronouncability of their own name. Their regimental numbers will suffice, their lack of distinction marked with a star. Then, by a sort of new reversal, Judaism is interpreted by its opponents as being a sign of God against his own people, as expressed in their own law. In Byzantine iconography, on the other hand, the portrayal of God in profile is forbidden. Conversely, several other subjects, including some profane scenes, Old Testament figures, and demons, are portrayed in profile: the woman carrying a pitcher, and the child and ass from the fifth-century mosaic pavement in Constantinople may be taken as illustrative examples.

Other examples of this phenomenon can also be found. In last judgment scenes of the twelfth century, sinners in hell are portrayed in profile. At Nerezi in Macedonia, Jews in profile can be seen entering Jerusalem, and a Jewish woman holds a kitchen utensil at the birth of the Virgin. In this connection as well, Leonid Ouspensky criticizes as uninspired a Roman medallion from the third century with Sts. Peter and Paul in profile. A fifteenth-century icon, by contrast, in which the same saints are frontally represented, he praises because it is truthful: "Generally [the saints] are turned to face the viewer frontally, or in a three-quarter view. This trait has characterized Christian art since its birth. . . . In addressing our prayer to a saint, we must do it face to face, we must converse with him. This is doubtless the reason that saints are almost never represented in profile. . . . The profile in some way interrupts direct contact."[7]

Why, though, were the Jews subjected to this prohibition on seeing the face and representing it? The reply is categorical: because they are a naturally idolatrous people. God only imposes this categorical prohibition in order to save his people from idolatry. But this will make no difference, and they will founder in the sin of idolatry, doomed to the sacrificial fate that is the mark of the idol.

The formal advantages of the profile are thus combined with gnoses on the exchange of the gaze. The circumscribable character of the profile disappears to the benefit of a face whose marks, linearity, are at the service of the gaze, and signs are deployed that are both anthropomorphic and conventional. The doctrine that supports this advent of God's face clearly states that the inscription of his gaze is the iconic equivalent of his speech. Here is Clément again:

> The icon is not a portrait. . . . It could be said that a portrait is a meeting at the periphery, even if "realistic" appearances are still visible. . . . The icon shows the person fully realized and open. . . . This is why one of the fundamental rules of iconographic representation is frontality. An icon represents somebody face-on. . . . A profile is already an absence. Or a domination: emperors and kings had themselves represented in profile on medals and coins. We speak of those who appear in profile in the third person: he, him, the master, or not without contempt, "that one, there." But the icon introduces itself by pointing to me; it calls out to me, says "you" to me, without itself being a me who is a subject. It is rather an interiority that is both effaced and luminous, and from which the infinite can shine

forth. . . . And last but not least, the Christian face gazes and welcomes. The duality of the gaze that has become good is maintained. Silence feeds the promise of a word, while the Buddhist non-face with its eyes closed gathers its thoughts in a silence that can have no further limits.[8]

There is not much point in commenting here on the Buddhist non-face, the contemplation of which Clément finds not very welcoming; what is important in this description of the Christian face is the immediate association that he makes with naming. He interprets the two-dimensionality of the face-to-face encounter as the union of the earth and sky, and the warding off of absence. Clément also speaks for the faceless sinner, *aprosopon*; whoever does not have God has no face. He speaks, too, of Christ's *maximum* face: whoever rejects Christ has a *minimum* face. All that remains to him is the wisp of life given him by the thread or line from which his existence sways, imageless and nameless, deprived of the gaze.

Psychoanalysis would be able to follow the imaginary development of the forbidden, wicked body step by step, and to explain its archaic roots quite clearly. Everything that has been said here about the impossible image of the Jew deprived of essential similitude could also be restated in terms of the pure and the impure. The Jew is a dividing spirit who can never mix the sacred and the profane together. His whole ritual consists in avoiding mixture and preserving what is holy from any contaminating contact and contagion. The things of this world to which he is said to be so passionately attached consequently become the sign of his true attachment to idolatry and the devil. A man of division, he cannot reconcile temporal interests with spiritual benefits. I would argue that it is most important today to link the dreadful construction of the Jewish body not to an unconscious, regressive will or animal fear, but on the contrary, to an ideological system powerfully formulated by the foundational authorities and institutions of the West: Greek thought and Christian vocabulary. It is certainly clear that both made unrestrained use of the frissons of horror aroused by a fear of bestiality and death. Thus it came about that the image of a body that had lost its rights in the name of humanity and in the gaze of God was created, using the most seemingly coarse methods.

We thus catch a glimpse of just what the image of the Jewish body was, and there was certainly nothing simple about it. We also see that it can only be understood on the basis of another imaginary body partly identified with the church, and partly with Reason. Although Nazi imagery in its most repugnant form is no longer explicitly widespread today, the underhanded and devastating hegemony of "ideal" images of the body spread by the different media still attacks us relentlessly, and in a universe filled with canons threatens the intimate perception that each of us has of ourselves. In 1993, while in Cracow to make a film about the ghetto, Steven Spielberg had a notice posted recruiting "extras with a Jewish profile." The reconstruction of the scene must have been convincing indeed, because, as *Le Monde* recounted the story, the producer shouted at the exhausted, frozen extras, "Who let these people out of the camp? Get back to your places immediately! From now on, the guards will lock the camp gates."[9] It can only be hoped that America the Redemptive will be able to provide American Jews with a harmonious body finally worthy of immunity and salvation.

Organized repulsion today stamps the paths of a standardized idealization and an aesthetic aimed at global forms of seduction. Far from the heterogenous forms that the essential similitude of the image tolerated, the exhibition of flawless bodies deprives us of the enigma of the flesh. *Visibility has taken the place of the image*, to the point of breaking the mirror in which those who were refused a gaze dared to look at themselves. The mirror is nothing more than a mimetic agent. Responsible for resemblance, it also kills similitude. In this way, resemblance becomes, paradoxically, a weapon of discrimination: not bearing resemblance can be a crime, and consensual thought comes to haunt uniform bodies.

Thus has the imaginal economy completely sunk beneath the industry of visibilities. But have we forgotten that it is in the mercantile belly of collective narcissism that the sordid beast has always laid its first eggs?

Conclusion

When one is still in the process of thinking through an issue, it always feels artificial, or even presumptuous, to end on a definite note, to close off the subject. This is all the more true here, because this study was conceived in the form of an open meditation, an ongoing questioning. This applies as much to the subject we have been examining as to the current, singular condition of the image. I had rather wanted to speak about the current condition of the visible, which ceaselessly demands that we reflect on what there is of the image in it at the heart of a world submerged by techniques of visualization. The image never allows itself to be fully grasped. There is always an uncircumscribability within it that the church fathers continually claimed was at the heart of the very inscription of the visible. What they religiously described as invisible is undoubtedly that enigmatic resistance to any closure. We will never succeed in subjugating it; in this sense, it shines like the figure of liberty. The extraordinary theoretical virtuosity of the first great thinkers about the image is to have tied this living insubordination of the image so closely to the visible inscription of temporal power, thanks to the concept of the economy. This was so successfully carried out that through iconicity a double-sided object was formed, a Janus of both liberty and despotism. Visibilities became the means to subjugate, and in many cases the wars prosecuted against idolatry were inspired by the sole concern of choking off the turbulent insubordination of troublesome or vanquished visibilities. The question that must be posed today is this: in the rising tide of things to see, what image will we be left with on the shore when it retreats? Where is that rebel who will be the embodiment of our current freedom?

Astonishingly, those who are delighted by this state of affairs are tempted to believe, and to have us believe, that what we see on the screen has the right to the name of image. The technical ability and digital precision that underpin these visual effects are almost enough to convince us that, from now on, a faultless image will produce a true image. By the same stroke, the screen becomes the site where the simulacrum of the truth is displayed. And to go into ecstasy about resemblance and simulation! Nothing is stranger to the image than this perfect intelligibility of a model that unreservedly gives itself up to iconicity. This equivalence of the visible to its model makes us believe in the equivalence of vision to the gaze, creating triumphant intoxication and anguish by turn concerning the loss of the sense of self. But inventions born of a *desire to see* should not be confused with scenes motivated by the *desire to show.* A nonenigmatic display can harbor no invisibility other than that of the procedures that produced it. It is only a trick of the professional magician, with the pleasure of the spectacle being shared between the spectator's belief and the complete power of the ringmaster showman; the issue is therefore one that concerns the relationship that ties belief to power. We have already seen the way this plays out in a secular context. The system is ecclesiastic, even if the church no longer has a monopoly over it. But it was the church that provided the model.

Against the new clergy of this economy of the visible, there arises a group of people who would like to return its enigma to it. Yet they find themselves reduced to the old standby, produced whenever a worldview is rejected, of crying idolatry. That, however, is a regressive reaction that will never be able to enrich our icons, to give them the free, creative dynamism that they need. It is even possible that this iconic inflation may also bring about a profound reevaluation of speech itself and of real contact.

The object of our inquiry has been the image, but we have been reduced to knowing it only in its perceptible manifestations, that is to say, in terms of whether its enigma is maintained or betrayed; always at a distance from the visible, it is also inscribed in our carnal reality. The image is inseparable from the incarnation, whereas simulacra make us doubt the flesh and deprive us by the same stroke of our mortality and our liberty. Visual communion, by contrast, is truly an incorporation.

What makes the image enigmatic is its absence of mystery. The invisibility within it is not hidden; on the contrary, it shows itself. Its enigma is not a secret; it does not rest on any hidden or private knowledge. It is the enigma of all living flesh haunted by the voice. That voice articulates the manifestation of what the very desire to see, in and of itself, produces: desire.

Christian thought has the major distinction of having provided a formulation for the linkage between our carnal intimacy and the imaginal voice, and therefore the world of the imaginary as well, for the very first time. But that is not its only merit: by the same stroke, it also produced a globalizing system for the administration and management of visible artefacts. The spiritual and political ambivalence of the iconic economy is not a perverse effect of that doctrine, but an intrinsic consequence of our relation to the visible. The reign established on the truth of the image cannot, in any way, be a reign of ontological truth. Truth is an image: there is no image of truth.

An economy of resemblance can only be based on the concept of a nonmimetic invisibility of similitude. This does not mean that it is an empty concept; rather, it is a concept of the image that requires an emptiness at the heart of visibility. Real resemblances are only ever relative to imaginary similitude and never its duplicate. The flood of modern visibilities and the most sophisticated technologies of simulation are still only the most naive tricks of duplication and substitution. Nonetheless, the financial and political power that these tricks mobilize turns them into lethal weapons arrayed against the world of the imaginary itself, as long as those apparitions empty us of our flesh instead of incarnating the emptiness that would allow our own image to arise. For some time at least, the desire to show and subjugate will prevail over respect for the desire to see and the requirement to incarnate. Perhaps it is there that the ethical question in the management of the visible lies.

What is the Christian church doing today in relation to the management of the iconic question, that is to say, of worldly visibilities? How can it remain faithful to the incarnational economy without thereby depriving itself of an instrument for spreading its message? For worldwide subjugation was always its primary concern. To be interested in ecclesiastic thought does not necessarily mean agreeing with the anxieties of the faithful or the concerns of the prelate, but rather rediscovering in the vocabulary of their questions and the economy of their reasoning a problem common to the entire world covered by the media. The church perfectly understood that whoever monopolizes visibility conquers thought itself and determines the shape of liberty. From the specific standpoint of provoking belief or obtaining obedience, there are no great differences between submitting to a church council or to CNN. Yet while CNN deploys its weapons through the obvious monopoly of its news and with the clear determination to dominate, the church continues to hold forth about the incarnation and the living enigma of the image. It is not looking for the simple effect of credulity, even if it is sometimes content with it; rather, it spreads its charisma liturgically, although it is a charisma in which faith is distinct from belief. Yet for several centuries, it has simultaneously managed both faith and belief. The producers of visibilities are themselves only interested in our belief, our powerful adherences, our consensus. The church still maintains a double discourse of spirituality and conquest. Overflowing with those who have followed it too closely for more than a thousand years, it can only fear losses on the same terrain where it had previously won it all. Will it have to remain faithful to its message, or will it adapt to a world that dictates new conditions of supremacy to it? Wanting to remain faithful to the desire to make manifest an enigma, it cannot resolve itself to abandoning the benefits of the visible. Parousia or spectacle? Communion or communication? The ecclesiastic economy thus faces a major problem whose formulation and solution concern the entire human race, whether Christian or not. What becomes of human bodies, of their participation in an imaginary life of similitude, what becomes of their desire to see, and in what place can they still constitute a face for themselves to make manifest their intimate and existential resistance to large-scale resemblance? In a world of simulation, what does our flesh become? What can we resemble? What appearance of ourselves are the screens screening? We saw earlier that the incarnation is not the materialization of thought, but on the contrary, the transfiguration of the flesh that gives substance to the imagination. Long ago, ghosts were figures of death; from now on, ghosts will form the flesh of the living. If the pope can bless one of the faithful on his knees in front of the television set, if the eucharist can radiate its grace simply by digitizing or cloning the image of an officiant, it is because the whole of our world has tipped over into a new worldwide Docetism. The era of simulacra has taken the place of the era of the image, of icons, and the word, all of which were originally indistinguishable from each other.

Between the praise of those who believe without seeing and the celebration of those who docilely adhere to everything that they see, everything that they are shown, Christian thought finds itself in the difficult situation of having to renounce either its message or its authority. This is a purely economic problem that the hierarchy will undoubtedly be able to resolve through encyclicals and pastoral warnings, just as it did a thousand years ago when it became necessary to negotiate between doctrinal rigor and the imperatives of reality. Our concern does not lie there. It relates, rather, to meeting our philosophical responsibility within the doctrinal edifice that has shaped our world, which consists in thinking through, at the very heart of visual tyranny, the management and administration of our incarnation and the vitality of our desire for the image. Can we ever emerge from the traditional network of the imaginal economy? The example of the Jewish face demonstrates that as long as one is within that economy, any distance from it is paid for at the cost of a massacre. The enemy of dominant visibilities is always expelled and sent to the camp of idolaters and idols destined for ritual sacrifice. *Have we not theatrically described as "holocaust" something that should only be labeled a crime, something that should never be allowed to evoke the sacred?* The collective unconscious remains subjugated to the reign of iconicity.

There is a great temptation in situations such as this to return to nature and to attempt to bring about in the domain of the image what ecology dreams of doing to save the planet. It is in this sense that I have spoken from the outset of an abrupt return to iconicity under the auspices of a return to an imaginal and redemptive truth, a sort of ecology of the image that would come to take over from the economy, or that would occupy the same conceptual terrain that the "spiritual" did at the turn of this century. Humanity will return to its similitude in the same way that the earth will be given back to humans, the forest to the trees, and the sea to the fish: an era of decontamination and global moralization conceived as the salvational hygiene of a return. Nature and icon will once again become a universal language, not without paschal tonalities. That, however, is the worst of the ideological consequences of the disarray engendered by the panicked despondency of philosophical thought. When the world changes, it must carry thought along with it; thought must follow the world and give it its living intelligibility. It must reformulate both its enigma and its meaning. Nikephoros interests me because, finding himself in the same situation, he threw himself into a struggle with his own system of thought at an inopportune moment. He created his object, he fashioned his enemy, he struggled with language and concepts. In his eyes, the imaginary power of the visible was under threat. The world's thought, and the world along with it, were at risk of disappearing. He feared for life as a whole more than for his own, and his motivation was passionate.

The imaginary annihilation of the realm of the visible can only relaunch the existential claims of the word more violently than ever; it is that which guarantees the presence of the enigma, or in other words, it is that which inspires the shape of new invisibilities in the visible. At present, everything can be seen, and the whole world devotes itself to itself as spectacle. In this new space, however, it is incumbent on thinkers and creators alike to devote themselves to fostering the emergence of sites where the image can curl up and await us to show itself. It is up to us to compose ourselves for the new face-to-face encounter, up to us to be done with belief and its "holocausts."

Extracts from the Iconoclast Horos *of Hieria*

[221 C–D] The aforesaid creator of evil, not wishing to see her [the church] being comely, did not refrain from using at different times different means of wicked ingenuity in order to subdue the human race to his power; thus, with the pretext of Christianity, he reintroduced idolatry unnoticeably by convincing, with his subtleties, those who had their eyes turned to him not to relinquish the creation but rather to adore it, and pay respect to it, and consider that which is made as God, calling it with the name "Christ."

[225 D] For this reason, therefore, Jesus, the author and agent of our salvation, as in the past he had sent forth his most wise disciples and apostles with the power of the most Holy Spirit in order to eliminate completely all these idols, so also now he raised his devotees, our faithful kings—the ones comparable to the Apostles, who have become wise by the power of the same Spirit—in order to equip and teach us, as well as to abolish the demonic fortifications which resist the knowledge of God,[1] and to refute diabolic cunning and error.[2]

[245 D] We considered it, therefore, right to demonstrate in detail, through our present definition [*horos*], the error of those who make and those who pay respect to the icons.[3]

[248 E] What is this senseless contrition on the part of the painter of caricatures[4] who, for the sake of cheap profiteering, has occupied himself in doing something that cannot be done, that is, with profane hands giving form to things that are believed with the heart and confessed with the mouth?[5]

[252 A–B] For he has made an icon that he has called "Christ."[6] But "Christ" is a name [indicative] of God as well as man; from which it follows that the icon must be an icon of God as well as man. Consequently, along with describing created flesh, he has either circumscribed the uncircumscribable character of the Godhead, according to what has seemed good to his own worthlessness, or he has confused that unconfused union, falling into the iniquity of confusion. Thus, in two ways, with the circumscription [*périgraphè*] and the confusion [*synkhysis*], he has blasphemed the Godhead. The one who has venerated them [the icons] is also responsible for the same blasphemies. Both [he who paints and he who venerates] are equally to be condemned because they have fallen into error along with Arius, Dioscorus, and Eutyches, and into the heresy of the Acephaloi.

[260 A] From those, therefore, who think that they are drawing the icon of Christ, it must be gathered either that the divinity is circumscribable and confused with the flesh or that the body of Christ was without divinity and divided; and also that they ascribe to the flesh a person with a hypostasis of his own—thus, in this respect, identifying themselves with the Nestorian fight against God.

[260 B] Those, therefore, who make, and those who desire, and those who pay respect[7] to the icon of Christ, which falsely is made and called so by them, should feel ashamed and embarrassed, and should be reproached for falling into such an impiety and blasphemy. Let them be far from us—Nestorius' division and Arius', Dioscorus', Eutyche's, and Severus' confusion—two evils diametrically opposite to each other, but equal in impiety.

[261 E] Let those who enact, desire, and respect the true [*apseudès*: nondeceiving] icon of Christ with a most honest heart, and who offer themselves to salvation, both soul and body, rejoice, exalt, and become outspoken. It is the celebrant himself and God who, when he assumed from us our entire composition, handed this [icon] down to his initiates, at the time of his voluntary passion, in place of [himself] and as a most visible remembrance [of him]. For, when he was about to offer himself voluntarily to his ever memorable and life-giving death, taking the bread, he blessed it, and, after he gave thanks, he broke it, and passing it on, he said: "Take, eat, for the remission of sins; this is my body." Similarly, passing on the cup, he said: "This is my blood; do this in remembrance of me."[8] He did so because there was no other kind or visible form under the sun selected by him which could depict his incarnation. Here is, therefore, the icon of his body, the giver of life, which is enacted honestly and which has the right to be honored. For what else did the all-wise God want to achieve through this? Nothing else but to show, to make abundantly evident to us, the mystery accomplished in his economy. That is, in the same way as that which he assumed from us is a mere matter of human substance, perfect in every respect, which, however, is not characterized as a Person with a hypostasis of its own—in this way no addition of a Person may occur in the Godhead—so did he command [264 B] that the icon also be matter as such; that is, he commanded that the substance of bread be offered that does not yield the shape of a man's form, so that idolatry may not be introduced indirectly. Therefore, as the natural body of Christ is holy, as it has been deified, so, obviously, is the one which is in its place [by convention]; that is, his icon is also holy as one which becomes deified by grace, through an act of consecration.[9] For this is what the Lord Christ specified, as we have said; so that, in the same way that he deified the flesh which he assumed by the union of it with the sanctity of his own nature, so did he the bread of the eucharist. He consented that this become a holy body—as a true [nondeceiving] icon of the natural flesh—consecrated by the descent of the Holy Spirit and through the mediation of the priest who makes the offer in order that the bread be transferred from the state of being common to that of being holy. Thus, the physical and cogitating flesh of the Lord was anointed with divinity through the Holy Spirit. Similarly also, the icon of his flesh, handed down by God, the divine bread along with the cup of his life-giving blood from his side, was filled with the Holy Spirit. This is, therefore, the icon that has been proven to be the true icon of the incarnate economy of Christ our God, as it has been stated before; and it is this one that the true Creator of the life of the world has handed down to us with his own words.

[268 B] The ill name of the falsely called "icon" neither has its existence [268 C] in the tradition of Christ, or the apostles, or the church fathers, nor is there any prayer of consecration for it to transpose it from the state of being common to the state of being sacred. Instead, it remains common and worthless, as the painter made it.

[277 C] How do they also dare to depict through the vulgar art of the pagans the all-praised mother of God, upon whom the fullness of the Godhead[10] cast his shadow and through whom the inaccessible light did shine on us—she who is higher than the heavens and holier than the cherubim? Or again, those who will reign[11] with Christ and sit along with him to judge the world,[12] and who will be as glorious as he[13] of whom, as the Word says, the world was not worthy?[14] Are they not ashamed to depict them through a pagan art? For it is not lawful for Christians, who have their hope in the resurrection, to use the customs of nations that worship demons, and to treat so spitefully, by means of worthless and dead matter, the saints who will be resplendent with such glory.

[324 C–E] Having been constituted firmly by these blessed scriptures inspired by God, and by the church fathers, and having fixed our feet with certainty on the stone of worshipping in spirit and in truth, we all, who have been vested with the office of the priesthood, having reached one opinion, we decree unanimously, in the name of the holy and supersubstantial Trinity, the principle of life, that every icon, made of any matter and of any kind of gaudiness of colors by painters, is objectionable, alien, and repugnant to the church of the Christians.

[328 B–C] No man should ever attempt to occupy himself with such an impious and unholy endeavor. He who from now on attempts to make an icon, or to venerate one, or to set one up in a church or in a private home, or to hide one, if [he be] bishop, presbyter, or deacon, let him be unfrocked; if monk or layman, let him be anathematized and subjected to the royal laws, as an opponent of the commandments of God and an enemy of the doctrines of the church fathers.

[336 E] If anyone endeavors, through material colors, to understand the divine impress of God the Word according to his incarnation, and not to offer adoration to him—who is beyond the brightness of the sun and is seated at the right side of God in the highest on a throne of glory—with his spiritual eyes and with all his heart, let him be anathema.

[337 C] If anyone endeavors to circumscribe with material colors in icons, in an anthropomorphic way, the uncircumscribable essence and hypostasis of God the Word, because of the incarnation, and not to predicate him as God—being not less uncircumscribable, even after the incarnation—let him be anathema.

[340 C] If anyone attempts to paint in an icon the undivided hypostatic union of the nature of God the Word along with that of the flesh—which two resulted in one, which is unconfused and undivided—calling this "Christ," while the name Christ implies God and man, and as a result of this one proclaims absurdly a confusion of the two natures, let him be anathema.

[341 A] If anyone sets aside the flesh that was united with the hypostasis of God the Word, thinking of it as mere flesh, and consequently, endeavors to describe it in an icon, let him be anathema.

[341 C] If anyone divides the one Christ into two hypostases, placing in one part the Word of God and in the other the Son of the Virgin Mary, and if he does not confess that there is one and the same Christ, but rather that there was only a nominal union between them, and if he consequently describes in an icon the Son of the Virgin, as if this had a hypostasis of its own, let him be anathema.

[341 E] If anyone depicts in an icon the flesh that was deified by the union with the divine Logos, let him be anathema, because he separates the flesh from the divinity that assumed and deified it, and as a consequence he renders it undeified.

[344 C] If anyone attempts to reform with material colors God the Word, who though he was in the form of God took upon his own hypostasis the form of a servant, and became like us in every respect, without sin, for being supposedly a mere man, and if one separates him from the inseparable and unchangeable divinity—this way introducing a fourth Person in the Holy Trinity, the principle of life—let him be anathema.

[345 A–B] If anyone does not acknowledge that the ever-virgin Mary is indeed and truly the mother of God, and that she is exalted above any creature, visible and invisible, and if he does not entreat her intercession with sincere faith, as having audience with our God to whom she gave birth, let him be anathema.

[345 C] If anyone endeavors to reinstate the effigies of the saints in inanimate and speechless icons made of material colors, which bring no benefit—for the idea [of the icon] is vain and an invention of diabolic cunning—and does not rather reproduce in himself their virtues through what has been written about them in books, like animate icons, consequently to incite in himself the zeal to become like them, as our church fathers inspired by God have said, let him be anathema.

Extracts from the Antirrhetics, *by Nikephoros, Patriarch of Constantinople*

[225 A] So the Iconoclast adds immediately: "and if the icon is good, it is consubstantial with what it is the icon of."[1] Therefore, you do not simply object that an image is made of Christ, but [you object] [225 B] that the iconic copy is heterogenous to him, because Christ is one thing and the material out of which his icon is made is another. Is it not ridiculous to focus on this? Because not even second-rate actors, or those entertainers that people strike on the head to make fun of would have talked such nonsense. But he, in the Bacchic drunkenness of an unbeliever, and being mad by the power of impiety, did say such things. But this is extreme sophistry and everything that has been done by him is in vain. Yet there are some who have reached such a degree of ignorance and irrationality that they think that they have observed something interesting in it. Therefore, it is necessary for us to examine things that are really unnecessary. Indeed, what is more irrational or [225 C] more unintelligible than the things that have been said? For they are not from a man who respects logical coherence. If his intention were the natural image, which is absolutely opposed to the artificial image [icon], and I mean the Son who is the image of the Father, his argument might have been tenable. He has failed, though, by using the copy here in an unintelligent way, because there is no need here for copies nor for objects to be aimed at by our sight. This is not the place to talk about copies: this is more unintelligible and more impious than that. He explicitly appears to make his argument starting from strange and irreconcilable premises.

Now, because his argument is about copies and artificial images, which consist of [225 D] the material base, and the technique and the talent of the artisan, who among sensible people will tolerate hearing him saying that the copy and the icon are consubstantial with the prototype? First, he is mistaken in regarding as one and the same thing essence and art, which differ from each another considerably. Indeed, the creator and the craftsman of all things, God, brought nature from nonbeing into being. Art imitates nature without the former being identical to the latter. On the contrary, having taken the natural, visible form as a model and as a prototype, art makes something similar and alike, as is possible to see in most artworks. But then he is diverted away from plausible reason when he asserts in his definition that the animate does not differ at all from the inanimate, that their essence is identical. [228 A] Thus, because man, for example, is animate, so must his icon also be animate, and so must his copy. Both the colors and the remaining inanimate material from which the icon has been made must have exactly the same nature as man. It would be necessary, then, according to this argument, that the man and his icon share the same definition and be related to each other as consubstantial things. So, just as a man falls under the same definition as another man, so does the copy. And if man is a rational animal, mortal, capable of intelligence and knowledge, then the icon will be a rational animal, mortal, and in a similar way capable of intelligence and knowledge without the slightest difference. But it is impossible that what only resembles something else can entirely reach the whole truth of the model. This is confirmed by truth itself and also by the best theologians.[2] Truthful discourse knows that man himself differs from himself, for he is composed of heterogeneous natures, by which I mean the soul and the body, [228 B] even if the man composed of those two elements is one and the same. Each of these elements has its own proper definition. The definition of the soul differs from that of the body, and each of them has its own differences and accidents. For we are composite, but we are also opposite to ourselves and also to one another. But he believes that copies do not differ in anything at all from the models that they are the copies of, and that the identity of nature and substance between elements that share only resemblance is purely maintained. But how could someone distinguish the image from the copy if there is no difference between them, resulting from their different natures? He has therefore been completely separated from the truth, this wisest man of all, and he has failed greatly in his understanding of reality. It is worthwhile to say to him: "It has escaped your notice, you, the greatest philosopher, [228 C] that here you are caught in your own arguments." Indeed, according to you, insofar as the image must be consubstantial with the prototype, and insofar as you yourself will agree in every way that the image is circumscribable (for none would be as mad as to argue that this is not the case), then you will agree that the prototype must be circumscribable, because it is consubstantial with the image. For it is absolutely not possible that consubstantial things differ from one another as far as the principle of substance is concerned, unless you yourself subsume both the circumscribable and the uncircumscribable under the principle of substance. So, if you maintain the principles of your doctrine, your contrivance is ruined and your arguments are thrown to the ground, mercilessly overthrown by the slingshot and weapons of truth. Indeed, it would have to be the case that the disciples [228 D] who have emerged today from teachers like these are similar to them. "The crops are similar to the soil from which they emerge; the worst come from bad soil, and the foulest come from foul soil."

Having still the same ideas, or to put it better, the same madness, he says: "in order to save the totality, there must be no icon."[3] All these result from his insanity and his stupidity. Indeed, those who have sane minds and who maintain coherence and congruity in their words will argue, rather, the opposite—that if the totality is saved, it is not the icon but what is itself depicted in the icon [that is saved]. [The icon and its model's] identity is only manifest in the visible form, not in their underlying substance. It is assumed by him that if the icon is not animate and does not move itself, [229 A] and if it does not have all the attributes of its archetype, it cannot be an icon. If all these attributes do not belong to the icon, then for him the raison d'être of the icon is altogether lost. What then is the consequence? It follows that one and the same thing is at the same time both one and two, but also that icons and archetypes find themselves identified with each other, and that the icon resembles the archetype and, inversely, the archetype resembles the icon. As if, for example, when talking about a man, it were said not that his icon resembles him but that he resembles his icon. It is as though even if the existing relationship between the icon and the archetype were reversed, their relationship would remain the same and unchangeable, and it could be said that not only is there an icon of a man, but also that there is a man of an icon. On this premise, from this point on, one could wonder which of the two is the cause of the other and antecedent to the other. All these clearly prove his intelligence! [229 B] Do such inventions not result from a dishonest and misled mind? Such a risk he took of being so inattentive to the true nature of things and of inhabiting places so far from the truth. These [inventions] are not better than the rambling tales sung by drunken old women in the *gynaecium*,[4] in endless verses.

[277 A] It is clear to those who are sober that it is possible to say, with respect to the topic under discussion, that the archetype is the principle and the model underlying the visible form that is made from it, as well as the cause from which the resemblance derives. This is the definition of the icon such that one could use it for all artificial icons: an icon is a likeness of the archetype, and on it is stamped, by means of its resemblance, the whole of the visible form of what it is a likeness of, and it is distinct from its model only in terms of a different essence because of its material. Or [another definition]: an icon is an imitation of the archetype and a copy differing [from the model] in its essence and in its underlying substance. Or [it is] a product of art portraying the visible form of the archetype by imitating it, but it differs from the model in its essence and its underlying substance. Indeed, if the icon does not differ in anything [from the archetype], then it is not an icon, but nothing other than the archetype itself. Thus the icon is a likeness and a replica of beings who have their own existence.

[277 B] But the idol is the formation of nonexistent and insubstantial things, forms that the Hellenes, because of their stupidity and atheism, invented, such as tritons, centaurs, and other nonexistent phantoms. This is why the icon and the idol differ from each other, so that those who do not accept the difference between them could justly be called idolaters. But icons can be icons of both good and bad people, and so the honor that is due to them is variable. The icons of the good are to be honored, but those of bad people are to be dismissed and to be avoided as much as idols, above all, those which some ancients, immersed in evil and atheism, venerated impiously, [277 C] failing to recognize the God of the universe and the primary cause. Such is the result of the obsession of those addicted to their passions and to material things, and it is also the result of the tyranny that transgresses the institutional limits of the honor that he deserves.[5] This is why one cannot use the word *idol* for a good icon, because that term is specifically reserved for the pagan cult rendered to demons through sacrifices, as the Apostle says.[6]

It is not inopportune now, I think, to add to my speech that the icon is related to the archetype and that it is the effect of a cause. Therefore, it is necessary that the icon both be one of these relatives and be called such. The relatives, these very same things, depend on things other than themselves and change their relationships reciprocally.[7] [277 D] For example, the father is called the father of his son, and inversely, the son is called the son of his father. In a similar way we can talk about the friend of a friend, and about the right of the left, and, inversely, about the left of the right. Similarly, the master is the master of the slave and inversely, and the same can be applied to all similar cases. Anyone who asserts that the icon does not concern a relation could no longer assert that it is an icon of something. The icon and the archetype are introduced and are considered simultaneously, the one with the other. Even if the archetype is absent, the relation does not in the least cease to exist.

[280 A] Indeed, the principle of the simultaneous abolition of the terms of the relationship does not apply to all such cases. There are times, indeed, when relationships are maintained unchanged, even when they are torn away from and deprived of the real terms of that relation, as in the case of the father and son, and in similar relations. Making visible, as if it were present, what is absent through similitude and memory of the outward form, the icon preserves the relationship with its model, which is extended in time. Consequently, then, the resemblance is a kind of middle relation that mediates between the extreme terms: I mean the thing resembled and what resembles it, uniting them by the visible form and relating them, even if the terms are different in nature. For one of them is "one thing" and the other is "another thing" in nature.[8] But we cannot talk about one person and another person, because [only] the model itself is one (other) person. Indeed, the knowledge of the primary visible form emerges by means of the graphic impression, and [280 B] the hypostasis of the inscribed person can be seen in this impression.[9] This is the very thing that is not possible to see in some other cases, as in that of the father, the son, or the friend. Exactly the opposite happens here, for it is not one thing here and another there, because they participate in the same essence. But there is one person here and another person there, each having different hypostases. If, then, the relationship between the terms of the preceding examples does not completely vanish, the relationship between [the icon and its model] will be maintained to a far greater extent. Moreover, the resemblance confers homonymy [on them]. The name is one and the same for both [the icon and the model]. The icon of the king is called "the king." The icon could say: "the king and I are one thing," despite the evident fact that they are different in essence. We have said these [things] in order to demonstrate the way in which the image, which is considered together with the archetype, is related to it. [280 C] Neither has the image acquired the same identity as the archetype in terms of its essence, nor are the properties that are attributed to the archetype said to belong to the icon. It is not the case, anyway, that attributes that belong to the icon can be attributed to the archetype. Indeed, the model may be animate, but the icon is inanimate. The model may be rational and able to move, but the icon is without reason and motionless. Consequently, these two are not identical, but they resemble each other in their visible form and differ from each other in essence. It is because the icon is one of the relatives that it is glorified jointly with the glorified model, and, inversely, why it is dishonored along with the dishonored model. Thus, once the difference between them has become known by means of reason and of definition, and because inscription [*graphê*] shows the external form and does not participate in the least in the definition of essence, then why are our adversaries so vainly agitated, preaching that things that are naturally united are separated here? They will be justly considered as mad and deranged.

[280 D] And it is necessary to say where the term *icon* derives from and how it was formed according to its etymology, we say that it comes from the verb *eikô*, which has other meanings, but properly means: "I am similar." Thus, the letter "n" is added to the verb *eikô*, resulting in the word *eikon*, which signifies likeness. That is why the enemies of truth treat [the icon] that resembles Christ spitefully. From this verb, exactly from one principle and one root, the verb *eoike* is formed, which itself means "to be (or to make) similar." [281 A] Because this is the case, who among the knowledgeable is not aware of the fact that the icon of Christ is different from Christ himself? Only that "wisest" of all men, ignoring things that everybody knows, who follows his own personal impulses and personal instructors; but if he had the least sense of conventional propriety, he should venerate and embrace this icon of Christ, at least on account of the relationship that Christ's icon has with the archetype, if for no other reasons. It seems clear, then, that his impiety and his ignorance make him not only tolerate, but also proclaim, such absurdities. In fact, it would be necessary to use the terms *similar* and *dissimilar*, which are included in what we have said, and which relate to the category of quality, as those who have devoted themselves to learning about these matters would say; and from that position, [281 B] he would be able to express his arguments on this subject. Instead, however, he introduces identity, which is yoked together with alterity and which is considered in terms of the essence. But none of these is necessary to demonstrate what has preceded it. It seems to me that he does not talk about the alterity of things, which distinguishes between different natures, but introduces the alterity of persons. Because he emphasizes the hypostases (according to which one person is distinguished from another), he will necessarily have to give many hypostases, and there will be as many Christs as there are icons. And so the sons will be multiplied, and the name Only-begotten will be removed. How should one feel about these arguments: criticize them for their impiety—or, rather, laugh at their folly?

[313 A] Because he talks triflingly and repeats what has been said, we too intend to talk triflingly with him about his own proposals. And because he repeats the same arguments on the same topics, so we too will again make the same objections to him. The case is as follows: according to him, "How can we give the name of both God and man to the icon, [this name] which designates both the divine and human nature, because the icon can portray only the human nature and not the divine and incomprehensible one?"[10] This "how"—to converse with you as if you were here, if the ears of your soul had not grown deaf, if the eyes of your soul were not blinded, if your mental faculties were not corrupted, if your rationality were not perverted, if you preserved the limits of religiousness intact, if you maintained the tradition of the catholic church unblemished, [313 B] if you retained at least some spark of faith within your heart and were not enraged against our blameless and impeccable confession, persuaded by those who lead you towards the precipice of faithlessness and ruin—this how would be demonstrated to you in the most obvious way, if there were really such a query, and if it were not rather kept only as a means of trickery or crafty dishonesty.

Thus, in order to take up the same arguments on the same questions again, as the crucifixion and the passion and the tomb and all the rest (in order not to be prolix, violating reasonable limits, and in order not to wear out the ears of the audience) are said to be Christ's, we do not say in any way like you that, [313 C] because of the fact that the name of Christ designates the duality of [his] natures, what is attributed to one nature must be always attributed to the other. The cross can torture only the human nature, yet it is called "the cross of Christ." Let the one who says the following convince you: "May I never boast of anything except the cross of our Lord Jesus Christ."[11] Circumcision can divide human flesh, and the tomb can circumscribe this same flesh, enclose it, and keep it hidden from sight, but all these things are said to be Christ's. Nevertheless, none of them will be properly and essentially said about the divine and ineffable nature, for this divine nature is pure and impassive, and completely free [313 D] from any such concept whatsoever. If such a thing is apparently said, it is said either in the way of reciprocity or appropriation, something with which you do not agree now, because you ignore it altogether. But it is said that Christ suffered the passion not as God but as a human being, even though he is one and the same, united as far as hypostasis is concerned. Thus, because the body, which he took from us, is called Christ's body, in which body it is believed that he suffered all [this passion], and because this body had absolutely and in every way a precise form (it could not be without form, because then it would not be a body), it is necessary that both the form of the body and the resemblance be called Christ's. [316 A] As indeed that body is Christ's own body, so it does not have any relation with the nature of the Word, about which we know that it is without visible form, has no relation and no configuration, but [it is related] to the body of the Word, the human nature and its visible form itself, from which Christ is composed. That is why the figure is designated with the homonym, manifesting itself according to its resemblance to the prototype.

But the name taken by Christ, which demonstrates that there exist two natures, urged you on to swell up and to boast about your doctrines, and to believe that neither of the two natures that this name manifests can be expressed by name without the other, in whatever practice or doctrine, or in whatever way it is used, or that if the one is isolated from the other, they are separated completely. How do we respond to this? At this point it could be proposed to you that Christ is called only a simple man or only the son of a human, [316 B] so he could be designated with a simple name. But if you do not believe in anyone else, you could (if you wish, of course) at least believe in Christ himself when he said to the Jewish people: "Why are you trying to kill me, a man who has told you the truth?"[12] and also, "Unless you eat the flesh of the Son of Man,"[13] and "Now the Son of Man will be glorified,"[14] and "The Son of Man is going to be betrayed,"[15] and also "For the Son of Man came to seek out and to save the lost,"[16] and finally, "They called him the Son of David."[17] And many phrases similar to these can be found in the Gospels, if, of course, you do not consider the words of the Gospels childish and mere nonsense.

Thus, because what is designated with the simplicity of a name given to a man is not one double thing but one singular thing, as is the case with the name *Christ* [316 C] (because this word designates to us only one nature, the human one), what will happen to you next, and what will you add as something new and great and admirable? Being an adversary of

Christ even more than of his name, you are allowed to preach that the Lord is only a common man and one of us, something that you have done zealously both in the past and now, and that that man was accused and tried in a court of justice, that he suffered the tortures of criminals and was condemned to violent death. And I deliberately omit the rest for fear of blasphemy. You might say that that man is also a God. Thus the problem has been solved, because that God is also a man. But if, on the contrary, when you hear only God being mentioned—"In the beginning [316 D] was the Word, and the Word was with God, and the Word was God,"[18] and "We saw his glory, the glory that he has from the Father,"[19] and "just as the Father raises the dead and gives them life, so also the Son gives life to whomever he whishes,"[20] and "Father, glorify your Son, so that your Son may glorify you,"[21] and "The Father and I are one,"[22] and to the one who was born blind this is said: "Do you believe in the son of God?"[23] and other similar things to this—[if] you understand God [in all this] only as deprived of our [human] essence, you also deprive him completely of the body and you take away from him everything human. Therefore, clearly, you are allowed to get rid of the entire economy.

[428 C] In view of the contentiousness and shamelessness of these fools, we consider that it is necessary to examine those points in a more elaborate way. Without conferring any dishonor on anything [neither the icon nor the cross] and as results from the examination of the following, we shall prove in a short time and in a particular way that is preeminent between them. So in order to start from the [issue of] resemblance, because the icon is also this, we say that:

1. The icon of Christ is a likeness of him, and it resembles his body, and it sketches out for us the form of his body, and it provides the visible form and it expresses clearly by imitation quite often the mode of his action, of his teaching and [428 D] of his passion. The form of the cross, on the other hand, neither resembles his body, nor does it make visible to us any of the aforementioned [things]. But what is similar is closer and more appropriate [to the model] than that which is not similar, because, thanks to the resemblance, it makes the model more familiar and therefore worthier of honor. Therefore, because the icon of Christ is more appropriate [to him] and makes him more familiar, and because the form of the cross deserves to be honored and venerated by us, that icon should be even more honored and more venerated.

2. The icon of Christ, primarily and immediately, and from the first look, manifests to us his visible form, and conveys his recollection. Indeed, we behold him [429 A] who is placed in the icon [as] being reflected, as in a mirror.[24] But it is not the same with the cross. For, when we look at the cross, in the first place we fix our mind on appearances. Then we reflect on what it is, and examine carefully how it is sanctified and by whom. Then, in the second place, we turn toward the one who was crucified and who sanctified the cross. What passes over to something in a primary way and makes it familiar in a primary way is worthier of honor than that which does so in a secondary way; thus the icon of Christ is worthier of honor than the cross that is indeed worthy of honor.

3. It is agreed by all those who are intelligent that what sanctifies is better than what is sanctified. Indeed, the Apostle's speech says, "It is beyond dispute [429 B] that the inferior is blessed by the superior."[25] Thus if the body of Christ sanctified the cross when he was lying on it at the crucifixion, he also implanted sanctification in us by means of the cross, which was sanctified by him. Those things whose prototypes are worthier of honor are themselves worthier of honor too. Because there are two forms, and because the form of the sanctified cross is worthier of honor, so the form of the body that sanctified it is even more worthy of honor.

4. Also, the form of the extension of Christ's hands and the form of his positioning is holy. As the body differs from its positioning, so those that derive from them will differ from each other. Those things whose archetypes are worthier of honor are themselves worthier of honor too. In fact, the positioning and the extension [of the crucifixion] exist on account of the body of Christ and not, contrariwise, the body on account of its positioning. For the body is essence and underlying substance while the positioning is accident and consequence. As the essence is superior to the accident, or as the soul is superior to knowledge, so the body is superior to its positioning. [429 C] It can be said that the body has been positioned, but none among the wise will say that the positioning has been given bodily existence. Thus, it could be also said that the body has been colored, but we cannot talk about the body of the color, nor about color to which bodily existence has been given. Thus, what belongs to the body is superior to what belongs to its positioning, and if this is the case, the form of the body is worthier of honor than the form of its positioning.

5. The cross conveys to us the passion of Christ in a simple and unadorned way. To the rustics, the cross could hardly be understood as a sym-

bol of the passion. But the sacred forms not only adorn with [429 D] colors and depict in detail the passion, but they also indicate to us in fuller detail and more clearly the miracles and the prodigious feats that Christ accomplished. Thus, things that manifest to us these prodigious achievements in a more explicit and more obvious way are more honorable and more praiseworthy than the ones that show them to us in a more obscure way.

6. Also, the cross is a symbol of the passion, and it hints at the way in which the one who suffered the passion endured it. [432 A] Indeed, what else does the following mean to express: "Lift and take your cross and follow me,"[26] if not that the one who is transfixed with the fear of the Lord,[27] and who renounces the vanities of this world is ready to suffer patiently everything for the love for him? So he who bears on his flesh the stigmata of Christ boasts,[28] and thinks highly of the passion, says: "May I never boast of anything except the cross of our Lord Jesus Christ,"[29] indicating to us in this way the crucifixion, that is to say, the passion of Christ. But the icon of the person himself who suffered is an impression and a likeness, and what depicts a person him or her self is more proper and worthier of mention than what indicates only the exterior and the periphery of that person. Thus, the icon, because it manifests to us Christ himself, is worthier of mention than the cross, which indicates to us the way of the passion.

[432 B] 7. The name *Christ* is also used homonymously to express the icon of Christ himself because the icon is also called "Christ," as the icon of a king is called "king." But it is impossible to say this about the cross. Indeed, nobody among sensible people would in any way call the cross "Christ." Thus, what shares the same name and what equally already has in common the form of the body is worthier of honor than that which does not share any of these. Therefore, the icon deserves more honor than the form of the cross.

8. The cause precedes the effect, and even more so the efficient cause. But what precedes something is worthier of honor than [432 C] what follows. Thus, because the cause of the form of the cross is the passion of the body of Christ, and because his body is the antecedent cause[30] of the form of the cross, consequently, the icon of the body of Christ, as the efficient cause, is worthier of honor than the form of the cross.

9. Moreover, what exists on account of something else is inferior to the one on account of which it exists. Thus, if the cross exists on account of the body of Our Lord, it is necessary that the inferiority of the form of

the cross be transferred to its signs, because the things whose antecedents are inferior are themselves inferior too. Consequently, it has been shown in numerous ways that the icon of Christ, in accordance with the [reasonable] sequence of the arguments given and with our examination, is even worthier of honor than the form itself of the life-giving cross, which is [also] honored by us. Thus, he who professes to honor the cross will then honor the icon of the Lord. And if he does not honor this icon, he is far from honoring the cross.

[432 D] 10. We see in a great number of places the crucifixion of the Lord depicted in an icon, and, as is reasonable, in accordance with the way in which the act was carried out, [we see] the body suspended, the hands stretched out and pierced by nails; by means of all these, the most marvelous miracle and the most significant way in which we have been saved, that is, the saving passion of Christ, is shown to us. What could the enemies of the cross of Christ[31] do in front of this? One of two things must be done: either prostrate themselves before the cross [433 A] and also prostrate themselves before the icon, if they do not want their profession of faith to fall apart, or, by destroying the icon, throw down the cross at the same time. But those who have chosen the second option, because they have at the same time completely drawn a line through both the cross itself and the whole economy of Christ, are rejected as accepting no economy at all, and they make the falsehood of their profession of faith public. Indeed, if there were just a little truth in them, it would be necessary for them to honor the icon in the first place as the efficient cause and producer of the cross. For everything that is said on account of something is inferior to that on account of which it was produced. And if the cross is worthy of honor, as it really is, the icon must be even more worthy of honor because it is the cause in relation to the cross. Indeed, the cross exists on account of the icon, and not, inversely, the icon on account of the form of the cross. In fact, in the first place, the icon was drawn and marked out, and then the cross itself was formed along with it, [433 B] with the position of the upright body of Christ and the stretching out of both of his hands. It follows that the cross by necessity and in consequence displays at the same time the shape of the body. And one would not be led astray from the truth by saying that someone who scratches the icon of the Lord in this way also scratches the form of the cross, even if he does not want to. How is it, then, that on account of all this, the insanity and the impiety of those Christomachs is not obvious? On the one hand, they pretend to venerate the form of the cross as worthy of honor, but on the other hand, they despise what is more honorable than it. But it is not in honoring the cross that they do such things: indeed, how [could they honor it], those people who throw down everything and burn up and trample everything under their profane and impure feet? But in order [433 C] not to give the impression that they disturb at their foundation all the things venerated by the church, they prefer opportunely and inopportunely[32] to remove the divine form of Christ, because Christ is a burden for them, even seen in his icon. As someone who wants to get rid of his natural ugliness makes himself up with ornaments for embellishment, [in the same way] they put forward the principle of the cross as the most gracious pretext.

Notes

INTRODUCTION

1. ["*Le trait.*"—Trans.]

2. "A new political and ideological orientation dominates the period that stretches from the beginning of the eighth century to the middle of the ninth. This period is known by the misleading name of iconoclasm. In effect, the controversy over images constitutes, in my opinion, only an exterior aspect of, or even a simple pretext for, the changes and profound convulsions that put the Byzantine empire, its state, its church, and its society to the test for more than a century." H. Ahrweiler, *L'Idéologie politique*, 25.

3. G. Ladner, "Origin and Significance"; and "Concept of the Image."

4. P. Lemerle, *Premier Humanisme byzantin*, 108.

5. Mansi, XIII. See the translation in the *Horos* at the end of this book.

6. These questions, or *Peuseis*, in the *Antirrhetics* were cataloged by G. Ostrogorsky in *Studien zur Geschichte den byzantinischen Bilderstreit*, then by H. Hennephof in *Textus byzantinos*. They are also provided at the end of my translation of the *Antirrhetics*, 297–302.

7. ["*La ruse*": this word has generally been rendered as *guile* throughout this book, except for the rare occasion where *trick* or *ruse* is better suited to the context.—Trans.]

8. R. Khawam, *Livre des ruses*.

9. On the life of Nikephoros, see *Vita Nicephori*, by Ignatios the Deacon (BHG 1335), in *Nicephori Archiepiscopi Constantinopolitani opuscula historica*, 139–217; PG 100, 41–160; P. J. Alexander, *Patriarch Nicephorus*.

CHAPTER 1

1. G. Dagron, "La Règle et l'exception," 4, 14.

2. 1 Cor. 11:7; 2 Cor. 4:4; Col. 1:15.

CHAPTER 2

1. Aristotle, *Economics*, II.1.

2. Hippocrates, *Corpus Hippocraticum*, Épidém. VI.2.24.

3. Dionysios of Halicarnassus, *De compositione verborum*, 25, *Epistula ad Cn. Pompeium*, 4.2.

4. Sophocles, *Electra*, 190.
5. ["*Économe*" in French.—Trans.]
6. Aeschylus, *Agamemnon*, 155.
7. Plato, *Phaedrus*, 256e.
8. Theodore of Stoudios, *Antirrhetics*, II, PG 99, 353 D.
9. Pseudo-Dionysios, *Celestial Hierarchy*, II.3.141A.
10. Hippolytos, *Against the Heresy of One Noetus*, 3, PG 10, 808A.
11. John Chrysostom, *On the Providence of God*, 21 and *passim*.
12. St. Augustine, *Trinity*, XV.vi.9.
13. Eph. 1:10, 3:9.
14. Hippolytos, *Against the Heresy of One Noetus*, 8, PG 10, 816 B.
15. J. Moingt, *Théologie trinitaire*, vol. 3, chap. 4, 852–932.
16. G. L. Prestige, *Dieu dans la pensée patristique*.
17. Tertullian, *Against Marcion*, V.17.
18. Tertullian, *Against Praxeas*, II.
19. "Oikonomia sacramentum, quae unitatem in trinitatem disponit."
20. Moingt, *Théologie trinitaire*, 927.
21. St. Augustine, *Trinity*, XII.vi.6. The citations are from Gen. 1:26–27.
22. 1 Cor. 13:12. [This is a slightly unusual rendering of the famous quotation. The New Revised Standard Version translates the first phrase as "For now we see in a mirror, dimly." In this respect, I follow the author, who forgoes the standard French translation of *obscurément*, using instead the phrase "*en énigma*." In this respect, she is following the Greek original, which is "*en ainúgmati*." She returns several times to the terms *enigma* and *enigmatically*, always in reference to this key text.—Trans.]
23. 2 Cor. 3:18.
24. St. Augustine, *Trinity*, XV.viii.14.
25. Ibid., XV.ix.16.
26. Basil of Caesarea, *On the Holy Spirit*, XII.28.
27. Athanasios, PG 26, 635 A.
28. Basil of Caesarea, *On the Holy Spirit*, XVIII.
29. 2 Cor. 2:15.
30. Basil of Caesarea, *On the Holy Spirit*, XIII.30.
31. Ibid., XVIII.45.
32. Ibid., XVIII.45.149 B.
33. All the following quotes are from Cyril of Alexandria, *Two Christological Dialogues*.
34. Athanasios, *On the Incarnation of the Word*, 8, 3.
35. John Chrysostom, *On the Providence of God*, IV.1–2.
36. Ibid., VII.6.
37. Ibid., II.6; citing Rom. 11:33.
38. Ibid., II.7.
39. Ibid., III.7; citing 1 Cor. 2:7.

40. Ibid., IV.13–17.
41. Ibid., XII, 3–4; citing 1 Cor. 11:19.
42. Ibid., XII.4–5 and 7.
43. Ibid., II.16.
44. Ibid., XVII, 9–10.
45. Ireneaus of Lyon, *Against the Heresies,* V.2–3.
46. Ibid., V.3.2.
47. Meletios, *Peri tou anthropou kataskeuès,* PG 64, 1082–1310.
48. Ibid., 1213.
49. Ibid., 1214.
50. Ibid., 1260.
51. Ibid., 1276.
52. Eusebios, *Martrydom of Polycarp,* PG 5, 1032 A.
53. John of Damascus, PG 96, 1309 A.
54. See Gregory of Nazianzos, letter 101 to Kleidonios, in *Lettres théologiques*; and Tertullian, *La Chair du Christ.*
55. Garnerius of Saint-Victor, *De homine, patrologia latina,* 193. Thus in chap. 34, "De Carne," the word *caro* is enumerated in the following way:

"*Carnis nomine natura humana designatur . . .* "(Human nature, in opposition to God.)

"*Carnis nomine, cordis sensibilitas . . .* "(Sensitivity with respect to the insensitivity of minerals.)

"*Carnis nomine, vita carnalis . . .* "(Carnal life submitted to corruption and pleasure with respect to the spiritual life.)

"*Carnis nomine, delectatio carnalis . . .* "(The temptation and pleasure of the body in opposition to contemplation.)

"*Carnis nomine, carnalitas . . .* "(The carnal state that one must turn away from in order to turn towards spirituality.)

"*Carnis nomine, infirmitas operis . . .* "(The imperfection of our works in opposition to the perfection of creation.)

"*Carnis nomine juxta naturam . . .* "(Nature in opposition to the creator.)

"*Carnis nomine reprobi, carnes enim diaboli sunt . . .* "(The devil, then the disciples in the act of betrayal, etc.)

The flesh and muscles are thus progressively excluded from the plan of salvation.

56. Ibid., chap. 1: "Viscerum nomine hi qui spiritualibus sacramentis in Ecclesia deserviunt designantur. . . . Quid enim aliud Sanctae Ecclesiae viscera debemus accipere nisi eorum mentes, qui ejus quaedam in se mysteria continent?"
57. John of Damascus, *On Female Vampires* (Peri Stryggon, De Strygibus), PG 94, 1604 A.
58. H. Sorlin, "Stryges et géloudes."
59. Eph. 1:10 ff.
60. Col. 1:25 ff.

61. ["*Parler par economie.*" Note the related English phrase "to be economic with the truth."—Trans.]

62. Matt. 10:16.

63. Rom. 3:7–8.

64. Plato, *Republic*, II.378d–e.

65. 1 Cor. 9:20.

66. Origen, *Commentary on the Gospel According to Matthew*, X.1.34–38.

67. St. Augustine, *Commentary on the Lord's Sermon on the Mount*, I.1, PL 34, 1231.

68. Origen, *Commentary on the Gospel According to Matthew*, X.25.

69. Origen, *Contra Celsum*, II.67.28.

70. Matt. 7:6.

71. Basil of Caesarea, *On the Holy Spirit*, French ed., p. 79. Emphasis added.

72. Theodore of Stoudios, PG 99, 1661 C.

73. Athansios, letter to Palladios, PG 26, 1168 D.

74. Basil of Caesarea, letter 113, PG 32, 528 A.

75. Basil of Caesarea, *On the Holy Spirit*, XXX.78–79. The quotation is from Matt. 7:6.

76. [*Apateis* in the Greek original, translated in the French as *ruse.*—Trans.]

77. John Chrysostom, *On the Priesthood*, I.6–8.

78. "*Prévoyance.*" [The English translation renders the word as "good management."—Trans.]

79. John Chrysostom, *On the Priesthood*, II.I.1–4.

80. Ibid., II.I.57–60.

81. Ibid., IV.3.13–16.

82. Ibid., IV.3.44–46.

83. Athanasios, *Dogmatic History*, PG 25, 488 B-492 C.

84. [This is what is known to philosophers and logicians as "kettle logic." The author provides the following explanation: "You tell me that I returned to you the kettle that you had lent me with a hole in it. First, there was no hole in it when I returned it to you, second, it already had a hole in it when you lent it to me, and third, you never lent me a kettle at all. This 'absurd' argument is often cited to illustrate syllogisms made in bad faith, which render the interlocutor guilty in all cases, even contradictory ones."—Trans.]

85. [The text here plays on the fact that in French, *glace* means both *ice* and *mirror*. The author comments on this in the following paragraph.—Trans.]

86. See above, 39–44.

87. ["*Gouvernement.*"—Trans.]

88. ["*Prévoyance.*"—Trans.]

89. John Chrysostom, *On the Priesthood*, III.11. [The English translation renders the word here as *stewardship.*— Trans.]

90. Ibid., VI.7.41.

91. ["*Puissance.*"—Trans.]

92. ["*Pouvoir.*"—Trans.]

93. John Chrysostom, *On the Priesthood*, IV.1.126.

94. Ibid., IV.2.96–114.

95. Titus of Bostra (fourth century) uses it in this same sense in book 3 of his work, *Against the Manichaeans* (PG 18, 1216 B): "Christ came not to break the law but to fulfill it; he enters the temple to drive out the reprehensible economies." He thus drives out those who pervert the purpose and function of the temple. Christ, considered as a steward [*économe*], that is to say the Father's administrator, causes justice and the true law to reign.

96. Basil of Caesarea, in letter 76 to Sophronios, calls *oikonomia* administration (PG 32, 452 A). In letter 31 (PG 32, 313 C) the same word refers to what the church distributes; footnote 65 specifies: "Saepe apud Basilium oikonomia dicitur id quod pauperibus distribuitur," and refers to Basil's *Commentary on the Prophet Isaiah* (PG 30, 212 A), where he talks of and condemns those who make use of the money of the poor. In the same author (PG 32, 593 C, 669 B), *oikonomia* refers to the ecclesiastic administration and the management of the *pecuniae sacrae*, that is, not only the sacred character of charity but also the sacredness of the goods of the clergy.

97. *Encyclopédie théologique*, 1855, vol. 5.

98. Ibid., 28.

99. Gregory of Nazianzos, letter 58, in *Correspondence*, 1:75–76.

100. ["*Économe*" in French.—Trans.]

CHAPTER 3

1. On this subject, see N. Baynes, "Icons Before Iconoclasm"; and E. Kitzinger, "Cult of Images." The remarkable article of P. Brown, "Dark Age Crisis," presents the benefit of linking the intensive development of the iconic cult closely to the social and spiritual history of the holy man in Byzantine society, starting in the seventh century.

2. ["*Graphe*."—Trans.]

3. G. Ladner, "Concept of the Image," 5.

4. [*Mammon* is the term by which Nikephoros routinely refers to his enemy, Constantine V.—Trans.]

5. Nikephoros, *Antirrhetics*, I, 225 A–C. [Translated by V.D.]

6. Ibid., I, 225 D–228 A. [Translated by V.D.]

7. É. Hugon, *Mystère de la Sainte Trinité*, 336.

8. Aristotle, *Fragments*, 178.1507b.36.21.

9. Gregory of Nazianzos, *Discourse*, 29, PG 36, 96.

10. Akakios of Berroia, PG 94, 83, n. 33.

11. Cyril of Alexandria, *Dialogue on the Holy and Consubstantial Trinity*, PG 75, 868.

12. John of Damascus, *Orthodox Faith*, PG 94, 837.

13. Aristotle, *Categories*, 6b.2, 7b.15.

14. PG 31, 914, 919, 946, 961 . . .

15. Aristotle, *Categories*, 6b22.

16. Plato, *Timaeus*, 29b, 37c.

17. G. Florovsky, "Origen, Eusebius," 77 ff.
18. *Painter's Manual*, 4 and 12.
19. Aristotle, *Categories*, 8b.20.
20. E. Kuryluk, *Veronica and Her Cloth.*
21. See Chapter 7.
22. Nikephoros, *Antirrhetics*, I, 227 A. [Translated by by V.D.]
23. Ibid., I, 277 A. See my article, "Autour de quelques concepts philosophiques," 135 ff.
24. Ibid., I, 277 C-278 D. [Translated by V.D.]
25. Aristotle, *Categories*, 6a.37–38.
26. Nikephoros, *Antirrhetics*, I, 277 D.
27. Ibid., I, 229 A. [Translated by V.D.]
28. Aristotle, *Categories*, 7b.10.
29. Thomas Aquinas, *Summa Theologica*, Quod 1.9.a.4.
30. Ladner, "Concept of the Image," 16.
31. John of Damascus, *On the Divine Images*, PG 94, 1317.
32. E. H. Kantorowicz, "Deus per naturam."
33. W. Kandinsky, "On the Question of Form."
34. See E. Kitzinger, "Byzantine Art," in which he notes constant divergences and interferences between what he names classicism and abstraction. What astonishes him, however, yet what confirms our hypotheses, is that on the eve of the inconoclastic crisis, the tendency that prevailed was what he calls abstract. In effect, Kitzinger believes that only an excessive development of the realistic, Hellenistic image would have been able to justify such anti-iconic reactions. But if, as we have attempted to do, the icon is approached in terms of an existential relation, it becomes clear that its power increased with its very "abstraction," owing to the power of its theoretical status.
35. W. Worringer, *Abstraction and Empathy.*
36. Phil. 2:7.
37. [*Bourrelet*: "roll" as in "roll of flesh" or "roll of fabric."—Trans.]
38. See below, "Idols and Veronicas."
39. *Painter's Manual.*
40. Nikephoros, *Antirrhetics*, III, 432 D.
41. PG 180, 8, 9.
42. John Chrysostom, *Homily on the Epistle to the Hebrews*, PG 63, 1.
43. John of Damascus, Second Apology of *On the Divine Images*, PG 94, 1316 A.
44. Cyril of Alexandria, PG 77, 217 B.
45. J. Paris, "L'or de Byzance," *Esprit*, March 1964.
46. Pseudo-Dionysios, *Ecclesiastical Hierarchy*, PG 3, 473 C.
47. Mansi, XI, 977E, 980A. This injunction was repeated at Nicaea (Mansi, XII, 1123 E, and XIII, 400 E ff.).
48. The question of the symbol is obviously tied to what would become of the image. Before the iconoclastic crisis, the church fathers dealt extensively with the

relations that perceptible signs maintain with the heavenly world. Pseudo-Dionysios is the major figure who dominates this theoretical tradition; on this, see J. Pepin, "Aspects théoriques du symbolisme." We must, however, disagree with the appendix devoted to the iconoclast controversy. In effect, according to the author, the iconoclasts privileged the symbolism of the dissimilar, although as Pepin also recognizes (32), they never stated this explicitly. Conversely, the iconodules, by opting for a symbolism of the similar, distanced themselves from the Dionysian tradition. The problem loses its contradictory character, however, if one envisages it from the aspect of *mimésis* in the Nikephorian sense. The iconodules, by instituting a doctrine of the image, gave a new meaning to the very term of *symbola*. Nikephoros uses *symbolikôs* and *skhètikhôs* frequently in the same way. Thus *symbola* becomes *pros tí* by nature, no longer semiologically, but ontologically. The figure of Christ in the icon no more *resembles* the real Christ than did the lamb; on the contrary, it is more abstract. Losing all of its metaphoric and narrative character, its formal codification means that it participates not in the rhetoric of distances separating sign and signified (Old Testament writings), but the new economy concerning the relationship of contemplator and contemplated who continually exchange gazes across iconic space. The linguistic analogies that symbolism today lends itself to are linked to a psychology of representation that was not yet at work when Nikephoros, John of Damascus, and Theodore of Stoudios developed their defense of the icon.

49. See Chapter 7.

50. On the *épigraphè*, see below.

51. Gregory of Nazianzos, letter 101 to Kleidonios, in *Lettres théologiques*.

52. Nikephoros, *Antirrhetics*, III, 389 B. The text quoted (Prov. 1:8) says: "Hear, my child, your father's instruction, and do not reject your mother's teaching [*torah*]."

53. John 1:23.

54. ["*Dessaisissement*": a term referring specifically to the removal of a case from a court or a judge.—Trans.]

55. Nikephoros, *Antirrhetics*, I, 280 B. [Translated by V.D.]

56. Athanasios, *Discourse Against the Arians*, 3.5, PG 26, 332 A.

57. Matt. 3:17; Mark 1:11; Luke 3:22.

58. Aristotle, *Categories*, 1a.1–2: "*Homônouma legetai hô onoma monon koinon, ho de kata tounoma logos tès ousias heteros oion xôon ote anthropôs kai to gegramménon.*"

59. E. Martineau, "La *Mimésis* dans *La Poétique*."

60. "*Allos kai allos . . . allo kai allo*"; see Gregory of Nazianzos, letter 101 to Kleidonios, in *Lettres théologiques*.

61. Nikephoros, *Antirrhetics*, III, 397 A.

62. The noninstrumental character of Byzantine music also meets up with the question of the incarnation. Christ's body cannot in any way be considered as the instrument (*organon*) of the incarnation. Thus Cyril writes clearly in his Epistle to

the Nuns: "However, if someone assigns to him only a simple instrumental service, he deprives him (without wanting to) of being truly the Son. Let us take as an example a man who has a son who knows how to play the lyre and who sings well. Would this man rank the lyre and the instrument on the same level as his son? For one takes up the lyre to show one's art; but the son is still the son of his father even without the instrument" (PG 77, 32 D).

63. All the insults cited are translated from the Greek. The lexicon of these terms can be found at the end of my translation of the *Antirrhetics.*

64. This is a late (twelfth century) epithet that refers either to Constantine's taste for excrement and manure or to a story according to which he dirtied the baptismal font. See G. Gero, "Byzantine Iconoclasm."

65. A. J. Festugière, *Les Moines d'Orient,* 1:163 ff.

66. Nikephoros, *Antirrhetics,* III, 505 A–B.

67. Ibid., II, 516 D.

68. Ibid., II, 396 C–397 B. See Chapter 5.

CHAPTER 4

1. É. Benveniste, *Le Vocabulaire des institutions indo-européens.*

2. Ibid., 196.

3. Ibid., 206. See also G. Dumézil, *Idées romaines,* 33 ff.

4. Nikephoros, *Antirrhetics,* I, 212 C.

5. See below, "Extracts from the Iconoclast *Horos* of Hieria."

6. Mansi, XIII, 268 B–C.

7. Nikephoros, *Antirrhetics,* III, 457 A.

8. Ibid., III, 453 C.

9. Mansi, XIII, 328 C: "*ois basilikois nomois hupeuthunos esto, hos enantios ton tou theou prostagmaton kai ekhthros ton patrikon dogmaton.*"

10. Ibid., XIII, 261 E–264 B, and 268 B.

11. Nikephoros, *Antirrhetics,* II, 332 D–340 B.

12. Ibid., II, 261 E.

13. Ibid., II, 264 B.

14. See below.

15. Nikephoros, *Antirrhetics,* I, 213 E, 249 C, 264 C, 264 B; II, 353 C.

16. Ibid., II, 336 B.

17. Ibid., II, 340 A: "*pothen to hiereion to mega, to amômon kai sebasmion, to katharsion thuma kai pantos tou kosmou sotiriou.*"

18. Ibid., II, 337 C.

19. Ibid., I, 217 B.

20. Ibid., I, 334 A.

21. Ibid., I, 213 A.

22. Ibid., I, 300 C.

23. Mansi, XIII, 232 E, 332 B.

24. Nikephoros, *Antirrhetics,* I, 212 A–C.

25. Ibid., I, 220 D.
26. Ibid., III, 388 D.
27. Ibid., III, 388 C.
28. J. Kotsonis, *Problèmes de l'economie ecclésiastique.*
29. Photios, *Ta Amphilochia,* questions 1 and 14.
30. Kotsonis, *Problèmes de l'economie ecclésiastique,* 44.
31. Theodore of Stoudios, letter 48 to Athanasios, PG 99, 1077.
32. Ibid., letter 10, 99 to Naukratios, PG 89, 1085 (quoted in Kotsonis, *Problèmes de l'economie ecclésiastique*).
33. Photios, *Ta Amphilocha,* questions 1 and 14.
34. Photios, letter 32, PG 111, 212.
35. Gregory of Nazianzos, *Homily 20 for Saint Basil,* PG 30, 493.
36. Ibid., III, 385 D.
37. Ibid., III, 388 B.
38. Ibid., III, 389 B.
39. Ibid., III, 377 B–C.
40. Ibid., I, 292 B.
41. Ibid., III, 380 D.
42. Ibid., III, 381 D–384 B.
43. See R. Cormack, *Icônes et société à Byzance.* This work, which inventories a great number of texts about icons, repeats over and over again that the issue concerns "iconolatry." Nikephoros himself is not spared, being labeled "the iconolatrous Patriarch"!
44. Nikephoros, *Antirrhetics,* III, 464 A–465 C.
45. Ibid., III, 464 C–D.
46. A. Grabar, "L'Esthetisme d'un théologien humaniste byzantin."
47. Nikephoros, *Antirrhetics,* III, 464 D–465 B.
48. Kitzinger, "Cult of Images."
49. Ibid., 100–101.
50. Plotinus, *Enneads,* II.9.16.
51. The expression recurs continuously in the Life of Steven the Younger, a martyr of iconoclasm. In the passage that we are currently analyzing, Nikephoros uses it as well: "*ho de tôn septôn morphomatôn.*"
52. P. Brown, "Dark Age Crisis," 31.
53. Ibid., 21.
54. Ibid., 13.

CHAPTER 5

1. E. H. Kantorowicz, "La Souveraintè de l'artiste."
2. Rom. 13:6–7.
3. A. Grabar, *L'Empereur dans l'art byzantin.*
4. M. J. Mondzain-Baudinet, "Autour de quelques concepts philosophiques."
5. Gregory of Nazianzos, letter 101 to Kleidonios, in *Lettres théologiques,* I.16.

6. Origen, *Commentary on the Epistle to the Romans*, 3.29.

7. A. Grabar, *L'Iconoclasme byzantin*, 254 ff.

8. P. J. Alexander, "The Iconoclast Council of St. Sophia."

9. St. Jerome, *Tractatus in librum psalmorum*, LXXXI, 1, edited by G. Morin (Maredsou; 1897), vol. III-2, p. 77; cited in Kantorowicz, "Deus per naturam, Deus per gratiam."

10. Eusebios, *In Psalmos commentaria*, LXXXI, PG 23, 988 B.

11. Kantorowicz, "Deus per naturam, Deus per gratiam."

12. Basil of Caesarea, *On the Holy Spirit*, XVIII.45.149 C.

13. G. Ladner, "Origin and Significance."

14. John 18:36.

15. Matt. 16:18 confers on Peter only a spiritual authority, and entrusts the keys of the kingdom of God to him.

16. Nikephoros, *Antirrhetics*, II, 396 A–397 B.

17. Isa. 40:6–8.

18. Gregory of Nyssa, PG 45, 140 B.

19. Isa. 45:23.

20. Ps. 95:4.

21. Ps. 2:8.

22. Ps. 47:8.

23. Matt. 21:5, citing Zech. 9:9.

24. Zech. 9:9.

25. Zeph. 3:5.

26. Ps. 146:10.

27. See Chapter 8.

28. S. Gruzinski, *La Guerre des images*, 331.

CHAPTER 6

1. To Christians, of course, such an unconditional adoption of portrayal could only lead to an extremely idolatrous perversion of iconicity.

2. J. Pouillon, "Fétiches sans fétichisme."

3. J. -P. Vernant, *Mythe et pensée chez les Grecs*, 325–38.

4. Ibid., 330.

5. See Chapter 7.

6. M.-J. Mondzain, "Le Destructeur était idolâtre," in the catalog of the Musée d'Ixtelles, 1983.

7. What can be said of this recent sentence by a judge condemning Bernard Tapie with these words: "He who lived by the image will perish by the image?" That very evening, that image was shown on television, shattered.

8. I. Goldberg, "Jawlensky ou le visage promis."

CHAPTER 7

This chapter is an adaptation of a paper given at Rennes in 1992, which was published in *La Photographie inquiète de ses marges* (Rennes: Éd. Le Triangle, 1993).

1. A. Legrand, *Linceul de Turin.*
2. Evagrios, *Church History*, IV.27, PG 86, 2745–2748.
3. Eusebios, *Church History*, I.13.1 ff.
4. W. Cureton, *Ancient Syriac Document.*
5. Kuryluk, *Veronica and Her Cloth*, 44.
6. [I.e., after having been enclosed in the wall for some time, its location was lost to the inhabitants, before being rediscovered thanks to Eulalios's dream.—Trans.]
7. P. Pedrizet, *Seminarium Kondakovianum*, 5:1–15.
8. Mgr. P. Savio, *Ricerca storica sulla Santa Sindone.*
9. I. Wilson, *Le Suaire de Turin.*
10. J. Calvin, *Traité des reliques.*
11. Quoted in Legrand, *Linceul de Turin.*
12. Ibid., 10.
13. Dr. P. Barbet, *Passion de Jésus-Christ.*
14. P. Claudel, "Toi, qui es tu?" letter to M. G. Cordonnier, acheiropoiete, Paris, 1936.
15. ["*Revelateur*," which is also related to *revelation.*—Trans.]
16. [Le Centre national de la recherche scientifique, approximately equivalent to the National Science Foundation in the United States.—Trans.]
17. A. Loth, *Photographie du Sainte Suaire.*
18. [In English in the text.—Trans.]

CHAPTER 8

This chapter was previously presented at the colloquium Judaïsme et Judaïcités, held at Centre national de la recherche scientifique (CNRS), 1984, and was published in *Traces*, special number 9–10, 170–182.

1. [Nouvelles Éditions Françaises, a publishing company.—Trans.]
2. A. Leroi-Gourhan, *Le Geste et la parole.*
3. Ibid., 71.
4. Ibid.
5. F. W. J. Schelling, *Philosophy of Art*, II.4.124.
6. O. Clément, *Visage intérieur*, 54–56.
7. L. Ouspensky, *Théologie de l'icône dans l'église orthodoxe*, 217.
8. Clément, *Visage intérieur.*
9. *Le Monde*, May 11, 1993.

EXTRACTS FROM *HOROS*

Mansi, XIII, 208 D and following. [The following text is drawn from the translation of the *Horos* of Hieria by Daniel Sahas, which appears in his *Icon and Logos*—Trans.].

1. 2 Cor. 10:4–5; Eph. 4:11–12.
2. Eph. 5:12.
3. Wisd. of Sol. 15:6.
4. *Skaiographè.* A play on the word *Skiagraphè* (the writing in shadows of the Old Testament prefiguration).
5. Rom. 10:10.
6. This is the problem of the homonymy and pseudonymy of artificial images.
7. Wisd. of Sol. 15:6.
8. Matt. 26:26–28; Mark 14:22–24; Luke 22:19–20.
9. *Apseudès.* Truth is thus directly linked to consubstantial homonymy.
10. Col. 1:19; Col. 2:9.
11. 2 Tim. 2:12.
12. Acts 17:31.
13. Rom. 8:29.
14. Heb. 11:38.

EXTRACTS FROM *ANTIRRHETICS*

The following text is translated by V.D.

1. First *Peusis* of Constantine V. See Ostrogorsky, *Studien zur Geschichte den byzantinischen Bilderstreit,* 8, fragment 2; Hennephof, *Textus byzantinos,* 52, fragment 142.
2. For example, Gregory of Nazianzos, *Oratio,* 23.11: "*mèdemia eikôn phthanei pros tèn alèthian*" (PG 35, 1164 A).
3. First *Peusis* of Constantine V. See G. Ostrogorsky, *Studien zur Geschichte den byzantinischen Bilderstreit,* 3, fragment 3; H. Hennephof, *Textus byzantinos,* 52, fragment 143.
4. 1 Tim. 4:7; 2 Tim. 3:6.
5. Wisd. of Sol. 14:15–20.
6. 1 Cor. 10:19–21.
7. Aristotle, *Categories,* 6a.36–37; 6b.28–29.
8. Gregory of Nazianzos, letter 101 to Kleidonios, in *Lettres théologiques,* I.20–21.
9. Athanasios, *Discourse Against the Arians,* III.5 (PG 26, 332 A).
10. First *Peusis* of Constantine V. See Ostrogorsky, *Studien zur Geschichte den byzantinischen Bilderstreit,* 9, fragment 15; Hennephof, *Textus byzantinos,* 54, fragment 161.
11. Gal. 6:14.
12. John 8:40.
13. John 6:53.

14. John 13:31.
15. Matt. 17:22; Mark 9:31; Luke 18:32.
16. Luke 19:10.
17. Matt. 9:27.
18. John 1:1.
19. John 1:14.
20. John 5:21.
21. John 17:1.
22. John 10:30.
23. John 9:35. The Byzantine text allows the reading "Son of God." The reading usually accepted today is "Son of Man."
24. 2 Cor. 3:18.
25. Heb. 7:7.
26. Matt. 16. 25; Mark 8. 34; Luke 9. 23.
27. Ps. 119:120.
28. Gal. 6. 17.
29. Gal. 6:14.
30. An expression borrowed from Stoicism. See Chryssippuss, *Stoicus*, 2.292; Sextus Empiricus, *Pyrrhonian hypotyposes*, II.13.
31. Phil. 3:18.
32. 2 Tim. 4:2.

Bibliography

Aeschylus. *Agamemnon.* Paris: Les Belles Lettres, 1935.

Ahrweiler, H. *L'Idéologie politique de l'Empire byzantine.* Paris: Presses Universitaires de France, 1975.

Alexander, P. J. "The Iconoclast Council of St. Sophia (815) and Its Definition." *Dumbarton Oaks Papers* 7 (1953): 35–66.

———. *The Patriarch Nicephorus of Constantinople: Ecclesiastical Policy and Image Worship in the Byantine Empire.* Oxford: Oxford University Press, 1958.

The Ante-Nicene Fathers: Translations of the Writings of the Fathers down to AD 325. Edited by Alexander Roberts and James Donaldson. Grand Rapids, MI: W. R. Eerdmans, 1978.

Aristotle. *The Complete Works of Aristotle.* Revised Oxford translation. Princeton: Princeton University Press, 1984.

Athanasios. *On the Incarnation of the Word.* Text and French translation by C. Kannengiesser. Sources chrétiennes, vol. 199. Paris: Éd. du Cerf, 1973. English translation in *Nicene and Post-Nicene Fathers,* 2nd ser., 4:36–67.

Augustine. *Commentary on the Lord's Sermon on the Mount.* In *Patriologiae cursus completus, Series latina,* edited by J. P. Migne. Paris, 1844–55. Translated by D. Kavanagh in *The Fathers of the Church,* vol. 11.

———. *The Trinity.* Translated by S. McKenna in *The Fathers of the Church,* vol. 18.

Auzépy, M. F. "Traduction et commentaire de la Vie d'Étienne le Jeune." Ph.D. thesis, Paris, Sorbonne, 1976.

———. "Une Lecture 'iconoclaste' de la Vie d'Étienne le Jeune." *Travaux et Mémoires* 8 (1991).

Barbet, Dr. P. *La Passion de Jésus-Christ selon le chirurgien.* 9th ed. Paris: Médiaspaul, 1982. Originally published by Issoudun, 1950.

Basil of Caesarea. *On the Holy Spirit.* Text and French translation by B. Pruche. Sources chrétiennes, vol. 17. Paris: Éd. du Cerf, 1968. English translation in *Nicene and Post-Nicene Fathers,* 2nd ser., 8:1–50.

Baynes, N. "The Icons Before Iconoclasm." *Harvard Theological Review* 44–45 (1951).

Benveniste, É. *Le Vocabulaire des institutions indo-européens.* Vol. 2. Paris: Éd. du Minuit, 1969.

Brown, P. "A Dark Age Crisis: Aspects of the Iconoclastic Controversy." *English Historical Review* 88 (January 1973): 1–34.

———. "The Rise and Function of the Holy Man in Late Antiquity." *Journal of Roman Studies* 61 (1971).

Calvin, J. *Traité des reliques.* In *La Vraie Piété: Divers traités de Jean Calvin et confession de foi.*

Clément, O. *Le Visage intérieur.* Paris: Desclée de Brouwer, Stock, 1978.

Cormack, R. *Icônes et société à Byzance.* Paris: Éd. Gerard Montfort, 1993.

Cureton, W. *Ancient Syriac Document Relative to the Earliest Establishment of Christianity in Edessa and the Neighbouring Countries, from the Year After our Lord's Ascension to the Beginning of the Fourth Century.* 1864. Reprint, Amsterdam: Oriental Press, 1967.

Cyril of Alexandria. *Two Christological Dialogues.* Text and French translation by G. M. Durand. Sources chrétiennes, vol. 97. Paris: Éd. du Cerf, 1964.

Dagron, G. "La Règle et l'exception." In *Religiöse Devianz, Untersuchungen zur sozialen, rechtlichen und theologischen Reaktionen auf religiöse Abweichungen im westlichen und östlichen Mittelalter.* Frankfurt, 1990.

Dionysios of Halicarnassus. *De compositione verborum.* Leipzig: Usener-Radermacher, 1899–1904.

Dumézil, G. *Idées romaines.* Paris: Gallimard, 1969.

Encyclopédie théologique. Edited by J. P. Migne. Paris: J. P. Migne, 1847–53.

The Fathers of the Church. Washington, DC: Catholic University of America Press, 1949–. 106 vols.

Festugière, A. J. *Les Moines d'Orient.* Vol. 1, *Culture ou Sainteté.* Paris: Éd. du cerf, 1961.

Florovsky, G. "Origen, Eusebius and the Iconoclastic Controversy." *Church History* 29 (1950).

Gero, G. "Byzantine Iconoclasm During the Reign of Constantine V." In *Corpus Scriptorum christianorum orientalium,* 52:169–75. Louvain: Peeters, 1977.

———. "Byzantine Iconoclasm During the Reign of Leo III." In *Corpus Scriptorum christianorum orientalium,* 41. Louvain: Peeters, 1973.

Goldberg, I. "Jawlensky ou le visage promis." PhD thesis, Université de Paris-I, 1991.

Grabar, A. *L'Empereur dans l'art byzantin.* Fasc. 75 of Publications de la Faculté des Lettres de l'Université de Strasbourg. Strasbourg, 1936.

———. "L'Esthetisme d'un théologien humaniste byzantin du IXe siècle." *Revue des Sciences religieuses* (1956). Special issue, "Mélanges Andrieu."

———. *L'Iconoclasme byzantin, Dossier archéologique.* Paris: Klincksieck, 1957.

Gregory of Nazianzos. *Correspondence.* Text and French translation by P. Gallay. Paris: Les Belles Lettres, 1965.

———. *Lettres théologiques.* Text and French translation by P. Gallay. Sources chrétiennes, vol. 208. Paris: Éd. du Cerf, 1974.

Gruzinski, S. *La Guerre des images: De Christoph Colomb à "Blade Runner" (1492–2019).* Paris: Fayard, 1990.

Hennephof, H., ed. *Textus byzantinos ad iconomachiam pertinentes.* Leyden: E. J. Brill, 1969.

Hippocrates. *Corpus Hippocraticum.* Paris: Éd. Littré, 1839–61.

Hippolytos. *Against the Heresy of One Noetus.* English translation in Roberts and Donaldson, *Ante-Nicene Fathers,* 5:223–31.

———. *Philosophumena.* French translation by A. Siouville. Milan: Archè, 1988. English translation of select works in Roberts and Donaldson, *Ante-Nicene Fathers,* vol. 5.

Hugon, É. *Le Mystére de la Sainte Trinité.* Paris, 1920.

Ignatios the Deacon. *Nicephori Archiepiscopi Constantinopolitani opuscula historica.* Edited by C. De Boor. Leipzig: 1880.

Ireneaus of Lyon. *Against the Heresies.* Text and French translation by A. Rousseau. Paris: Éd. du Cerf, 1985.

John Chrysostom. *On the Priesthood.* Text and French translation by A. M. Malingrey. Sources chrétiennes, vol. 272. Paris: Éd. du Cerf, 1980. English translation in *Nicene and Post-Nicene Fathers,* 1st ser., 9:33–83.

———. *On the Providence of God.* Text and French translation by A. M. Malingrey. Sources chrétiennes, vol. 79. Paris: Éd. du Cerf, 1961.

John of Damascus. *On the Divine Images: Three Apologies Against Those Who Attack the Divine Images.* Translated by D. Anderson. Crestwood, NY: St. Vladimir's Seminary Press, 1980.

Kandinsky, W. "On the Question of Form." In *The Blaue Reiter Almanac,* edited by W. Kandinsky and F. Marc, 147–87. New York: Viking, 1974.

Kantorowicz, E. H. "Deus per naturam, Deus per gratiam." *Harvard Theological Review* 45 (October 1952): 253–76.

———. "La Souverainté de l'artiste." In *Mourir pour la Patrie,* 31–57. Paris: Presses Universitaires de France, 1984.

Khawam, R. *Le Livre des ruses: La Stratégie politique des Arabes.* Paris: Phébus, 1976.

Kitzinger, E. "Byzantine Art in the Period Between Justinian and Iconoclasm." In *Akten des XIen Internationalen Byzantinistenkongress.* Munich, 1958.

———. "The Cult of Images in the Age Before Iconoclasm." *Dumbarton Oaks Papers* 8 (1954): 83–150.

Kotsonis, J. *Problèmes de l'economie ecclésiastique.* Collection "Recherches et synthèses." Gembloux: Duculot, 1971.

Kuryluk, E. *Veronica and Her Cloth.* Cambridge, MA: Blackwell, 1991.

Ladner, G. "Der Bilderstreit und die Kunstehren der byzantinischen und abendländischen Theologie." *Zeitschrift für Kirchengeschichte* 50 (1931).

———. "The Concept of the Image in the Greek Fathers and the Byzantine Iconoclastic Controversy." *Dumbarton Oaks Papers* 7 (1953): 1–34.

———. "Origin and Significance of the Byzantine Iconoclastic Controversy." *Medieval Studies* 2 (1940): 127–49.

Legrand, A. *Le Linceul de Turin.* Paris: Desclée de Brouwer, 1980.

Lemerle, P. *Le Premier Humanisme byzantin.* Paris: Presses Universitaires de France, 1971.

Leroi-Gourhan, A. *Le Geste et la parole.* Paris: Albin Michel, 1965. Translated by A. Bostock Berger as *Gesture and Speech.* Cambridge, MA: October, 1993.

Loth, A. *La photographie du Sainte Suaire.* Paris, 1902.

Mansi, J. D. *Sacrorum conciliorum nova et amplissima collectio.* 31 vols. Florence and Venice, 1759–98.

Martineau, E. "La *Mimésis* dans *La Poétique.*" *Revue de métaphysique et de morale* 4 (1976): 438–66.

Moingt, J. *Patriologiae cursus completus, Series graeco-latina.* 161 vols. Paris, 1857–66. Abbreviated PG.

———. *Théologie trinitaire de Tertullien.* Paris: Aubier, 1966.

Mondzain-Baudinet, M.-J. "Autour de quelques concepts philosophiques de l'iconoclasme et de l'iconodoulie." In *Nicée II, 787–1987: Douze siècles d'images religieuses.*

———. "Économie et idolâtrie durant la crise de l'iconoclasme byzantin." In *Image et Signification: Rencontres de l'École du Louvre.* Paris: La Documentation française, 1983.

———. "La Relation iconique à Byzance au IXe siècle d'après les *Antirrhétiques* de Nicéphore le Patriarche: Un destin de l'aristotélianisme." *Études philosophiques* (January 1978). Special issue, "Aristotle."

———. "L'Incarnation, l'image et la voix." *Esprit* 2 (February 1982). Special issue, "Le Corps."

———. "Visage du Christ, forme de l'Église." In *Du visage,* edited by M. J. Baudinet and C. Schlatter. Lille: PUL, 1982.

Nicée II, 787–1987, Douze siècles d'images religieuses. Actes du colloque international Nicée II. Edited by F. Boespflug and N. Lossky. Paris: Éd. du Cerf, 1987.

Nicene and Post-Nicene Fathers of the Christian Church. Edited by Philip Schaff. 1st and 2nd ser. Grand Rapids, MI: W. R. Eerdmans, 1978.

Nikephoros, Patriarch of Constantinople. *Antirrhetics.* French translation by M. J. Mondzain in *Discours contre les iconoclastes.* Paris: Klincksieck, 1989.

Origen. *Commentary on the Epistle to the Romans.* PG 14.

———. *Commentary on the Gospel According to Matthew.* Text and French translation by R. Girod. Sources chrétiennes, vol. 162. Paris: Éd du Cerf, 1970.

———. *Contra Celsum.* Translated by H. Chadwick. Cambridge: Cambridge University Press, 1965.

Ostrogorsky, G. "Les Débuts de la querelle des images." In *Mélanges Charles Diehl.* Vol. 1. Paris, 1930.

———. *Histoire de l'état byzantin.* Paris: Payot, 1956.

———. *Studien zur Geschichte den byzantinischen Bilderstreit.* Historische Untersuchengun, vol. 5. Breslau: M. H. Marcus, 1929.

Ouspensky, L. *Théologie de l'icône dans l'église orthodoxe.* Paris: Éd. du Cerf, 1980.

Painter's Manual, The. Translated by Paul Hetherington. London: Sagittarius Press, 1981. First published 1900, 1909, by A. Papadopoulos-Kerameus, Saint Petersburg.

Pedrizet, P. *Seminarium kondakovianum.* Prague, 1932.

Pepin, J. "Aspects théoriques du symbolisme dans la tradition dionysienne, antécédents et nouveautés." In *Settimana di studio del Centro italiano di studi sull'alto medio evo.* Spoleto: Panetto and Petrelli, 1976.

Photios. *Bibliothèque.* French translation by R. Henry. Paris: Les Belles Lettres, 1991.

———. *Ta Amphilochia.* Athens: Soph. Oikonomos, 1858.

Pouillon, J. "Fétiches sans fétichisme." *Nouvelle Revue de psychanalyse* 2 (Autumn 1970): 135–47.

Prestige, G. L. *Dieu dans le pensée patristique.* Paris: Aubier, 1955.

Pseudo-Dionysios. *The Celestial Hierarchy.* In *Pseudo-Dionysius: The Complete Works.* Translated by C. Luibheid. Mahwah, NY: Paulist Press, 1987.

Roberts, Alexander, and James Donaldson, eds. *The Ante-Nicene Fathers: Translations of the Writings of the Fathers down to AD 325.* New York: Charles Scribner's Sons, 1899.

Sahas, Daniel. *Icon and Logos: Sources in Eighth-Century Iconoclasm.* Toronto: University of Toronto Press, 1986.

Savio, Mgr. P. *Ricerca storica sulla Santa Sindone.* Turin, 1957.

Schelling, F. W. J. *The Philosophy of Art.* Translated by D. Stott. Minneapolis: University of Minnesota Press, 1989.

Schönbrun, C. von. *L'Icône du Christ, fondements théologiques.* 2nd ed. Paris: Éd. du Cerf, 1986.

Sophocles. *Electra.* Paris: Les Belles Lettres, 1958.

Sorlin, H. "Stryges et géloudes: Histoire d'une croyance et d'une tradition." In *Travaux et mémoires,* 3:19–208. Paris: Éd. de Brocard, 1991.

Tertullian. *Against Marcion.* English translation in Roberts and Donaldson, *Ante-Nicene Fathers,* vol. 3.

———. *Against Praxeas.* English translation in Roberts and Donaldson, *Ante-Nicene Fathers,* vol. 3.

———. *La Chair du Christ.* Text and French translation by J. P. Mahé. Sources chrétiennes, vol. 216. Paris: Éd. du Cerf, 1975.

Theodore of Stoudios. *On the Holy Icons.* Translated by C. P. Roth. Crestwood, NY: St. Vladimir's Seminary Press, 1981.

Thomas Aquinas. *Summa Theologica.*

Vernant, J.-P. *Myth and Thought Among the Greeks.* London: Routledge and Kegan Paul, 1983.

Wilson, I. *Le Suaire de Turin.* Paris: Albin Michel, 1978.

Worringer, W. *Abstraction and Empathy: A Contribution to the Psychology of Style.* New York: International Universities Press, 1953.

Cultural Memory in the Present

Marie-José Mondzain, *Image, Icon, Economy: The Byzantine Origins of the Contemporary Imaginary*

Cecilia Sjöholm, *The Antigone Complex: Ethics and the Invention of Feminine Desire*

Jacques Derrida and Elisabeth Roudinesco, *For What Tomorrow . . . : A Dialogue*

Elisabeth Weber, *Questioning Judaism: Interviews by Elisabeth Weber*

Jacques Derrida and Catherine Malabou, *Counterpath: Traveling with Jacques Derrida*

Martin Seel, *Aesthetics of Appearing*

Nanette Salomon, *Shifting Priorities: Gender and Genre in Seventeenth-Century Dutch Painting*

Jacob Taubes, *The Political Theology of Paul*

Jean-Luc Marion, *The Crossing of the Visible*

Eric Michaud, *The Cult of Art in Nazi Germany*

Anne Freadman, *The Machinery of Talk: Charles Peirce and the Sign Hypothesis*

Stanley Cavell, *Emerson's Transcendental Etudes*

Stuart McLean, *The Event and its Terrors: Ireland, Famine, Modernity*

Beate Rössler, ed., *Privacies: Philosophical Evaluations*

Bernard Faure, *Double Exposure: Cutting Across Buddhist and Western Discourses*

Alessia Ricciardi, *The Ends Of Mourning: Psychoanalysis, Literature, Film*

Alain Badiou, *Saint Paul: The Foundation of Universalism*

Gil Anidjar, *The Jew, The Arab: A History of the Enemy*

Jonathan Culler and Kevin Lamb, eds., *Just Being Difficult? Academic Writing in the Public Arena*

Jean-Luc Nancy, *A Finite Thinking*, edited by Simon Sparks

Theodor W. Adorno, *Can One Live after Auschwitz? A Philosophical Reader*, edited by Rolf Tiedemann

Patricia Pisters, *The Matrix of Visual Culture: Working with Deleuze in Film Theory*

Talal Asad, *Formations of the Secular: Christianity, Islam, Modernity*

Dorothea von Mücke, *The Rise of the Fantastic Tale*

Marc Redfield, *The Politics of Aesthetics: Nationalism, Gender, Romanticism*

Emmanuel Levinas, *On Escape*

Dan Zahavi, *Husserl's Phenomenology*

Rodolphe Gasché, *The Idea of Form: Rethinking Kant's Aesthetics*

Michael Naas, *Taking on the Tradition: Jacques Derrida and the Legacies of Deconstruction*

Herlinde Pauer-Studer, ed., *Constructions of Practical Reason: Interviews on Moral and Political Philosophy*

Jean-Luc Marion, *Being Given: Toward a Phenomenology of Givenness*

Theodor W. Adorno and Max Horkheimer, *Dialectic of Enlightenment*

Ian Balfour, *The Rhetoric of Romantic Prophecy*

Martin Stokhof, *World and Life as One: Ethics and Ontology in Wittgenstein's Early Thought*

Gianni Vattimo, *Nietzsche: An Introduction*

Jacques Derrida, *Negotiations: Interventions and Interviews, 1971–1998*, ed. Elizabeth Rottenberg

Brett Levinson, *The Ends of Literature: Post-transition and Neoliberalism in the Wake of the "Boom"*

Timothy J. Reiss, *Against Autonomy: Global Dialectics of Cultural Exchange*

Hent de Vries and Samuel Weber, eds., *Religion and Media*

Niklas Luhmann, *Theories of Distinction: Redescribing the Descriptions of Modernity*, ed. and introd. William Rasch

Johannes Fabian, *Anthropology with an Attitude: Critical Essays*

Michel Henry, *I Am the Truth: Toward a Philosophy of Christianity*

Gil Anidjar, *"Our Place in Al-Andalus": Kabbalah, Philosophy, Literature in Arab-Jewish Letters*

Hélène Cixous and Jacques Derrida, *Veils*

F. R. Ankersmit, *Historical Representation*

F. R. Ankersmit, *Political Representation*

Elissa Marder, *Dead Time: Temporal Disorders in the Wake of Modernity (Baudelaire and Flaubert)*

Reinhart Koselleck, *The Practice of Conceptual History: Timing History, Spacing Concepts*

Niklas Luhmann, *The Reality of the Mass Media*

Hubert Damisch, *A Childhood Memory by Piero della Francesca*

Hubert Damisch, *A Theory of /Cloud/: Toward a History of Painting*

Jean-Luc Nancy, *The Speculative Remark (One of Hegel's Bons Mots)*

Jean-François Lyotard, *Soundproof Room: Malraux's Anti-Aesthetics*

Jan Patočka, *Plato and Europe*

Hubert Damisch, *Skyline: The Narcissistic City*

Isabel Hoving, *In Praise of New Travelers: Reading Caribbean Migrant Women Writers*

Richard Rand, ed., *Futures: Of Derrida*

William Rasch, *Niklas Luhmann's Modernity: The Paradox of System Differentiation*

Jacques Derrida and Anne Dufourmantelle, *Of Hospitality*

Jean-François Lyotard, *The Confession of Augustine*

Kaja Silverman, *World Spectators*

Samuel Weber, *Institution and Interpretation: Expanded Edition*

Jeffrey S. Librett, *The Rhetoric of Cultural Dialogue: Jews and Germans in the Epoch of Emancipation*

Ulrich Baer, *Remnants of Song: Trauma and the Experience of Modernity in Charles Baudelaire and Paul Celan*

Samuel C. Wheeler III, *Deconstruction as Analytic Philosophy*

David S. Ferris, *Silent Urns: Romanticism, Hellenism, Modernity*

Rodolphe Gasché, *Of Minimal Things: Studies on the Notion of Relation*

Sarah Winter, *Freud and the Institution of Psychoanalytic Knowledge*

Samuel Weber, *The Legend of Freud: Expanded Edition*

Aris Fioretos, ed., *The Solid Letter: Readings of Friedrich Hölderlin*

J. Hillis Miller / Manuel Asensi, *Black Holes / J. Hillis Miller; or, Boustrophedonic Reading*

Miryam Sas, *Fault Lines: Cultural Memory and Japanese Surrealism*

Peter Schwenger, *Fantasm and Fiction: On Textual Envisioning*

Didier Maleuvre, *Museum Memories: History, Technology, Art*

Jacques Derrida, *Monolingualism of the Other; or, The Prosthesis of Origin*

Andrew Baruch Wachtel, *Making a Nation, Breaking a Nation: Literature and Cultural Politics in Yugoslavia*

Niklas Luhmann, *Love as Passion: The Codification of Intimacy*

Mieke Bal, ed., *The Practice of Cultural Analysis: Exposing Interdisciplinary Interpretation*

Jacques Derrida and Gianni Vattimo, eds., *Religion*

The authorized representative in the EU for product safety and compliance is:
Mare Nostrum Group
B.V Doelen 72
4831 GR Breda
The Netherlands

www.ingramcontent.com/pod-product-compliance
Lightning Source LLC
LaVergne TN
LVHW050952080826
845145LV00005B/1478

* 9 7 8 0 8 0 4 7 4 1 0 1 9 *